# Secrets in the Stars of Ancient Egypt

John Bunker
Karen Pressler

Secrets in the Stars of Ancient Egypt

Copyright ©2021 by John M. Bunker & Karen L. Pressler

ISBN: 978-1-7325792-1-7 (Black & White edition)
ISBN: 978-1-7325792-3-1 (Color edition)

Bunker Pressler Books

"Two and a Guide"

The cover image is a partial representation of the rectangular zodiac from the Temple of *Hathor* at *Dendera*.

Questions regarding this book can be addressed to:

Bunker Pressler Books
8829 Heffelfinger Rd.
Churubusco, IN 46723

Email:
  Bunker.Pressler@gmail.com

Website:
  https://sites.google.com/site/edgarcayceandthehallofrecords/

# 𝔈𝔠𝔠𝔢 𝔔𝔲𝔞𝔪 𝔅𝔬𝔫𝔲𝔪

"Above all, keep an open mind. What may seem to be a proved fact to-day may wear a very different aspect to-morrow."

--- Prof. Salim Hassaan
*The Sphinx: Its History in Light
of Recent Excavations*
1949, page IX.

# Table of Contents

**PREFACE** ............................................................................................................................. 3
   How we Came to Know the Stars ............................................................................... 3

**PART I – STARS IN THE TOMBS** .......................................................................................... 5
   Tomb of *Seti I* (1279 BC) ............................................................................................ 7
      *Gemini - the Twins* ................................................................................................. 7
      *Taurus and the Ploughman* .................................................................................. 10
      *The Scales of Orion* ............................................................................................. 13
      *The Bow of Eridanus* ........................................................................................... 15
      *Cetus – The Hippo and the Crocodile* ................................................................. 19
      *Leo and Hydra - the Lion and the Serpent* .......................................................... 21
   Tomb of *Ramesses VI* (KV9, 1137 BC) .................................................................... 23
   Tomb of *Senmut* (1483 BC) ..................................................................................... 26
   Tomb of *Pedamenope* (circa 26th dynasty, 525 BC) ............................................... 30
   Ptolemaic Tomb at *Atfieh* (circa 150 BC) ................................................................ 34
   Balance ....................................................................................................................... 36

**PART II – THE CALENDAR** ................................................................................................ 39
   The Calendar and the Stars ...................................................................................... 41
   Length of the Year ..................................................................................................... 42
      *The Epagomens* ................................................................................................... 43
      *The Birth of the Five Gods* .................................................................................. 47
      *The Tomb of Hepzefa* .......................................................................................... 49

**PART III – THE ZODIAC OF *DENDERA*** ............................................................................ 55
   The Zodiac Ceiling in the Temple of *Hathor* ........................................................... 57
   The Hours of the Night .............................................................................................. 58
      *The First Hour of Night* ....................................................................................... 58
      *The Second and Third Hours of the Night* .......................................................... 60
      *The Fourth, Fifth, Sixth and Seventh Hours of the Night* ................................... 67
      *The Eighth and Ninth Hours of the Night* ........................................................... 72
      *The Tenth and Eleventh Hours of the Night* ....................................................... 76
      *Twelfth Hour of the Night* .................................................................................. 77

**PART IV – THE INVENTORY STELA** ................................................................................... 79
   Description of the Inventory Stela ............................................................................ 81
   Text of the Inventory Stela ........................................................................................ 83
      *Translation of the Four Registers by Selim Hassan* ............................................ 83
      *The Outside Edge and Base of the Inventory Stela* ............................................ 85
         The Egyptian word Hent ................................................................................... 86
         Translation of the Text ...................................................................................... 103
         The Tuat .............................................................................................................. 114
   Analysis of the Inventory Stela ................................................................................. 117
      *Line 1. The mother of the god* ............................................................................ 119
      *Line 2. The house, temple & the pyramid* .......................................................... 120
      *Line 3. The gods* .................................................................................................. 123
      *Line 4 & 5. The pyramids that Khufu built* ......................................................... 123
      *Line 6. The positioning of other buildings* .......................................................... 125
      *Line 7 & 8. The books* ......................................................................................... 126

    *Line 9 & 10. The purpose of Khufu's trip to the Giza Plateau* ........................................................... *126*
    *Line 11. Naming the Sycamore Tree* ............................................................................................... *127*
    *Line 12. The great book, Horus, and his likeness* ............................................................................ *127*
    *Line 13. The gazelles* ........................................................................................................................ *128*
    *Line 14. Entrance ground of the hill cemetery and inscribed memorial stela* .................................. *129*
    *Line 15. The circle of eternity in the Tuat* ....................................................................................... *131*
    *Line 16. The protection of the lion and the goddess* ...................................................................... *133*
  CHANGING HISTORY ................................................................................................................................ 136

**PART V – THE MYSTERY OF THE DEATH AND RESURRECTION OF *OSIRIS*** ............................................... **139**
  THE LEGEND OF *OSIRIS* ........................................................................................................................... 141
  FURTHER COMMENTS ABOUT THE DEATH AND RESURRECTION OF *OSIRIS* ................................................................ 150

**APPENDIX A - COMPLETE TRANSLATION OF THE INVENTORY STELA** ................................................... **153**

**APPENDIX B - SELIM HASSAN'S PRESENTATION OF THE INVENTORY STELA** ......................................... **169**

**BIBLIOGRAPHY** ................................................................................................................................... **175**

**INDEX** ................................................................................................................................................ **179**

# PREFACE

This book is a collection of research about the stars of ancient Egypt. The simple truth is, no one has been able to fully identify the star constellations in the tomb of *Seti I* until now. Likewise, no one has provided a reasonable explanation of the square zodiac images on the ceiling of the temple at *Dendera*. We have done both in this book. We also explain how the stories about the death and resurrection of *Osiris* originated as a description of the movements of star constellations in the sky. Finally, we provide a reliable translation and commentary of the inscribed text of the Inventory Stela found at Giza in 1858 by Auguste Mariette.

### HOW WE CAME TO KNOW THE STARS

When we first discovered Skyglobe computer generated astronomy program in 1998, one image seemed to stand out to us. It was the collective view of the combination of three star constellations that filled the sky: Centaurus, Hydra and Leo, shown below.

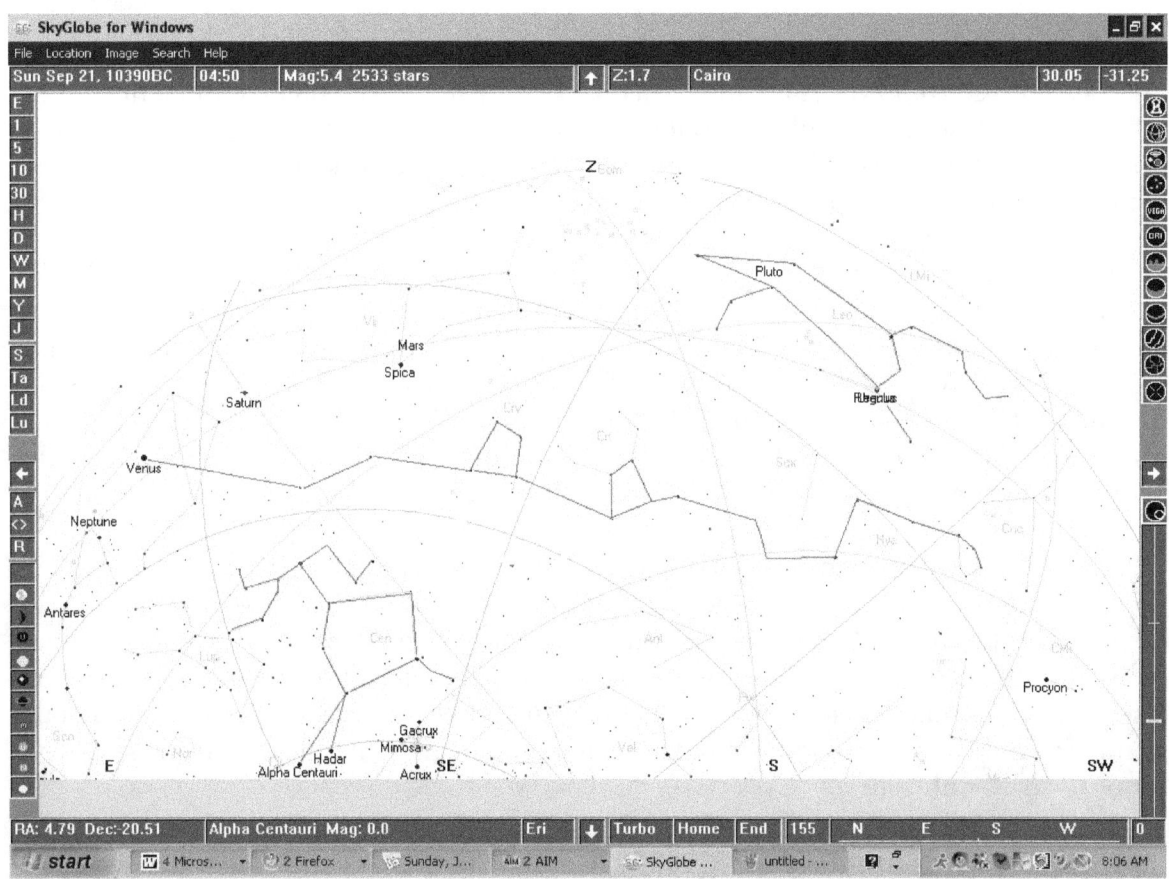

We had never studied astronomy before but to us this combination of constellations seemed to resemble a serpent with a lion on each side of it. Some time later we saw an image from an ancient Egyptian tomb that we thought must be a representation of these same constellations.

# PREFACE

From the tomb of Rameses VI [1]

We could not help but notice the apparent shape of a pyramid in the tomb of *Ramesses VI*. This reminded us that Edgar Cayce, 20th century healer and prophet, had said that the construction of the Great Pyramid was begun in 10,490 BC and completed in 10,390 BC.

During the years of our research we found the same configuration of stars to be visible in the sky over Cairo, Egypt at about 4:50 A.M. on the autumnal equinox, September 21st, 10,390 BC. But the date of this configuration was outside the accepted approximations for civilization in Egypt. This is how we began to develop interest in Egyptian star constellations and their connection to ancient dates.

As we continued to be curious about Egyptian astronomy, we found the temple of *Hathor* at *Dendera* with its square zodiac ceiling. We wondered if there was also a connection between the equinox and the ceiling of this temple. Eventually we found that the ceiling configurations matched the sky of 2501 BC. But, unexpectedly, we found that various positions of the constellations and the hours represented were from the autumnal equinox, the winter solstice, the spring equinox and the summer solstice, all from 2501 BC. This may indicate that the Temple of *Dendera* dates back to 2501 BC.

When we turned our attention to the tomb of *Seti I*, we were faced with the enigma of the hippopotamus and crocodile constellation. Since *Seti I* died in 1279 BC, we decided to explore the positions of constellations on the equinox of that year. As we studied these constellations and compared the *Seti I* illustration with other tombs, and as we learned more about ancient Egyptian gods and hieroglyphic texts, we began to understand that the tomb drawings were star configurations commemorating specific dates. That is what we hope to share with you.

---

[1] Piankoff, A. *The tomb of Ramesses VI.*

# PART I – STARS IN THE TOMBS

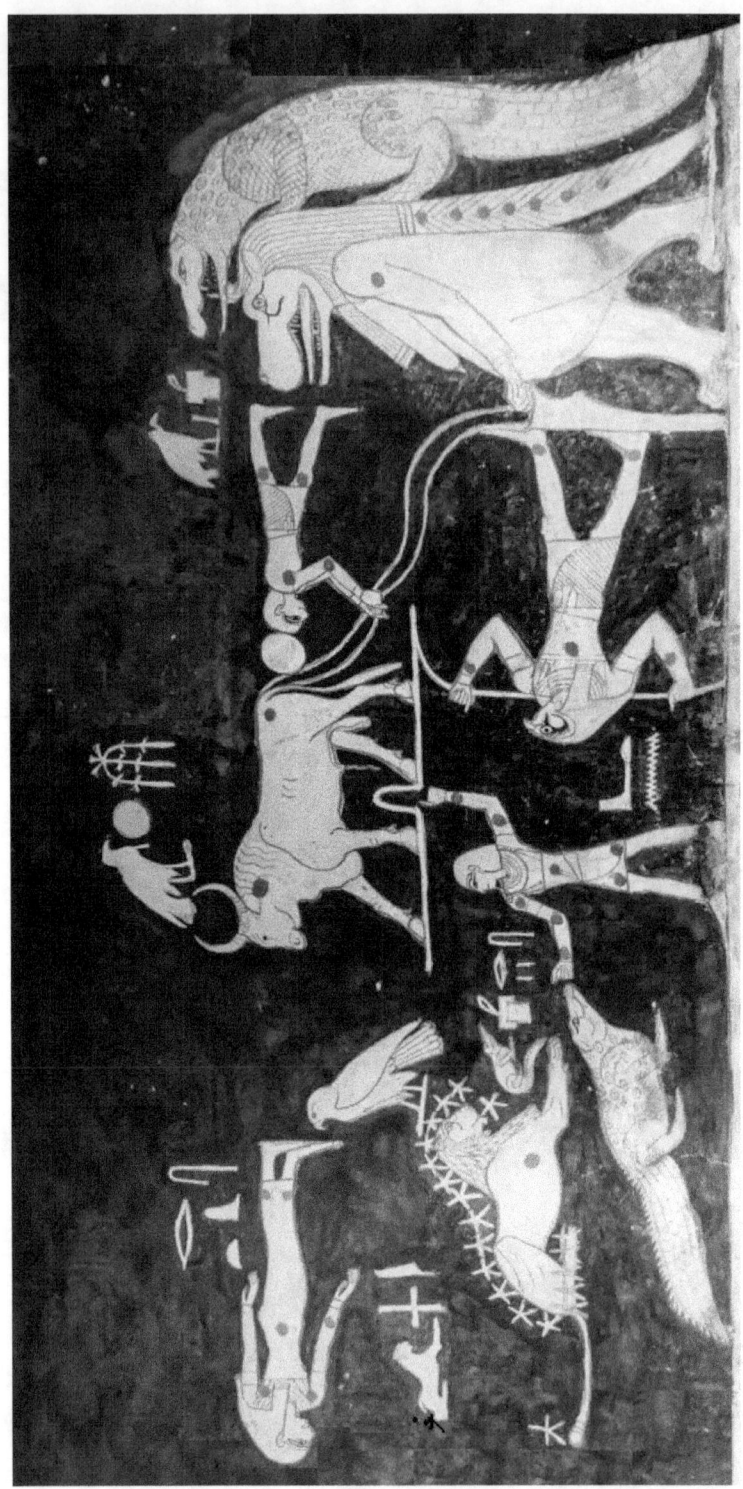

Scene from KV17 Tomb of Seti I Valley of the Kings

---

[2] https://www.flickr.com/photos/manna4u/36500349182

# TOMB OF *SETI I* (1279 BC)

We begin with the scene from the tomb of *Seti I* depicted on the facing page. A study of each figure and its celestial identity helps to clarify that the scene is of a group of stars together in the sky during the year of the death of *Seti I*. Let's look at who these characters actually are.

## Gemini - the Twins

In the image of the goddess, there are six stars marked with circles. In comparison with a modern star chart we can see a correlation in the placement of these circles with the stars of the Gemini constellation.

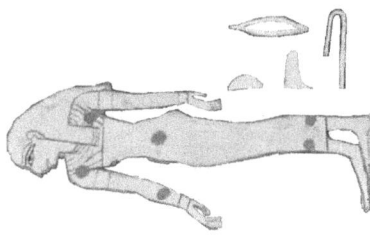

Matching stars have been emphasized in the image below.

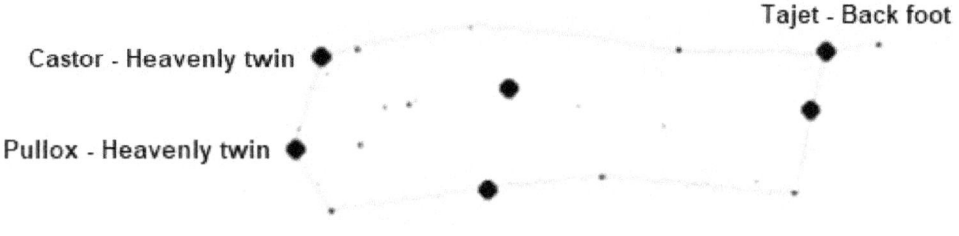

The hieroglyphic text above the horizontal goddess reads , *Serqit*, scorpion goddess. In the Ptolemaic temple inscriptions *Isis* is sometimes called "the scorpion" or "*Isis* the scorpion."[4]

---

[3] Noonan. *Fixed stars and judicial astrology,* page 39.
[4] Klasens, *A Magical Statue Base*, page 65.

# STARS IN THE TOMBS

Other tombs that include similar imagery contain variations of the same hieroglyphic text. For example, in the tomb of *Pedamenope*[5], prophet and chief lector priest of the 26th, dynasty, we see:

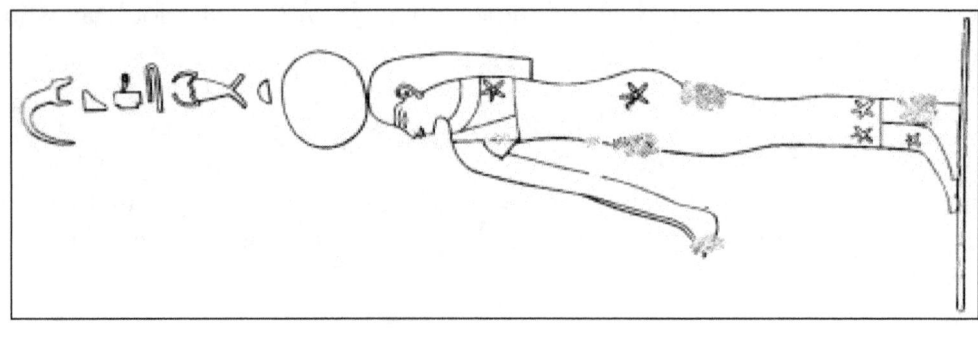

*saq*
to gather together, to assemble

*Serqit*
Scorpion goddess

From *Ramesses II* [6] we see:

*saq*
to gather together, to assemble

*Serqit*
Scorpion goddess

From the tomb of *Senmut* we see:

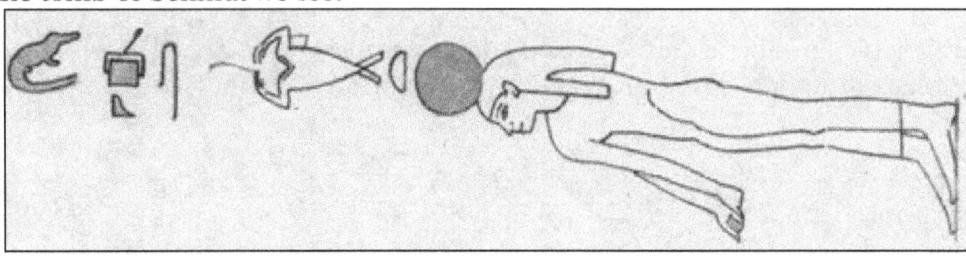

*saq*
to gather together, to assemble

*Serqit*
Scorpion goddess

---

[5] https://en.wikipedia.org/wiki/TT33_(tomb)

[6] Neugebauer and Parker, *Egyptian Astronomical Texts*, Volume III. Decans, Planets, Constellations and Zodiacs, Text, page 185.

# The Tomb of *Seti I*

All of these texts are about an assembly of star constellations at one particular time, and seem to have been referred to as *"the gathering."* The date is September 21, 1279 BC at 2:43 A.M.

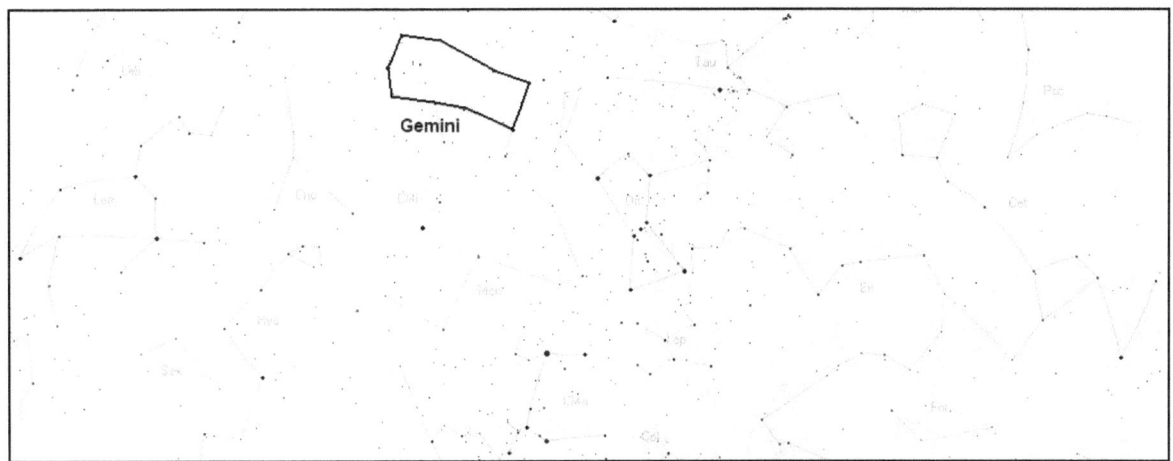

These are the stars of the first constellation we have identified on the autumnal equinox, September 21, 1279 BC at 2:43 A.M. (The year of the death of *Seti I*)

# STARS IN THE TOMBS

## Taurus and the Ploughman

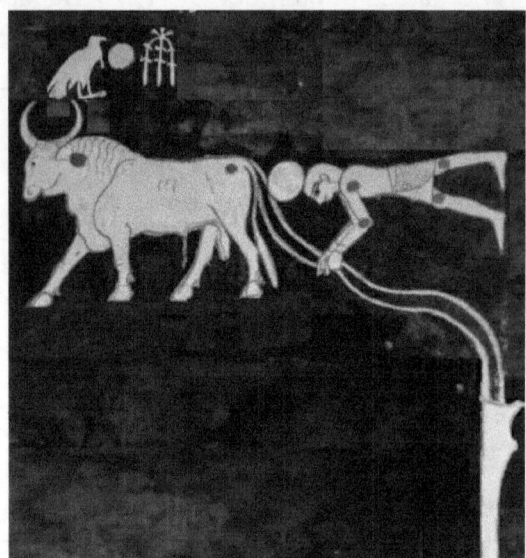

Bull and Ploughman
From the tomb of *Seti I*

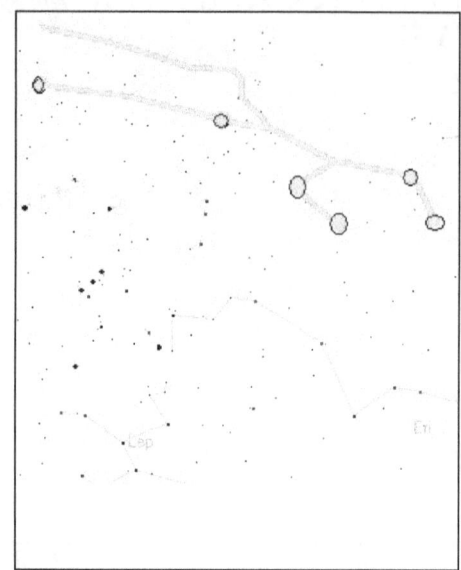

Taurus Constellation

Hieroglyphic text above the bull [glyphs] ⁷ reads *Meskhti*, thought to mean the great bear or Big Dipper, however our research shows that this image in the tomb of *Seti I* actually refers to the constellation of Taurus, the bull.

Here, the image of the constellation of Taurus overlays the bull and ploughman, and illustrates a similarity in the pattern of stars.

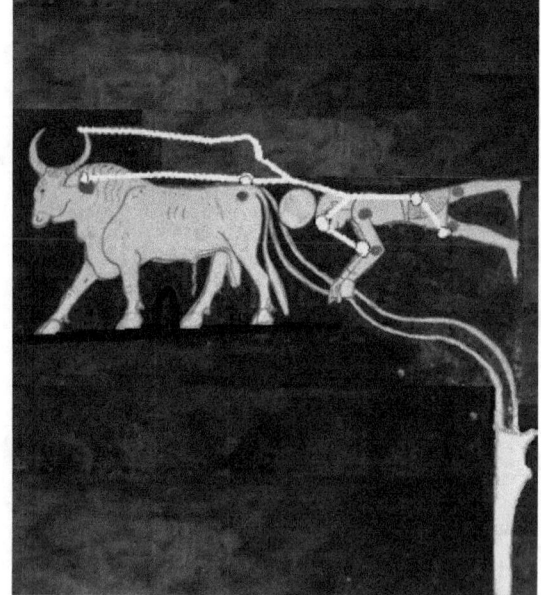

---

[7] Budge, *Egyptian Hieroglyphic Dictionary*, 326A, *Meskh-ti* [glyphs], Thes. 124ff, the Great Bear, depicted as a *bull-headed heart*, or a *bull-headed bull's haunch* with seven stars. [NOTE: Until now, *Meskh-ti* [glyphs] has been incorrectly identified as the Great Bear constellation, but the new information presented in *Secrets in the Stars of Ancient Egypt* prove that *Meskh-ti* [glyphs] indicates the constellation Taurus.]

# The Tomb of *Seti I*

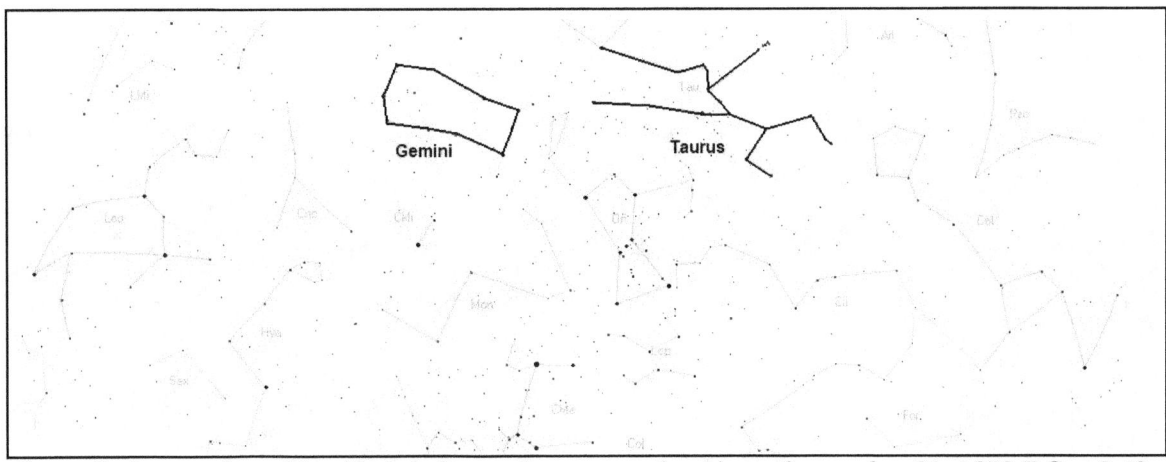

Constellations we have identified so far on the autumnal equinox, September 21, 1279 BC at 2:43 A.M. (the year of the death of *Seti I*)

# STARS IN THE TOMBS

To understand the next group of images, shown below, they need to be viewed individually. On the following pages we have separated them.

# The Tomb of *Seti I*

## The Scales of Orion

Image from *Seti I*

Orion

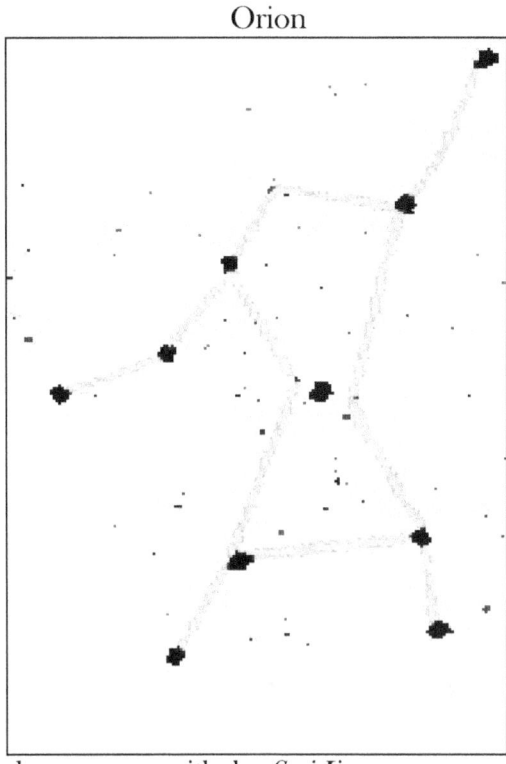

Above, the stars of Orion have been reversed to compare with the *Seti I* image.

Taurus is standing on a pair of stylized scale pans with Orion acting as the pivot or fulcrum of balance. This idea of balance in all probability symbolizes the equinox.

Parts of a scale

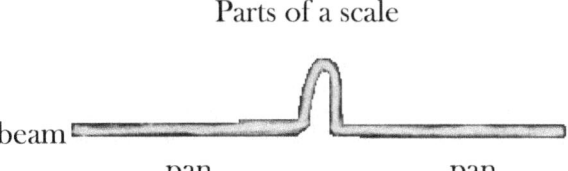

# STARS IN THE TOMBS

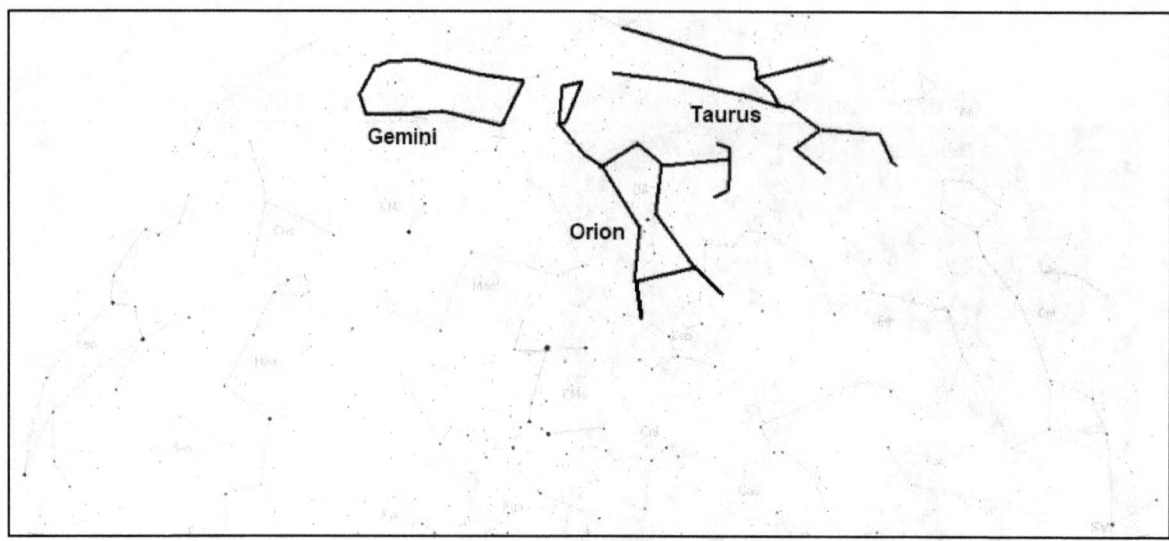

Constellations we have identified so far on the autumnal equinox, September 21, 1279 BC at 2:43 A.M. (the year of the death of *Seti I*)

# THE TOMB OF *SETI I*

## The Bow of Eridanus

The hawk-headed man ~~~ *An* is holding a stick over his shoulders. The first impression is that the stick appears to be bent, then twisted in an unusual manner, but we have already seen that the bull is balanced on a scale. So let's remove the bull and the scales and see what is left.

The back part of the bent stick appears to be missing. Perhaps there was not enough room in the allotted space within Seti's tomb to complete the drawing, so the artist was unable to include the missing piece of the bent stick being held by the hawk-headed man.

A close up view of the upper end of the stick reveals a grooved notch for a bowstring!

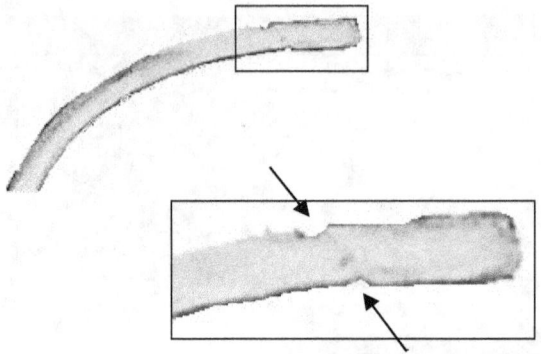

If the back of the bent stick is a duplicate of the front of the stick, then it becomes clear that *An* is carrying an unstrung bow across his shoulders.

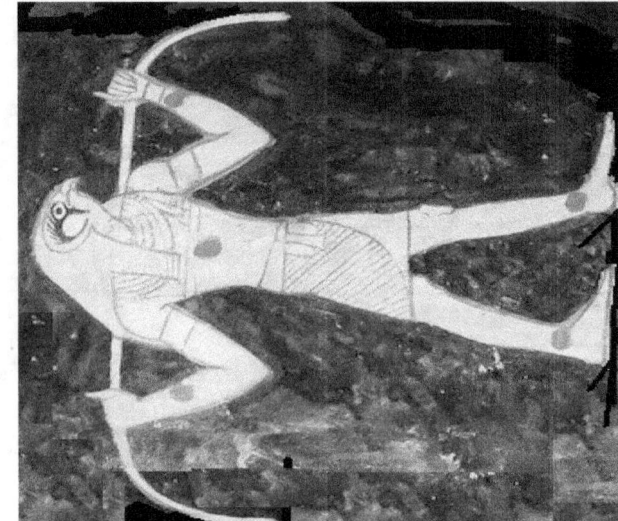

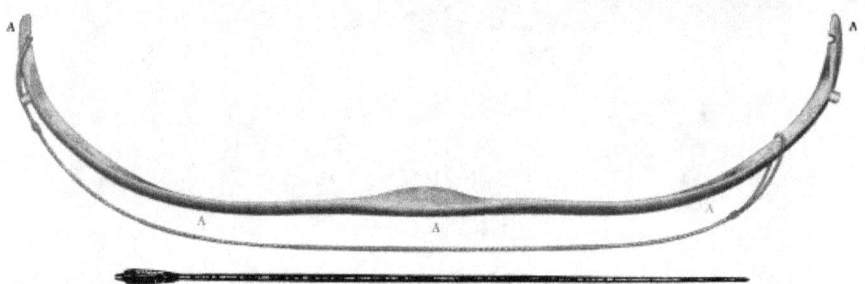

Unstrung reflex bow and arrow [8]

A poem written in Latin, published in 19 BC reads, *"They carry unstrung bows across slumped shoulders, ..."* [9]

---

[8] Payne-Gallwey, *A summary of the history, construction and effects in warfare of the projectile-throwing engines of the ancients*, page 2, Fig. 1A.

[9] Quinn, *Virgil's Aeneid*, page 250; also see https://en.wikipedia.org/wiki/Aeneid:
"The Aeneid is a Latin epic poem, written by Virgil between 29 and 19 BC, that tells the legendary story of Aeneas, a Trojan who travelled to Italy, where he became the ancestor of the Romans. It comprises 9,896 lines in dactylic hexameter."

# The Tomb of *Seti I*

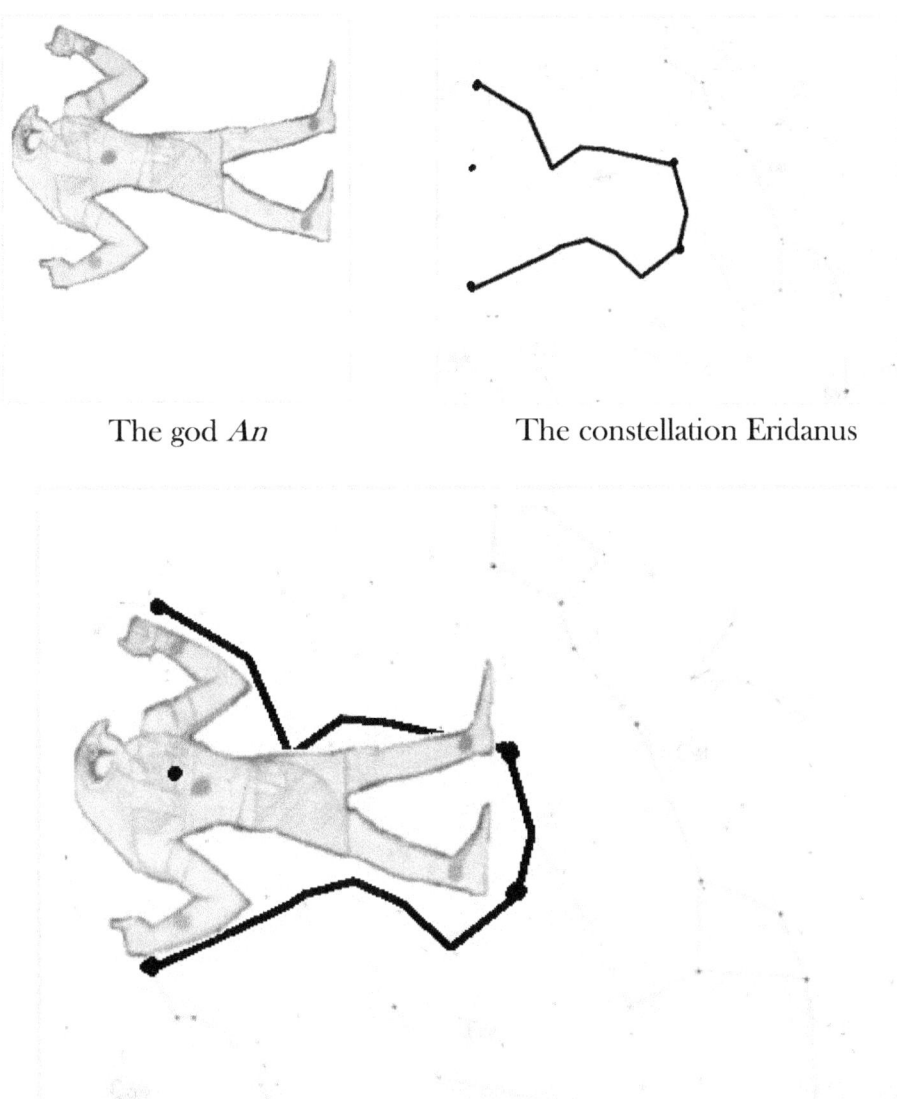

The god *An*       The constellation Eridanus

The god *An* overlays the constellation Eridanus

# STARS IN THE TOMBS

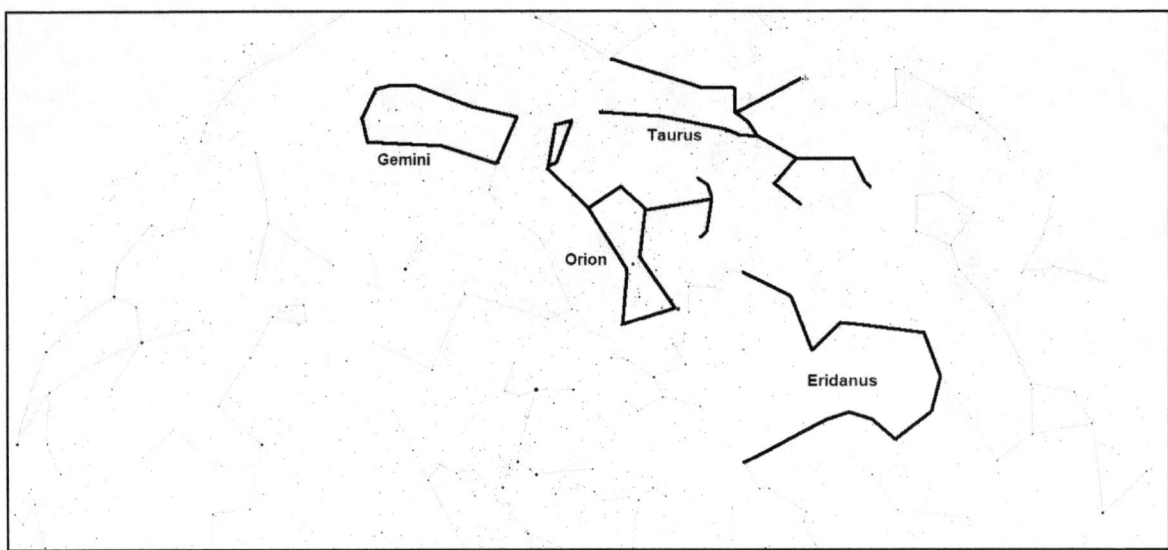

Constellations we have identified so far on the autumnal equinox, September 21, 1279 BC at 2:43 A.M. (the year of the death of *Seti I*)

# THE TOMB OF *SETI I*

## Cetus – The Hippo and the Crocodile

Let's look next at the hippopotamus and the crocodile. The outline of the constellation Cetus resembles a hippopotamus standing erect on its hind legs with its front paws extended and one foot forward. There is a fin on the back of Cetus, resembling the spiked crest on a crocodile's back. The "V" shaped line at the end of the fin suggests an upturned tail.

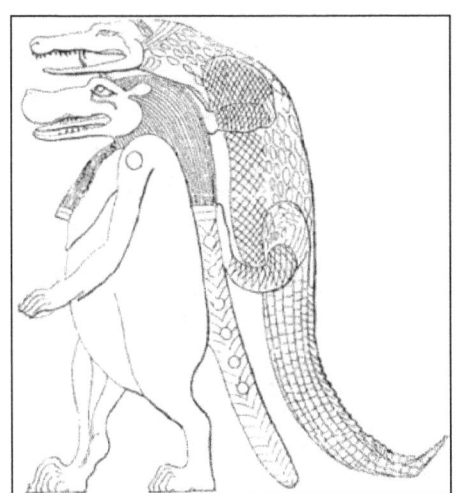 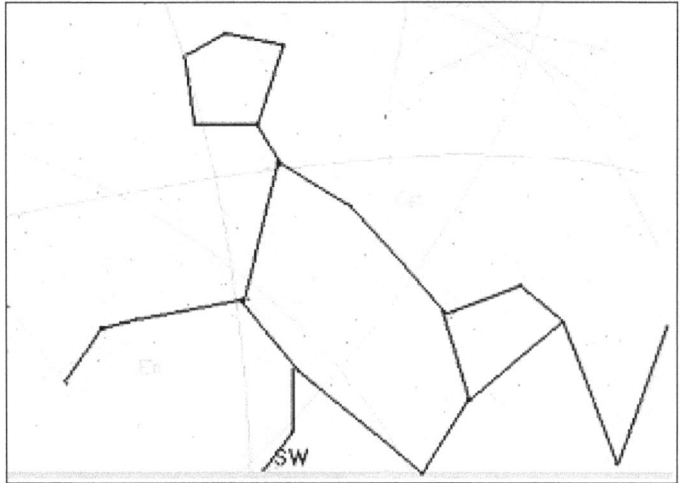

*sa mut*
*Hesamut*[10]
Hippopotamus goddess

---

[10] Budge, *Egyptian Hieroglyphic Dictionary*, 510B, *Hesamut*, Tomb of *Seti I*, the goddess of a constellation in the northern sky who appears in the form of a hippopotamus.

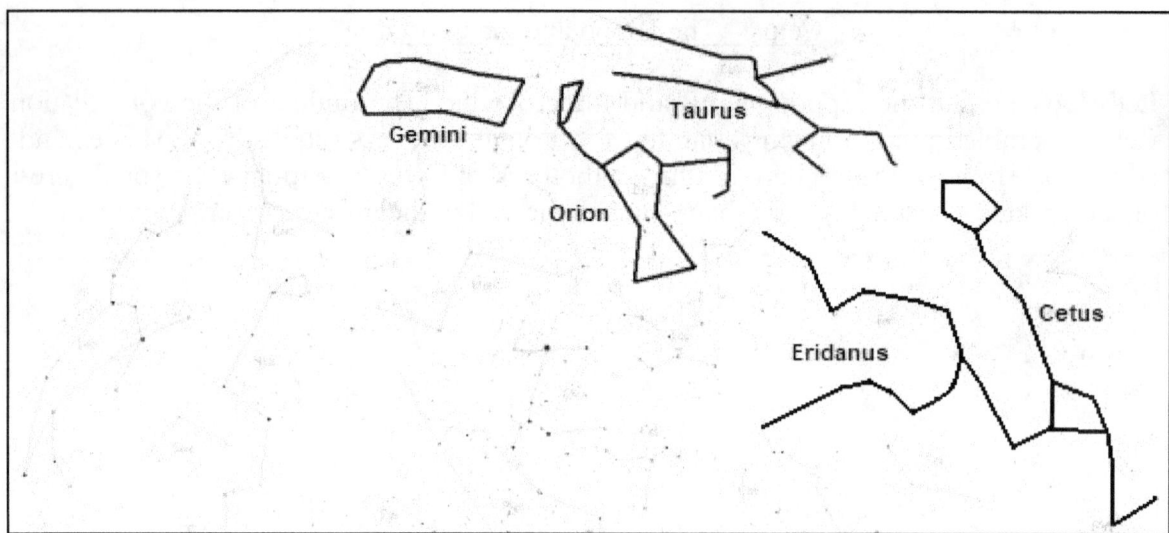

Constellations we have identified so far on the autumnal equinox, September 21, 1279 BC at 2:43 A.M. (the year of the death of *Seti I*)

# The Tomb of *Seti I*

## Leo and Hydra - the Lion and the Serpent

This segment from the Tomb of *Seti I* illustrates *Horus* and the lion-god with the serpent-god who sometimes took the form of a crocodile.

The hieroglyphic text reads:

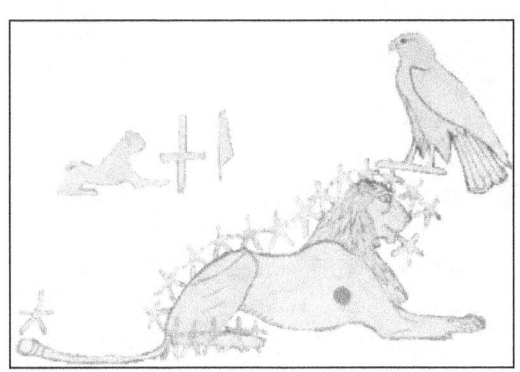   

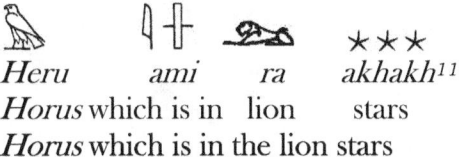

| Heru | ami | ra | akhakh[11] | | Sirsa[12] |
|---|---|---|---|---|---|
| Horus | which is in | lion | stars | | a star god |
| Horus which is in the lion stars | | | | | a star god |

---

[11] Budge, *Egyptian Hieroglyphic Dictionary*, page 8B, *akhakh*: 🦅⊙🦅⊙⊙★★★, flowers (of heaven) i.e. stars.

[12] Budge, *Egyptian Hieroglyphic Dictionary*, 647B, *Sirsa*, [glyphs] Thes. 129, a star god; var. [glyphs] (Thes. = Brugsch, *Thesaurus inscriptionum aegyptiacarum*)

## STARS IN THE TOMBS

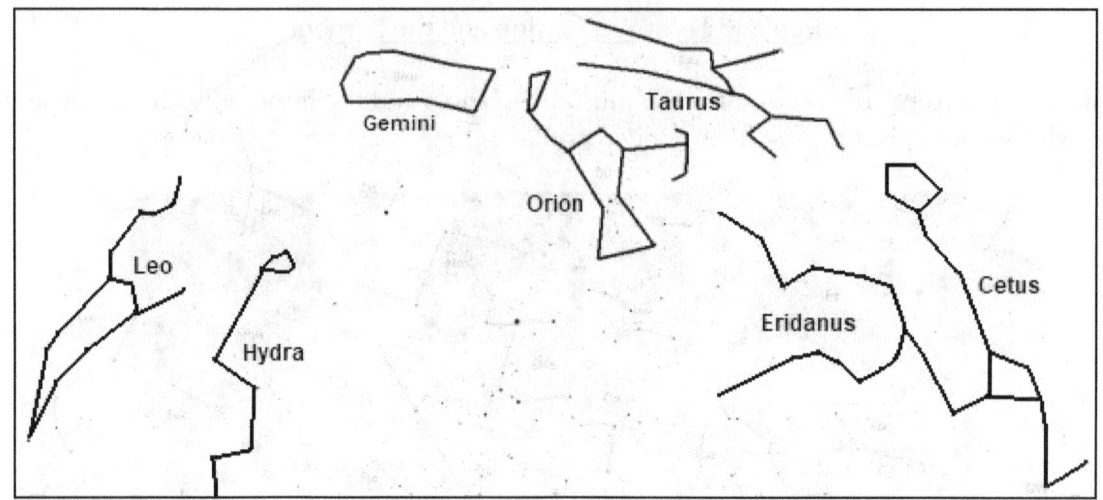

Constellations we have identified on the autumnal equinox, September 21, 1279 BC at 2:43 A.M. (the year of the death of *Seti I*)

They match the tomb images of *Seti I* below.

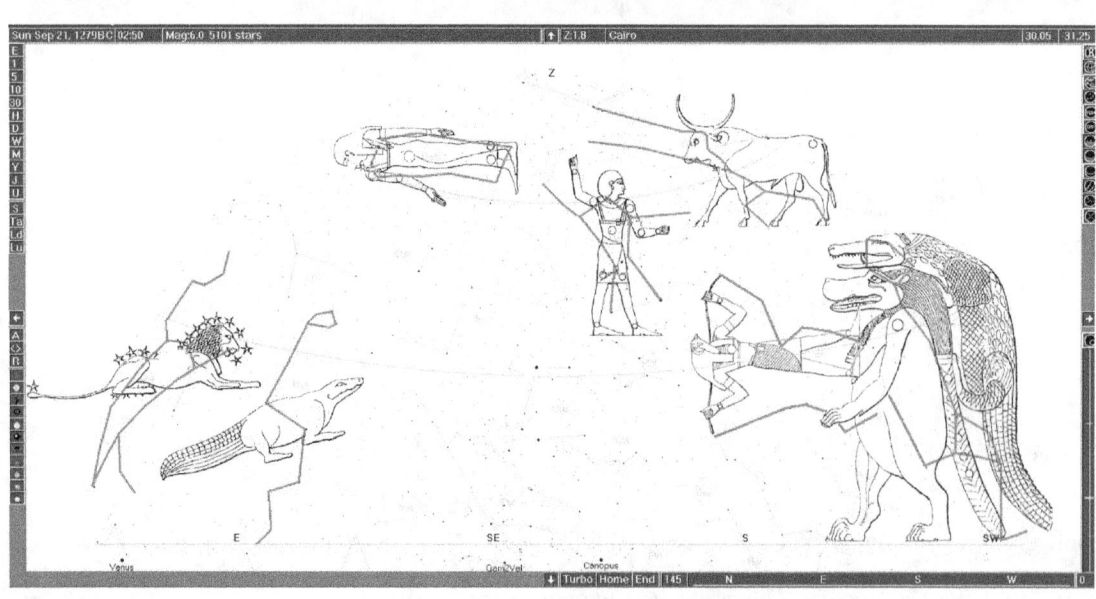

## TOMB OF *RAMESSES VI* (KV9, 1137 BC)

Moving to the tomb of *Ramesses VI* we find figures similar to those in the tomb of *Seti I*. Let's take a look at these individually.

The festival of the Hippopotamus goddess

The groups of hieroglyphic text in this image can be translated as follows:

| heb set | Hesamut [13] | | Serqit [14] |
|---|---|---|---|
| festival | Hippopotamus goddess | | Scorpion goddess |

**The festival of the Hippopotamus goddess.**   **The scorpion goddess.**

| Heru neter | Ra | nti | ami | seni [15] | sirsa [16] |
|---|---|---|---|---|---|
| Horus god | lion | who | is in | dual | a star god |

**The sun god who is in Leo & Centaurus**   **Hydra**

---

[13] Budge, *Egyptian Hieroglyphic Dictionary*, page 510B, *Hesamut*, Tomb of Seti I, the goddess of a constellation in the northern sky who appears in the form of a hippopotamus.

[14] Budge, *Egyptian Hieroglyphic Dictionary*, page 681B, *Serqit hetu*, Metternich Stele 23, Scorpion-Goddess.

[15] The scribe left out the letter. Compare to the spelling of in the tombs of *Senmut* and *Pedamenope*.

[16] Budge, *Egyptian Hieroglyphic Dictionary*, 647B, *Sirsa*, Thes. 129, a star god; var. (Thes. = Brugsch, *Thesaurus inscriptionum aegyptiacarum*)

# STARS IN THE TOMBS

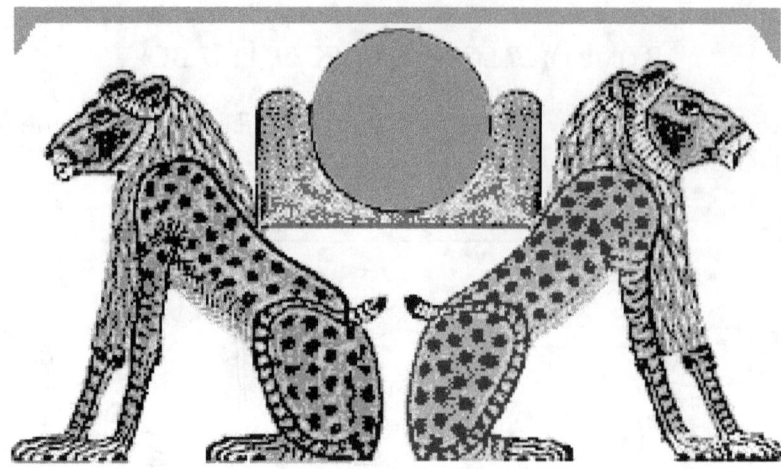

Horus, the sun god is the sun by day, and the double lion god by night, represented by the constellations of Leo and Centaurus. This is the mystery of the midnight sun, this meaning being a part of what was revealed in the mysteries, and *seeing of the sun at midnight*.[17]

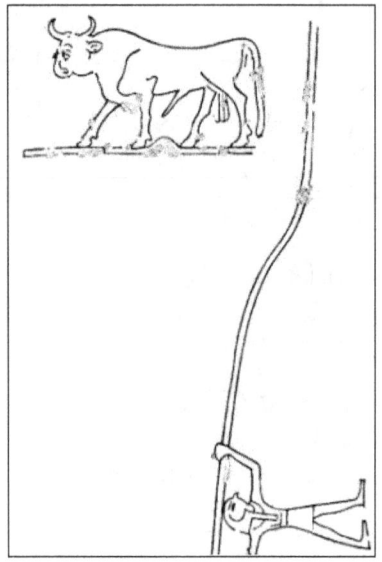

A bent stick is held by *An*
Taurus stands upon the scale pans.

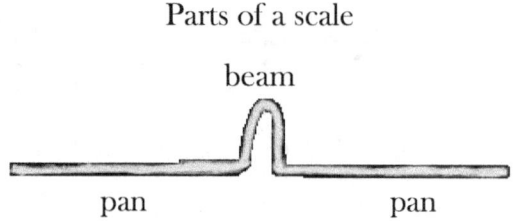

Parts of a scale

In this tomb, it appears that the scribe misunderstood the significance of the bent stick, and it was not given the shape of a bow.

---

[17] Knight, Richard Payne. *The symbolical language of ancient art and mythology*, page 96, paragraph 135 (1892). Translated into English by Alexander Wilder, M.D. [This book is Knight's attempt to correlate mythology with astronomy, and connects the appearance of the sun at night with star constellations.]

# Tomb of *Ramesses VI*

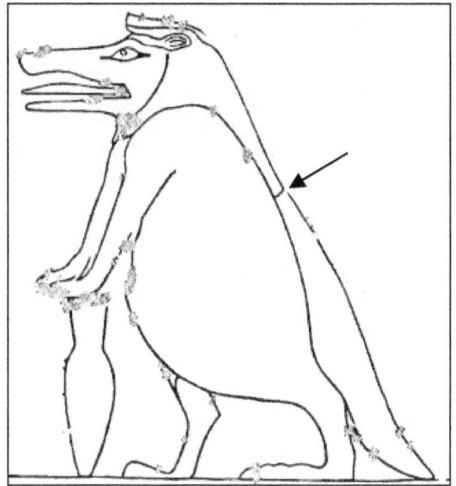 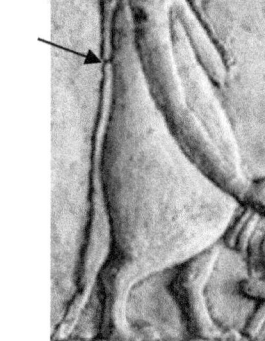

Tomb of *Ramesses VI*, KV9, 1137 BC        Temple of *Hathor*, 2501 BC

In both images above the tongue of the hippopotamus is prominently displayed, the hippopotamus rests against a vessel, and there is a distinct line where the head dress ends and the crocodile-like ridge of the tail begins. It is possible both images were made from the same source document, or the tomb of *Ramesses VI* may have been copied from the temple of *Hathor*.

---

[18] The two handled jug sits upon a three-legged stool.

## STARS IN THE TOMBS

### TOMB OF *SENMUT* (1483 BC)

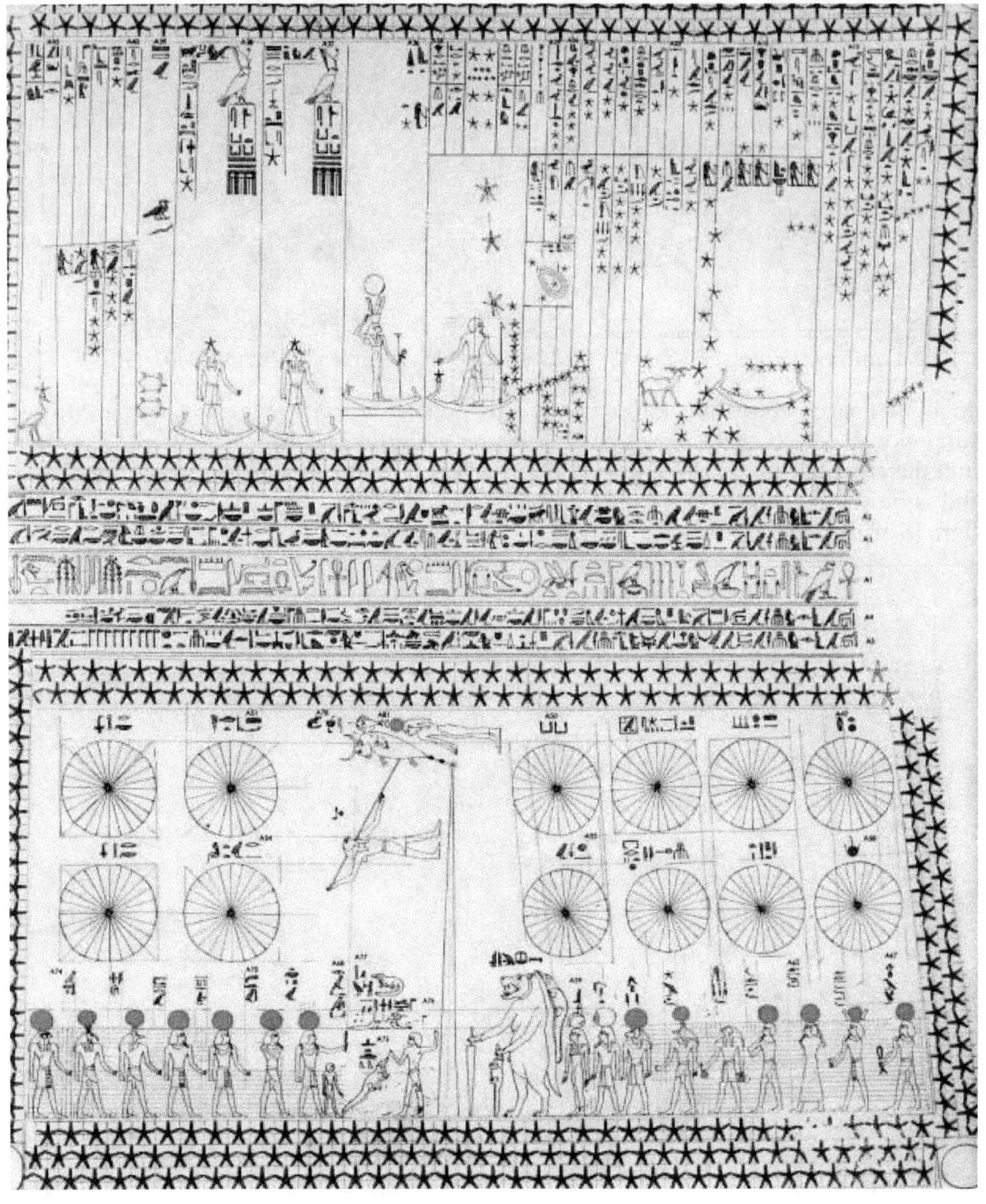

Below, we see Taurus, the bull, with Pleiades as the encircled tail star.[19] The goddess monitors the scales suspended from the Pleiades star cluster. The level position of her hands indicates the even position of the scale pans. The Egyptian word for the equinox was *Khekh*, which also meant balance or scales.[20]

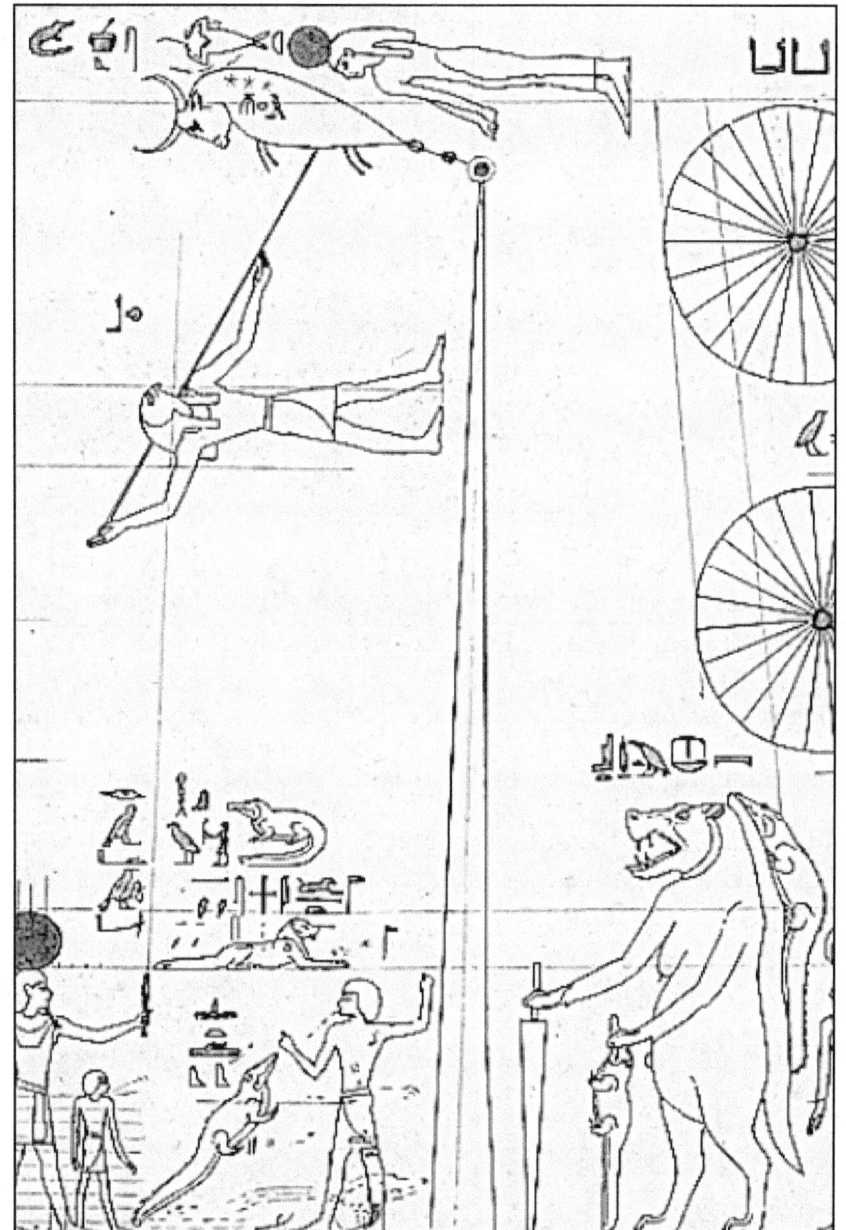

The Hippopotamus is standing on one side of the scales and the other gods are all on the opposite side to balance the level of the scales.

---

[19] Taurus is known for its bright stars Aldebaran, Elnath, and Alcyone, as well as for the variable star T Tauri. The constellation is probably best known for the Pleiades (Messier 45), also known as the Seven Sisters, and the Hyades, which are the two nearest open star clusters to Earth. https://www.constellation-guide.com/constellation-list/taurus-constellation/

[20] Massey, *The Natural Genesis*, volume 2, published in 1883, page 196.

Below is a star chart of Taurus and Eridanus with a circle surrounding Pleiades. We have added a line crossing Eridanus toward Taurus and a circle around Pleiades for the purpose of comparison. Beside it is imagery from the ceiling of the tomb of *Senmut*.

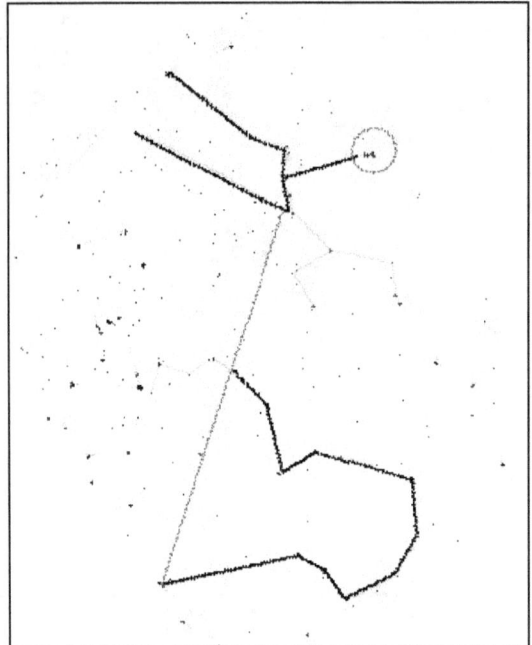 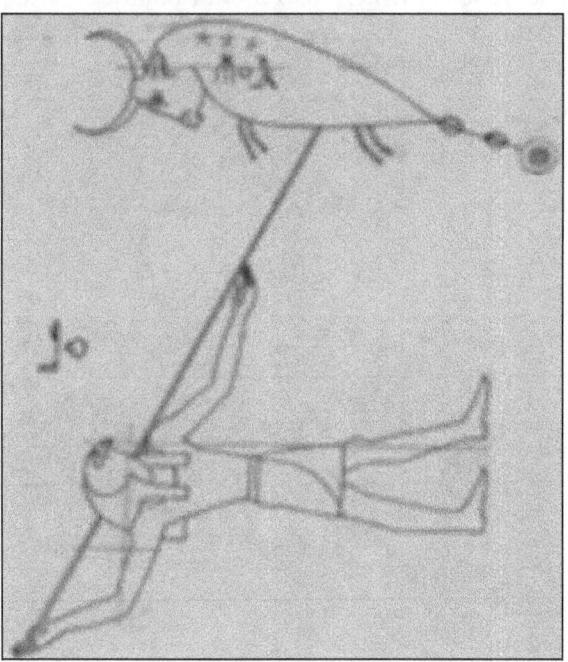

Taurus rises above the horizon pursued by Eridanus.

In Budge's *Hieroglyphic Dictionary* we can see that there is a similarity of the hieroglyphic spelling of the name of the god *An-her-t* ![glyphs],[21] and the illustration in *Senmut's* tomb, which also includes the image ![glyph], where the rod across Eridanus' shoulders (above right) resembles the slanted line crossing Eridanus and intersecting Taurus (above left).

---

[21] Budge, *Egyptian Hieroglyphic Dictionary*, 57A, *An-her-t*, ![glyphs].

## TOMB OF SENMUT

The Hieroglyphic text in the tomb of *Senmut* appears to form a statement when all of the text is considered collectively:

| saq | Serqit | Meskh-ti[22] | An-her-t[23] |
|---|---|---|---|
| to gather together | Scorpion goddess | Taurus | Eridanus |

The gathering. The Scorpion goddess, Taurus, Eridanus,

| heq | neter | ru | net | ami | seni[25] |
|---|---|---|---|---|---|
| power | god | lion | of | that which is in | dual |

and the power of the lion god which is in the dual.

| hetep-t | ta | qeq | s-tcha[26] | Mut | heb | pet |
|---|---|---|---|---|---|---|
| offering table | to set | to eat | to enjoy | mother goddess | festival | of the heaven |

The offering table is set to eat to enjoy the Mother Goddess festival of heaven.

---

[22] Budge, *Egyptian Hieroglyphic Dictionary*, 326A, Meskh-ti, Thes. 124ff, the Great Bear, depicted as a *bull-headed heart*, or a *bull-headed bull's haunch with seven stars*. [NOTE: Until now, Meskh-ti has been incorrectly identified as the Great Bear constellation, but the new information presented in *Secrets in the Stars of Ancient Egypt* prove that Meskh-ti indicates the constellation Taurus.]

[23] Budge, *Egyptian Hieroglyphic Dictionary*, 57A, An-her-t, Dêr al-Gab. 1, 18, , P.S.B. 7, 175, , Cairo Cat. 71, , , centre of whose cult was Abydos (This); Copt. ⲁⲛϩⲟⲩⲣⲉ, Gr. Ὀνοῦρις.

[24] Budge, *Egyptian Hieroglyphic Dictionary*, 512B, heq, heqa to rule, to govern, to direct, to guide, to reign; heq, heqi , rule, power.

[25] Budge, *Egyptian Hieroglyphic Dictionary*, 673B, seni, .

[26] Budge, *Egyptian Hieroglyphic Dictionary*, 716B, s-tchai , to be well, happy, amused, to enjoy oneself.

## STARS IN THE TOMBS

### TOMB OF *PEDAMENOPE* (CIRCA 26TH DYNASTY, 525 BC)

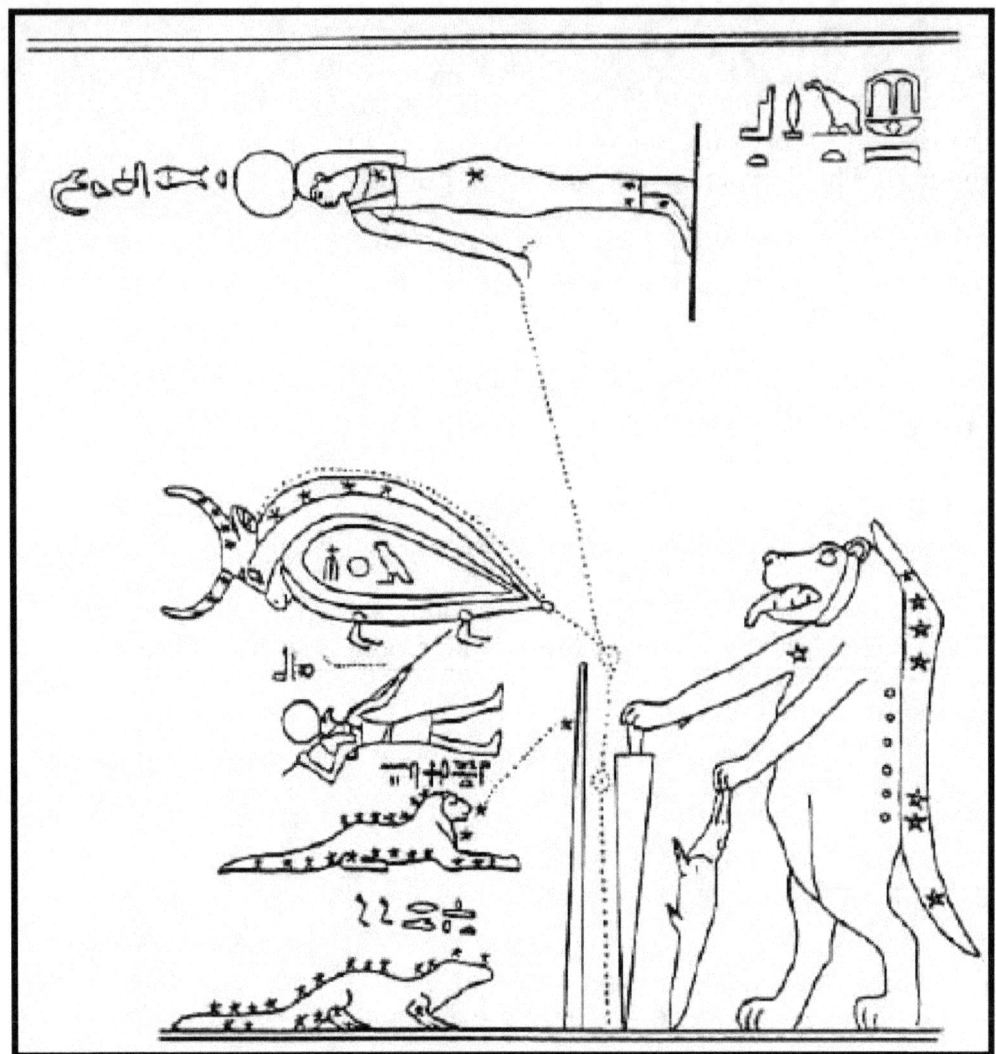

The theme of this drawing from the tomb of *Pedamenope* is *balance* (equinox). The goddess suspends the scales from a string of stars she holds in her hand. On one side of the scales is the hippopotamus. The combined weight of the other gods balances the scales against the weight of the heavy hippopotamus.

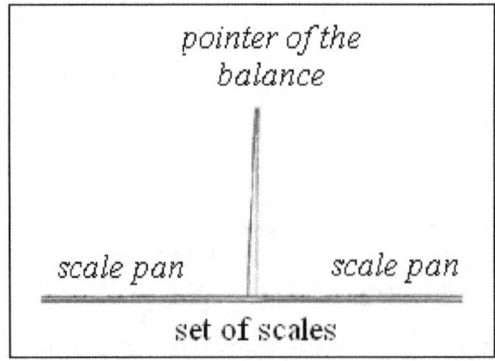

## TOMB OF PEDOMENOPE

The text reads:

| s-tcha²⁷ | Mut | heb | pet | saq | Serqit |
|---|---|---|---|---|---|
| to enjoy | mother goddess | festival | of the heaven | gather together | Scorpion goddess |

| Meskh-ti²⁸ | An-her-t ²⁹ |
|---|---|
| bull-headed haunch with seven stars | the god Onouris |

| neter | ru | neth | ami | seni ³⁰ | hotep | ret |
|---|---|---|---|---|---|---|
| god | lion | of | who are in | dual | rest | legs |

*Transliteration:* The gathering of Isis the scorpion goddess, Taurus, Eridanus, and one of the double lion gods (legs at rest), enjoy the Mother Goddess festival of heaven.

---

> The lion in each of these tombs is the constellation Leo, which taken together with the constellation Centaurus, forms the great double lion god constellation. Below is a list of references from these tombs that indicate these leonine constellations:
>
> Tomb of *Seti I* 1279 BC:
> "*Horus* which is in the lion stars."
>
> Tomb of *Ramesses VI*, KV9 1137 BC:
> "The lion god, which is of the dual".
>
> Tomb of *Senmut* 1483 BC:
> "Power of the lion god, which is in the dual".
>
> Tomb of *Pedamenope* circa 26ᵗʰ dynasty 525 BC:
> "The lion god who is in the dual"
>
> Ptolemaic Tomb at *Atfieh* circa 150 BC:
> "The leading lion of the sun god"

---

²⁷ Budge, *Egyptian Hieroglyphic Dictionary*, 716B, *s-tchai*, to be well, happy, amused, to enjoy oneself.

²⁸ Budge, *Egyptian Hieroglyphic Dictionary*, 326A, *Meskh-ti*, Thes. 124ff, the Great Bear, depicted as a *bull-headed heart*, or a *bull-headed bull's haunch with seven stars*. [Until now, *Meskh-ti* has been incorrectly identified as the Great Bear constellation, but the new information presented in *Secrets in the Stars of Ancient Egypt* prove that *Meskh-ti* indicates the constellation Taurus.]

²⁹ Budge, *Egyptian Hieroglyphic Dictionary*, 57A, *An-her-t*.

³⁰ Budge, *Egyptian Hieroglyphic Dictionary*, 673B, *sen* pronoun. Suffix 3ʳᵈ pers. plur., they, them, their; dual.

All of these statements bear a relationship to the illustration found in the fifth division of the ancient Egyptian book known as *Am Tuat*. In this image from the Am Tuat, *Horus* stands balanced upon a flying serpent between the double lion Gods. The leading lion is Leo on the right, the first of the double lion gods to rise in the sky. The lion on the left is Centaurus, the winged serpent is Hydra.

The oval of the horizon with a lion god at the East and the West

The Hippopotamus goddess balances a knife on the tip of its blade and balances a crocodile on the tip of its tail.

The text above the hippopotamus reads:

*s-tcha*[31]  *Mut*  *heb*  *pet*
to enjoy  the mother goddess  festival  of heaven

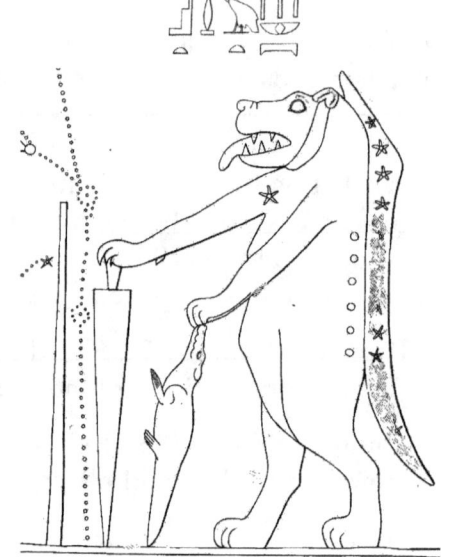

The text over the goddess reads:

*saq*  *Serqit*
to gather together  Scorpion goddess

---

[31] Budge, *Egyptian Hieroglyphic Dictionary*, page 716B, *s-tchai* , to be well, happy, amused, to enjoy oneself.

*Meskh-ti* is depicted as a bull-headed heart, or a bull-headed bull's haunch with seven stars.[32]

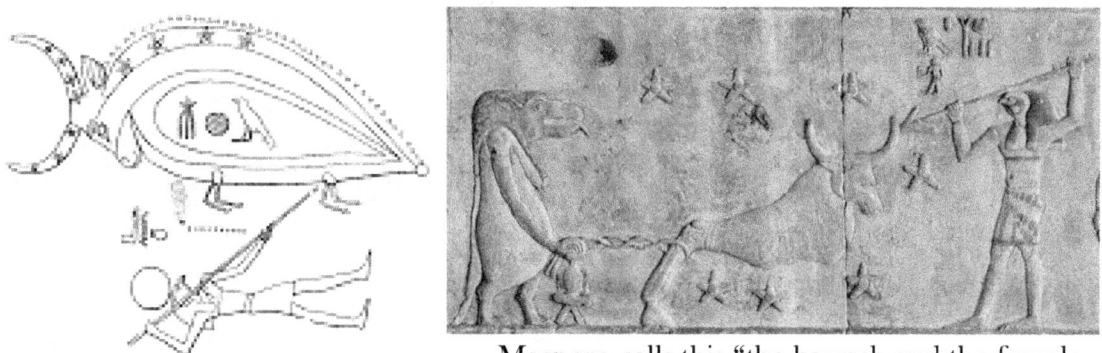

Maspero calls this "the haunch and the female hippopotamus" [33]

| *Meskh-ti* | *An-her-t* |
|---|---|
| Taurus | The god *Onouris* (Eridanus) |

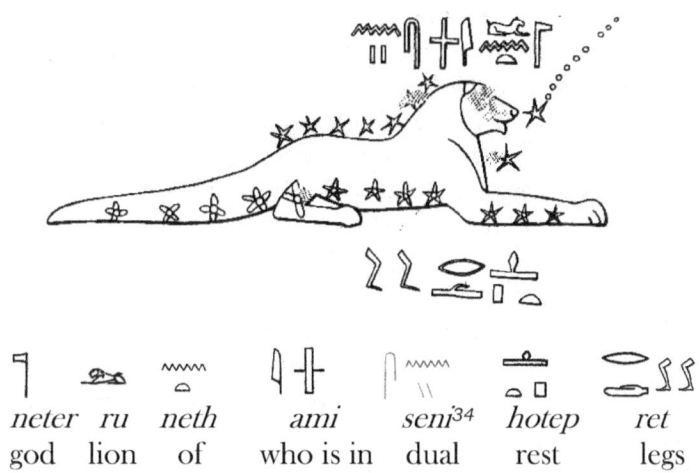

| neter | ru | neth | ami | seni[34] | hotep | ret |
|---|---|---|---|---|---|---|
| god | lion | of | who is in | dual | rest | legs |

The star image of the crocodile is surrounded by stars, but has no associated hieroglyphic text.

---

[32] Budge, *Egyptian Hieroglyphic Dictionary*, 326A, *Meskh-ti*
[33] This caption is from *The Dawn of Civilization* by Gaston Maspero, page 94.
[34] Budge, *Egyptian Hieroglyphic Dictionary*, 673B, sen ⌐⌐⌐, pronoun Suffix 3rd pers. plur., they, them, their; dual ⌐⌐

# STARS IN THE TOMBS

## PTOLEMAIC TOMB AT *ATFIEH* (CIRCA 150 BC)

This tomb probably dates from around the middle of the Ptolemaic era that lasted about 275 years, from 305 to 30 BC. Daressy's illustration and text is as follows: [35]

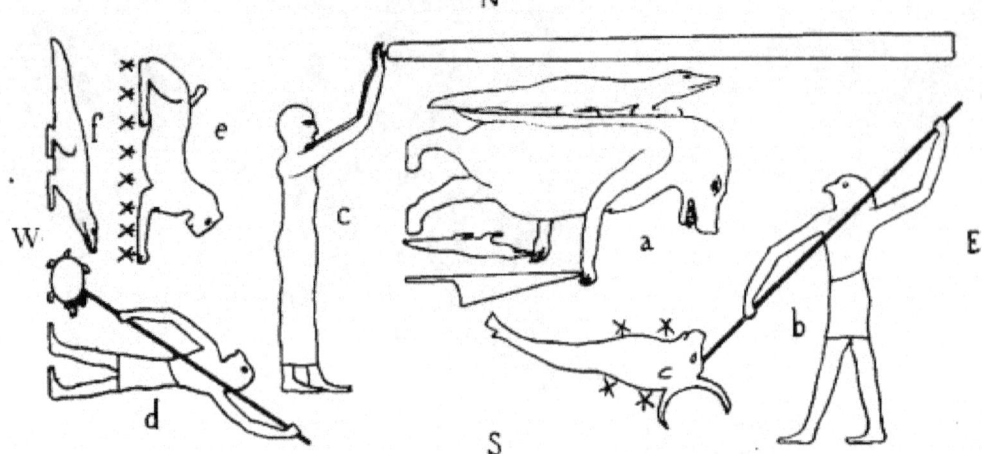

The relative arrangement of the characters can be indicated as follows:
  a. A *female hippo* standing on her feet, one hand placed on a *large knife*, the other on a small *crocodile* standing on its tail. A large *crocodile* is shown on the back of the *hippopotamus*. Above the head is inscribed the name ⬚ ⬚.
  b. *Horus with a hawk's head* placed at a right angle to the *hippopotamus*, piercing a *thigh ending in an ox's head* with its *lance*. Stars originally surrounded this figure but only four remain and the name has disappeared.
  c. A *standing goddess*, under the feet of the *hippopotamus*, facing east; the mutilated name is ⬚ (probably for ⬚) Her two arms raised in front of her lean against a *long, slightly triangular red band* which passes over the *hippopotamus* and goes to the eastern end of the painting.
  d. Towards the west a *hawk-headed Horus* turned towards the north, pierces a *turtle* with its lance.
  e. Facing this *Horus*, under the goddess *Selk*, is a *lion* lying on eight stars which is called ⬚ [36] star ( ᾽Αστήρ ) of Râ.
  f. In the northwest corner, below the *lion*, a large *crocodile* whose name is mutilated: ⬚

---

[35] Daressy, *Tombeau ptolémaïque à Atfieh. Annales du Service des Antiquités de l'Égypte,* 3, page 178.
  https://archive.org/details/annalesduservice03egypuoft

[36] We believe this should be read as:

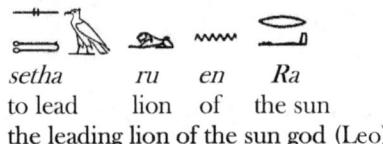

setha    ru    en    Ra
to lead  lion  of    the sun
the leading lion of the sun god (Leo)

Identification of the constellations represented by the figures in the tomb of *Atfieh*:
  a. *Hippopotamus* = Cetus
  b. *An* = Eridanus and Taurus
  c. *Goddess* = Gemini
  d. *Horus* with *pole* and the *tortoise* = position of Sun in Cancer[37]

To the Greeks, Cancer was initially represented by a turtle or tortoise. The modern symbol for Cancer represents the pinchers of a crab, but in the Egyptian records of about 2000 BC it was described as *Scarabaeus* (Scarab), the sacred emblem of immortality.[38] The images in this drawing represent star constellations: a-Cetus, b-Eridanus and Taurus, c-Gemini, d-Sun in Cancer, e-Leo, and f-Hydra. Letter d above indicates the Sun was in Cancer. This idea of the Sun in Cancer bears a distinct resemblance to the Zodiac of *Dendera*, not in form but in content. In other words they have the same meaning expressed differently.

Tomb at *Atfieh*          Temple of *Hathor*

 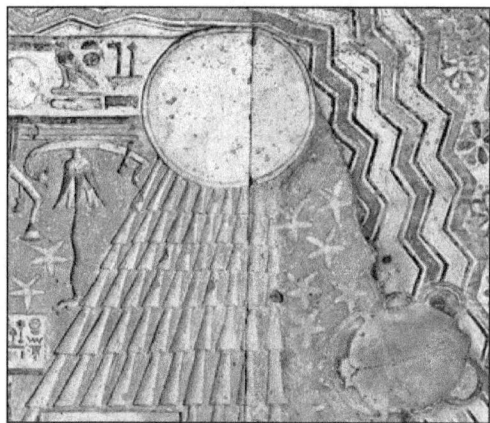

Both illustrations are of the Sun in Cancer on the Spring Equinox 2501 BC. On the left, hawk headed *Horus* the Sun holds a balancing pole resting on a tortoise which in Ptolemaic times represented the constellation Cancer. On the right, the sun is shown rising in the zodiac sign of Cancer, indicated by the scarab beetle (lower right side).

---

[37] instead of the usual figure of Orion/Osiris.
[38] Cancer the Crab - The historical background of the Zodiac Signs, https://en.wikipedia.org/wiki/Cancer_(constellation)

## BALANCE

In all of these tombs we have observed that they represent the balance of the equinox when day and night were of equal length. In these various tomb illustrations we saw a god holding a pole. A balancing pole may be as long as 12 meters (39 feet) [39] The pole also helps balance the tightrope walker[40] by lowering the center of gravity.[41] The feat of walking on a stretched rope dates back to the Greeks and Romans, and even beyond, to the ancient Egyptians. [42]

*An-her-t* [43]

The examples above express the idea of balance, which makes sense when we consider that the dates, according to the positions of the stars in the illustrations in these tombs, coincide with the equinox (which comes from the Latin words *aequus nox* or equal night).

The drawing on the facing page shows the sky goddess on the ceiling of the temple of *Hathor* at *Dendera*. The right half of the drawing shows the positions of the constellations and the Moon at different hours during 2501 BC. The left half shows the Sun in Cancer just before sunrise, where we see Gemini, Taurus, the Moon in Pisces, and Aquarius on the spring equinox of 2501 BC, illustrated on the following page.

---

[39] Tight Rope Walker – Daryl Science http://www.darylscience.com/Demos/TightRope.html
[40] Funambulist.
[41] https://www.mansfieldct.org/Schools/MMS/staff/hand/lawstightrope.htm
[42] Willoughby, *Super-athletes*, page 320.
[43] Budge, *Egyptian Hieroglyphic Dictionary*, page 57A, *An-her-t*.

# BALANCE

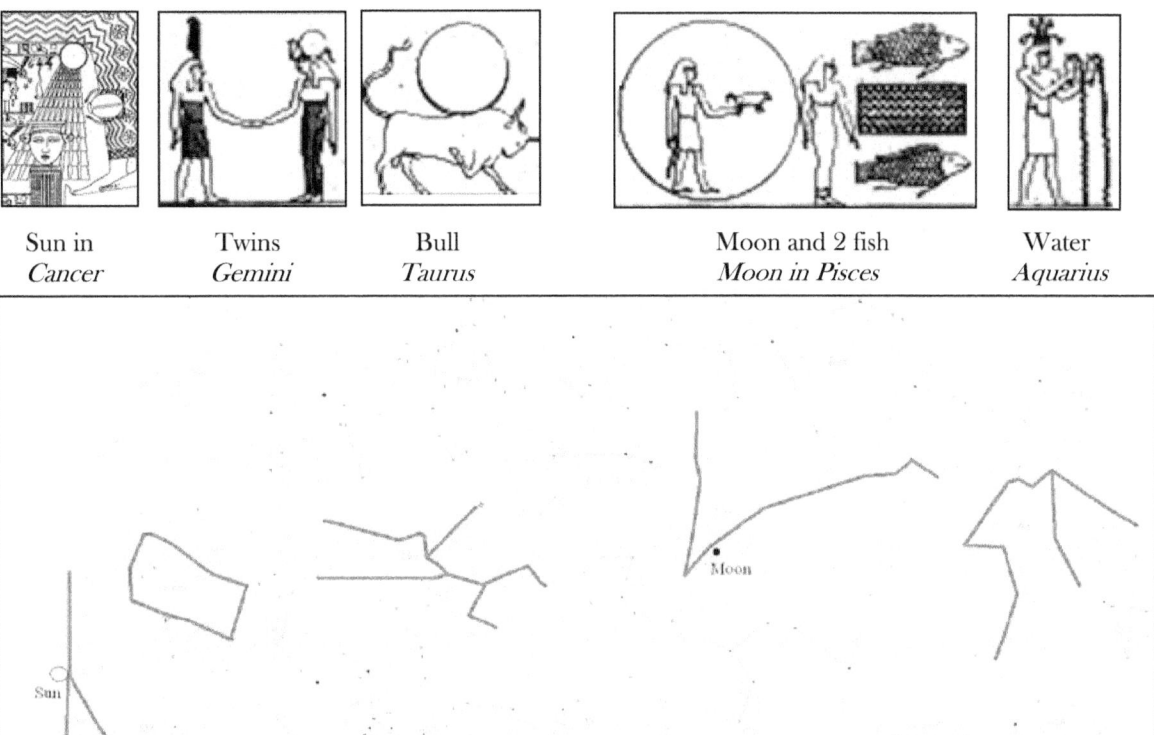

| Sun in<br>*Cancer* | Twins<br>*Gemini* | Bull<br>*Taurus* | Moon and 2 fish<br>*Moon in Pisces* | Water<br>*Aquarius* |

The presence of the temple of *Hathor* in this imagery may indicate that it existed at the time of this equinox in 2501 BC.

The sun shining on the temple of *Hathor* on the spring equinox of 2501 BC.

The face of *Hathor* identifies this structure as her temple.

# PART II – THE CALENDAR

# The Calendar

## The Calendar and the Stars

The ancient Egyptians were very good astronomers and that means they had a solid understanding of mathematics and an accurate calendar. They knew exactly how much time elapsed in one year. We can see by the positions of the constellations they drew that they possessed an accurate understanding of astronomy that matches our contemporary Skyglobe computer simulations over thousands of years. With the continued invasions and conquests of Egypt by foreign powers, their extensive astronomical knowledge was destroyed and forgotten. A few of the ancient texts were preserved in tombs. These times were the Dark Ages, when the accuracy of ancient astronomy and the calendar were forgotten. Records in tombs testify to the accuracy of the ancient Egyptian astronomy from the equinox of 10,390 BC to the equinox of 1279 BC.

Here's something! We are using Skyglobe computer program to see the positions of the stars over long periods of time to compare the consistency of the astronomical information from different tombs. These are three examples where the dating can be found by using the positions of the stars recorded by the ancient Egyptians:

- In the tomb of *Ramesses VI*, if we consider the images of the double sphinxes and the flying serpent with a head at its tail[44] as representing star constellations, we come up with the date of September, 21, 10,390 BC at 4:45 AM on the autumnal equinox.
- If we consider the positions of the stars on the zodiac ceiling of *Hathor* at *Dendera* during the second and third hours of the night we find the date is September 21st, 2501 BC for the autumnal equinox, which was 7,889 years later.
- And if we consider the stars 1,222 years later from the tomb of *Seti I*, we find the date to be September 21st, 1279 BC at 2:43 AM.

The ancient Egyptian astronomy matches our computerized astronomical program over a period of 9,111 years. But then something happened that changed things. It may have been that Egypt was repeatedly conquered by a variety of foreign powers that attempted to replace indigenous science and religion. During the reign of *Ramesses III* from 1186 to 1155 BC, for example, there was a decline of Egyptian political and economic power linked to a series of invasions and internal economic problems.[45] Evidently some things were forgotten and the calendar became inaccurate. After Rome invaded Egypt, in 247 BC, Ptolemy III reintroduced leap year into the calendar at the behest of the priesthood, by adding one day every four years to adjust the calendar. [46]

---

[44] The head at the tail represents Venus.
[45] https://en.wikipedia.org/wiki/Ramesses_III
[46] Budge, E. A. W. (1904). *The decree of Canopus*. London: Kegan Paul, page 29.

# THE CALENDAR

## Length of the Year

It has often been stated that the ancient Egyptians first thought there were 360 days in a year, but later realized their error and added 5 additional days. This seems to be a common misconception. But if it were true, their astronomy would not exactly match our computer generated astronomy program for more than ninety centuries, from 10,390 BC to 1279 BC.

There was never a time when the year was believed to be only 360 days.[47] We believe that the confusion of the importance of the number 360 has to do with the number of degrees in a circle. The number 365 is, of course, the number of whole days in a year. Further, we believe that since the sacred science of astronomy was by far the most important branch of science to the ancient Egyptians, it was correlated by and through their religious mythology and it was for this reason, in our opinion, that five days of the year were set aside for the end of the year festival, leaving the remainder of 360 days to be set aside to signify the number of degrees in a circle. So we followed this reasoning to see where it would take us in reconciling 360 with 365. Even though we had an idea of their relationship, we needed more facts. This meant we needed to delve into the past. This seems like an appropriate time to introduce some of the history concerning the background of the 360-day year and the 365-day year.

Plutarch, who lived from 46 AD to 119 AD, recorded an Egyptian fable using Greek names for some of the Egyptian gods and goddesses:

> "The Sun, having discovered the infidelity of his wife Rhea, prevented her by a curse from bringing forth her offspring on any of the 360 days of the year; but that Hermes, playing at dice with the Moon, won five additional days, on which Osiris and his brothers and sisters were born."[48]

In 1838, Edward Hincks wrote of Plutarch's 360 day year:

> "Such is the only ancient authority in existence for a year of 360 days having ever been in use; and it is evident that this authority, by throwing back the disuse of that year to the mythological epoch of the birth of Osiris, does in fact negative the supposition that a year of 360 days was ever used in the times of real history." [49]

In 1882 Adolf Erman writes:

> "Ed. Meyer draws my attention to the fact that such calculations are based on a fictitious year of 360 days. So one need not see here a reminder of an earlier division of time." [50]

---

[47] Erman, Adolph. *Zeitschrift*, page 172, footnote 1.
[48] Hincks. "On the Years and Cycles used by the Ancient Egyptians," vol. 18, part 2, of the *Transactions of the Royal Irish Academy*, page 157.
[49] Hincks. "On the Years and Cycles used by the Ancient Egyptians," vol. 18, part 2, of the *Transactions of the Royal Irish Academy*, page 157.
[50] Erman, Adolph. *Zeitschrift*, page 172, footnote 1.

# The Length of the Year

In 1890, James Frazier recounted Plutarch's story, using for the most part names of Egyptian gods:

> "Osiris was the offspring of an intrigue between the earth-god Seb (Keb or Geb, as the name is sometimes transliterated) and the sky-goddess Nut. The Greeks identified his parents with their own deities Cronus and Rhea. When the sun-god Ra perceived that his wife Nut had been unfaithful to him, he declared with a curse that she should be delivered of the child in no month and no year. But the goddess had another lover, the god Thoth or Hermes, as the Greeks called him, and he playing at draughts with the moon won from her a seventy-second part of every day, and having compounded five whole days out of these parts he added them to the Egyptian year of three hundred and sixty days. This was the mythical origin of the five supplementary days which the Egyptians annually inserted at the end of every year in order to establish a harmony between lunar and solar time." On these five days, regarded as outside the year of twelve months, the curse of the sun-god did not rest, and accordingly Osiris was born on the first of them."[51]

In 1904 Eduard Meyer published *Aegyptische Chronologie*, in which he wrote,
> "The twelve equally long months of 30 days, however, are inseparable from the five epagomens; both can only have arisen at the same time. A year of 360 days has of course always had a magical attraction on amateurs and will continue to do so in the future - belief in it is actually the touchstone of dilettantism in chronology-; but historically it has never existed"[52]

## The Epagomens

So what are the *epagomens*? The Greek word from which this word is derived is επαγόμενη and this is spelled *epagómeni* [53] using the English alphabet. The translation of επαγόμενη is "*induced*", a form of the word *induce,* which means *to bring about* or *give rise to.* So επαγόμενη applied to the 5 days outside the year means the days that gave rise to or brought about the new year.

But why was there so much confusion with the calendar and the numbers 360 and 365? Obviously the ancient Egyptians knew there were 365 days in a year, and they also knew there were 360 degrees in a circle.

One year ≈ 365 days[54]
One yearly cycle ≈ 360 degrees

---

[51] Frazer, *The Golden Bough*, Chapter 38: The Myth of Osiris
  https://en.wikisource.org/wiki/The_Golden_Bough/The_Myth_of_Osiris
[52] Meyer, Edouard, *Aegyptische Chronologie*, 1904, page 10 (translated to English).
[53] Επαγόμενη = induced
  Επαγόμ = induction
[54] The symbol ≈ means approximately equal.

# THE CALENDAR

To the astronomer a circle of the year was measured as 360 degrees. But to agriculturists the circle of a year was measured as 365 days. So the number of parts (*days*) in the circle of a year was 5 more than the number of parts (*degrees*) in a circle: 360 + 5.

This is translated from *Egyptian Chronology*, by Eduard Meyer, 1904, page 8:

> How strongly Egyptians felt the anomaly of these additional days can still be seen clearly. They are called [hieroglyphs] or [hieroglyphs] or [hieroglyphs], later also [hieroglyphs] (among others) written, dua hriu ronpet "the five that are on the year", ΑΙ ΠΕΝΤΕ ΑΙ ἘΠΑΓΌΜΕΝΑΙ; i.e. they stand outside the month as well as outside the year as a group of days that is attached to the year (or more precisely "superimposed"). Therefore the "final day of the year" celebrated as a feast day [hieroglyphs] is not the 5th Epagomene, but the 30th Mesori; and in the calendar of Medinet Habu, Ramses II and Ramses III, who copied it, calculate the daily offerings [hieroglyphs] to be delivered to the Temple of Amon by multiplying by 365 "for the year and the 5 days" [hieroglyphs] — strictly speaking, the "5 days" do not belong to the year, as this only consists of the 12 months. Thus, the formula "well, a temple day is 1/360 of the year" that is repeated in the contracts from the tomb of Hapzefa will be even easier to understand than I thought earlier.[55]

This merits attention. In astronomy, a circle was 360 degrees. The circle of the year was also 360 degrees, but it was comprised of 365 days. When we calculate $1/360$ of the year, we are calculating the $360^{th}$ part of one temple year and 5 days [hieroglyphs]. So we decided to divide a year of 365 days into 360 parts and we got this: $365/360 = 1.01388888889$, or $1^1/_{72}$, which is one temple day. We thought of it this way: to the priests, who were astronomers, a year was measured in degrees, but to the farmers and everyone else besides the astronomers, a year was measured in days. One year was 360 degrees in one perspective (not days), and 365 days (not degrees) in another perspective. When we calculated the proportion of days to degrees, the answer we got was $1^1/_{72}$ days per degree. This fractional day of $1/_{72}$, reminded us of the Greek fable as told by Plutarch during the $1^{st}$ century A.D[56]: *Thoth gambled with the Moon for $1/_{72}$ of its light ($360/_{72} = 5$), or 5 days, and won. During these 5 days, Nut and Geb gave birth to Osiris, Set, Isis, and Nephthys.*

This gave us confidence that we were on the correct path, because this Egyptian myth contained the fraction 1/72 and connected it with 5 days and connected it with the time of the birth of the 5 gods. We had also previously learned from our computer astronomy program that during the last night of the year at sunset, Orion (*Osiris*) was the first constellation to arise. This happened on the eve of the autumnal equinox, September

---

[55] Meyer, *Aegyptische Chronologie*, pages 8-9.
[56] Plutarch lived from 46 AD to 119 AD

# The Length of the Year

20th in 10,390 BC. Orion (*Osiris*) was followed by the Gemini (Twin Goddesses of Truth: *Isis* and *Nephthys*), Hydra (*Set*) was next, followed by the Sun (*Horus*). Thus we see that the gods were all star constellations "born" on the same day.

There is another curious text left us in the town of *Si'ut* (modern *Asyut*) in the tomb of *Hepzefa* (*Hptfaä*), a large rock grave from the Middle Kingdom of Egypt exhibiting a writing style that suggests it is older than the 13th dynasty: [57]

This translates to:

| renp-t | heru | heru tui | gerh | en | renpit |
|---|---|---|---|---|---|
| year | who are over | days five | night | of | opening of the year |

5 days that are over the year 5 days on the night of New Year's Eve

[NOTE: In the above translation indicates a year of 365 days (year + 5).]

It seems repetitious to say: , and then to say , which together would be "5 days over the year 5 days." Then, considering the remainder of this phrase , which means "night of new year's eve," it makes even less sense: "5 days over the year 5 days on the night of new year's eve."

We must consider that these hieroglyphs were not only thousands of years old, but the tomb environment was less than ideal for making copies. Adolf Erman tells us:

> "Unfortunately, copying these 64 lines is difficult to accomplish. The preservation is so sad that in many places it is necessary to look closely in order to find traces of the hieroglyphics at all; the room of the grave is also very dark. Whoever does not make up his mind to stand on a high ladder to illuminate and examine each sign individually will achieve nothing here, and even with such a procedure a large part of the signs remains questionable."[59]

---

[57] Erman, *Zeitschrift für Ageyptische Sprache* (Magazine for Egyptian Language), 1882, "Zehn Verträge aus dem mittleren Reich" (Ten Contracts from the Middle Kingdom), page 161: *"They are usually all placed in Dyn. XIII, probably only because the Ra-ka-mri king of tomb No. 4 is equated with the Ra-Mr-kau of the royal line of Karnak. I don't want to contradict this, but I notice that the texts of tomb I seem to me to be somewhat more ancient in orthography than the inscriptions of Benihassan."*

[58] Brugsch, *Thesaurus*, page 482.

[59] Erman, *Zeitschrift*, page 160.

# THE CALENDAR

With this in mind, there is another Egyptian symbol that closely resembles ⊙ that should be considered; it is this symbol for 'time' ⊛.⁶⁰ When it is written like this ⊛|| it means two times. When it is written like this ⊛|||| it means 4 times.⁶¹ So five times would be ⊛||||. In a dark environment, standing on a ladder with poor lighting, looking at deteriorated hieroglyphs that are thousands of years old, it might be quite easy to mistake ⊛|||| as ⊙||||. We found that if this were true and we used it in the phrase in question, it would look like this:

*Renp-t heriu*      *sepu*    *gerh*   *en* ⁶²    *up-t renpit*
Those who are over the year   five time's   night   of   New Year's Eve
**Those who are over the year five times on the night of New Year's Eve,**

*maa*    *pa*⁶³   *shen*     *tche-ti* ⁶⁴
to see   to fly   to go round   the "two children," ⁶⁵
see *Shu* and *Tefnut* fly and go round.⁶⁶

So now we consider that this ancient Egyptian celebration of the *Birth of the Gods over the Year* commemorated the completion of Giza and the sealing of the Hall of Records, and inaugurated the first New Year's Eve, the night of the beginning of the first year, on Saturday, September 20, 10,390 BC. For more information on this please refer to the introduction of our book *The Coffin Texts Resurrected*, volume I.

Next we will look at the birth of the five gods on the first New Year's Eve celebration and look at a series of five illustrations that support the foregoing translation.

---

60 In Budge's *Egyptian Hieroglyphic Dictionary*, Volume 1, page cxxiv, A List of Hieroglypnic Characters, XII, Heaven, Earth, Water, numbers 8,9 ⊙, O were used to mean the sun, the Sun-god, Ra, day, period, time in general. We also find In Budge's *Egyptian Hieroglyphic Dictionary*, Volume 2, page 595A, that ⊛ and ⊚ were also used to mean time. I say this because the tomb of *Hepzefa* was dark and the hieroglyphs were thousands of years old. The men who copied the text stood on ladders and worked under poor lighting conditions. With these contingencies in mind, it seems quite possible that ⊛ may have been ⊙. Nevertheless, both could mean time, and so ⊛≡ or ⊙≡ could be correct.

61 Budge, *A Hieroglyphic Vocabulary to the Book of the Dead*, page 341.
62 Budge, *A Hieroglyphic Vocabulary to the Book of the Dead*, page 191.
63 Budge, *Egyptian Language*, List of Signs, page 66, sign no. 73, **to fly**.
64 Budge, *Egyptian Hieroglyphic Dictionary*, 893A, *tche-ti*.
65 Naville, *La litanie du soleil*, Plates, Seti 1st, Litanie 61, i.e., *Shu* & *Tefnut* [Leo & Centaurus]
66 See image #5 on page 48 for illustration.

# THE LENGTH OF THE YEAR

## The Birth of the Five Gods

These are the five gods who were rising on New Year's Eve.

    1. Birth of *Osiris* at sunset                       7:00 PM
    2. Birth of *Isis*                                        7:30 PM
    3. Birth of *Nephthys*                            8:00 PM
    4. Birth of *Set*                                       11:00 PM
    5. Birth of *Horus* – *Shu* & *Tefnut* go round    5:05 AM

On the eve of the autumnal equinox, *Osiris* was the first to begin his appearance above the horizon. *Isis*, *Nephthys*, and *Set* followed.

### 1. Birth of *Osiris* at sunset 7:00 PM

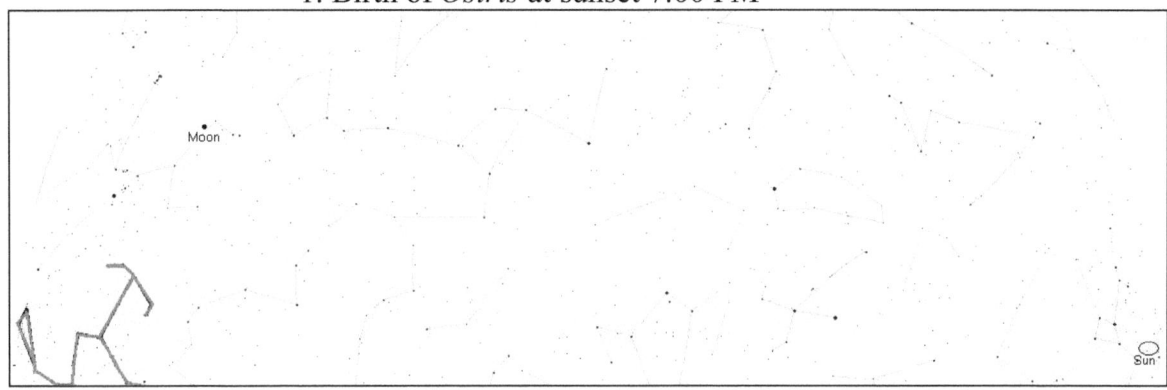

### 2. Birth of *Isis*     7:30 PM

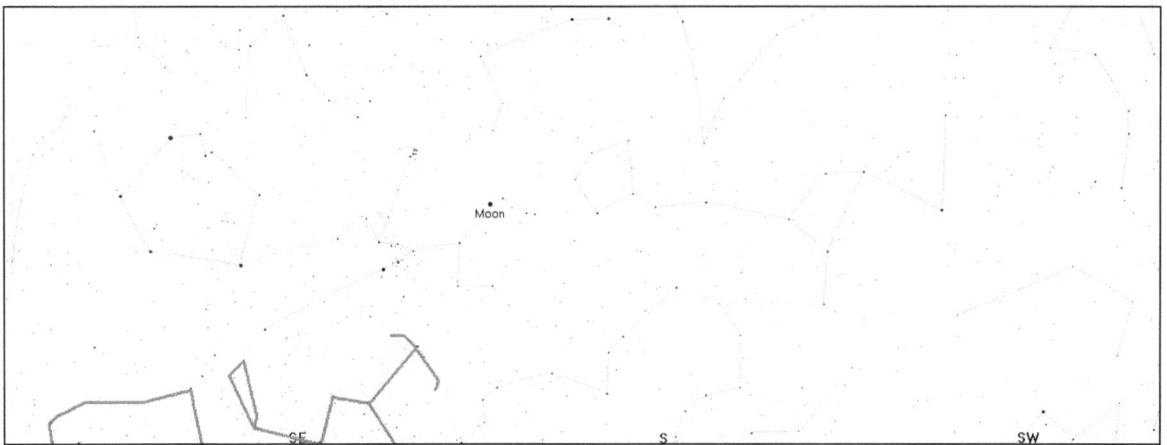

48

# THE CALENDAR

### 3. Birth of *Nephthys*  8:00 PM

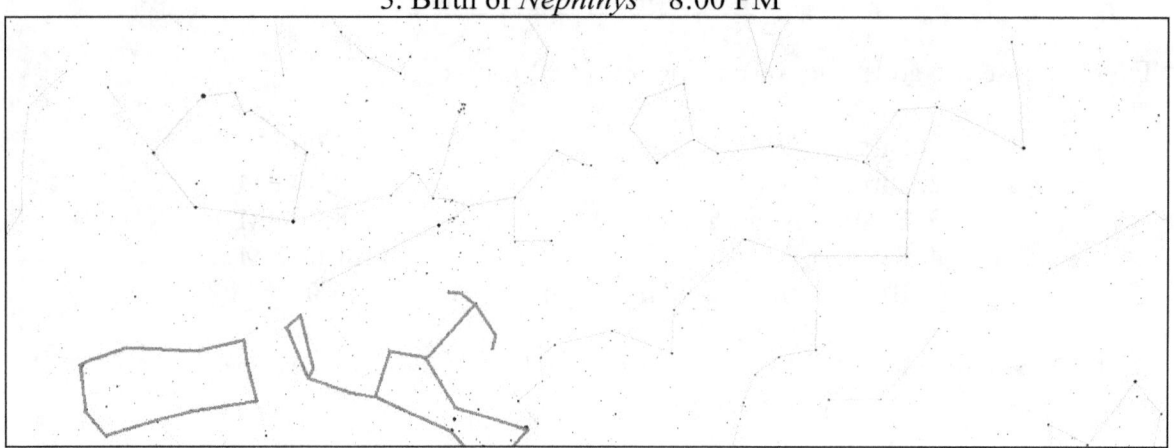

### 4. Birth of *Set*  11:00 PM

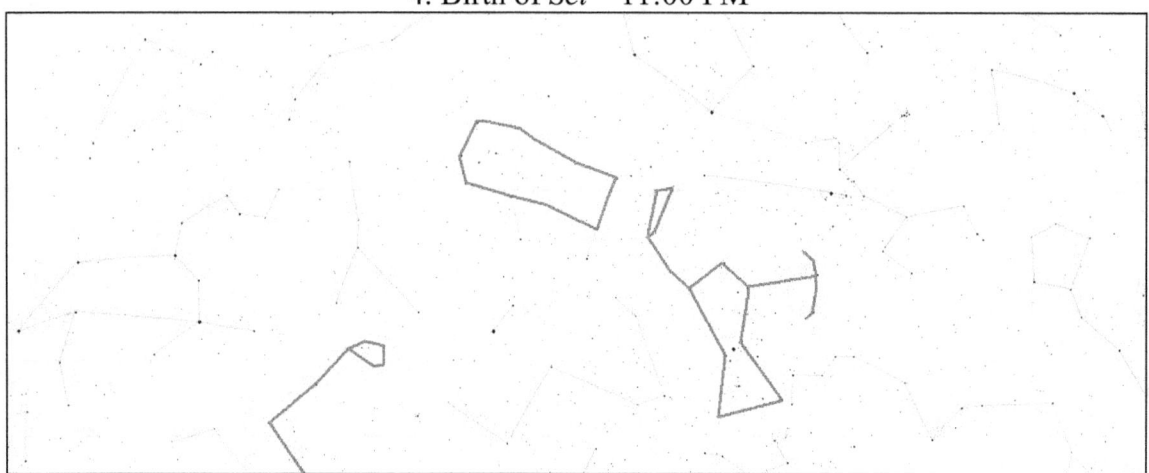

### 5. Birth of *Horus – Shu & Tefnut* go round 5:05 AM

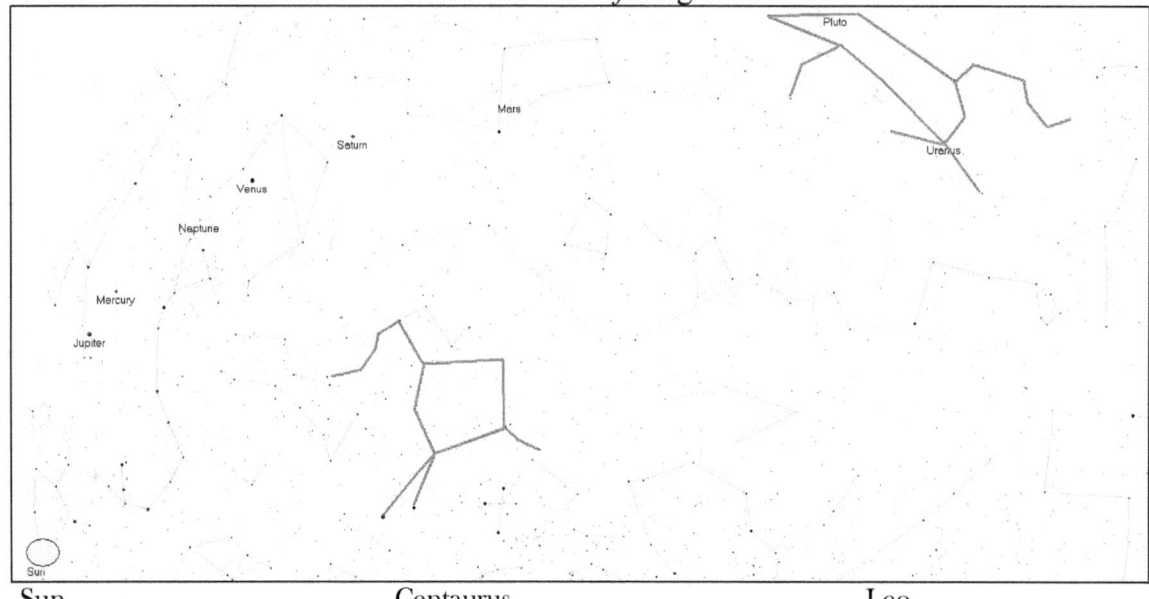

| Sun | Centaurus | Leo |
| *Horus* | *Tefnut* | *Shu* |

# The Tomb of *Hepzefa*

The gods included in the previous star charts are:
- *Osiris* - Orion
- *Isis and Nephthys* - Gemini, the twin goddesses of truth
- *Set* - Hydra, the god of evil
- *Horus* – the Sun
- *Shu* and *Tefnut* – Leo and Centaurus

The text from the grave of *Hepzefa* reads:
> With the appearance of a heavenly body above, to kindle a sacred fire, to conduct before the god of the year the five who are over the year five times on the night of New Year's eve, and to see Shu and Tefnut fly to go round.

*Shu* and *Tefnut* were the twin lion gods. The last line from the above text, "**See Shu and Tefnut fly to go round,**" really lets you know that the text is talking about star constellations and may help convince you of the ideas presented in this book.

## The Tomb of *Hepzefa*

Three places we have found information about the text from the tomb of *Hepzefa* are from Reisner, Breasted, and Erman. Below are complete references of these three sources.

It appears that Adolf Erman was the first to publish the hieroglyphic text and commentary in 1882. Then in 1906 James Henry Breasted wrote about this same text but did not show any hieroglyphic text. Later, 1n 1917 George Reisner wrote about the same text using his own words in giving his translation. To us it seems that both Breasted and Reisner relied upon Erman's work.

### James Henry Breasted Version (1906) [67]

[ ] = words so enclosed are uncertain in meaning: that is translation is not above question.[68]
( ) = numbers in parentheses indicate the line from the original document

## V. FIFTH CONTRACT

*Title*

559. (296) Contract, which the count, the superior prophet, *Hepzefi*, triumphant, made with the [keeper of the wardrobe] of the temple, concerning :

*What Hepzefi Receives*

560. Three [wicks] with which the fire is kindled for the god.

---

[67] Breasted, *Ancient records of Egypt*, volume I, page 265-266: The Contracts of *Hepzefi*, Twelfth Dynasty, reign of *Sesostris I*.
[68] Breasted, *Ancient records of Egypt*, page xlii.

*What He Pays*

561. While he (the count) has given to him (the keeper) for it: 3 temple-days. Now, these 3 temple-days shall be due to every future [keeper of the wardrobe], because (297) these 3 [wicks] are due to him (the count).

*Disposition of Wicks*

562. 1. Lo, he spake to him, saying: "One of them shall be given to my mortuary priest, when he goes forth, kindling the fire with it for the god, on the fifth of the 5 intercalary days, New Year's night[69], by the [keeper of the wardrobe]. He shall deliver it (298) to my mortuary priest after he does that which he does with it in the temple."

563. 2. "He shall give another on New Year's Day, in the morning, when the house makes gifts to its lord, when the lay priests of the temple give to me this white bread, which they give to me per individual priest (w'b), on New Year's Day. It shall be due (299) from my mortuary priest at my glorification."

564. 3. "He shall give another in the first month of the first season on the eighteenth day, the day of the Wag-feast, at the same time with the white bread, which they give to me per individual priest (w'b). This [wick] shall be due from my mortuary priest when glorifying me, together with the lay priests."

Lo, he said to him:

*Definition of "Temple-Day"*

565. (300) "Behold, as for a temple-day, it is 1/360 of a year.[70] When ye[71] therefore divide everything that comes into the temple, consisting of bread, beer, and everything for each day, that which makes 1/360 of the bread, of the beer, and of everything which comes into this temple, is the unit in these temple-days which I have given (301) to thee. Behold, it is my property, of my paternal estate, but not of the count's estate."

*Future Validity of Agreement*

566. "Now, these 3 temple-days shall belong to every future [keeper of the wardrobe,] because these 3 [wicks] are due to him, which thou hast given to me for these 3 temple-days, which I have given to thee."

*Conclusion*

567. Lo, he was satisfied with it.

---

[69] Really the evening before New Year's Day

[70] "A temple day is 1/360 of a year" = 365/360 days = 1 1/72 days.

[71] Although speaking to the keeper of the wardrobe, as the conclusion (1. **301**) shows.

# The Tomb of Hepzefa

## George A Reisner Version (1917) [72]

The ten contracts have been translated and discussed by Prof. Erman[73], as well as by Prof. Breasted[74]. For convenience sake, I give the translation in my own wording, with a few departures from the earlier versions. I have to thank Dr. Gardiner for a series of notes which I have used in the translation.

### Contract V (ll. 296—301).

Contract which (a) the nomarch, the chief priest, *Hepzefa*, true of voice, made with (b) the wardrobe-keeper (*šndwty*) of the temple (of Wepwat),

(1) for three wicks with which the lamp (? torch) is to be lighted for the god.

(2) That which he (*Hepzefa*) gave to him (the *šndwty*) in return was three temple days. Now these three temple days shall be due to every future wardrobe- keeper (?) because these wicks are to be due to him (*Hepzefa*).

(3) And he spoke, saying: One of them (the wicks) shall be given to my *ka*-priest when he goes forth at the lighting of the lamp (? torch) with it for the god

(c) on the fifth intercalary day, the eve of the New Year. As for the wardrobe-keeper (?), he shall hand it (the wick) to my ka-priest after he has done that which he has to do with it in the temple.

He shall give another

(c) on New Year's day in the early dawn (*diw*), when the house is given to its lord after the hour-priests of the temple have given me this white bread which they are to give to me individually on New Year's day. It shall be issued through my ka-priest at my glorification (i.e., given to him and used by him).

He shall give another

(c) on the 18th day of the first month of the first season, the day of the wa'g-festival, at the same time as the white bread which the individual wa'b-priests give to me. This wick shall be issued through my *ka*-priest at my glorification (attended) by the hour-priests of the temple.

And he (*Hepzefa*) said to him : See, as for a temple day, it is 1 /360th of a year. Ye shall divide all the daily rations which enter the temple, (consisting) of bread, beer and everything ; for a daily ration is reckoned at 1 /360th of the bread, beer, and every thing which enters the temple, for each of these temple days which I have given to thee.

(d) See, it is my personal property from the estate of my father, not from the estate of the nomarch.

Now these three temple days shall pass to every future wardrobe-keeper (?) because to him (*Hepzefa*) are to be due these wicks which thou hast conveyed to me on account of these three temple days which I have conveyed to thee .

(4) And he was satisfied therewith.

---

[72] Egypt Exploration Fund, *The Journal of Egyptian Archaeology*, Volume IV, 1917. Reprinted from *The Journal Of Egyptian Archaeology*, volume 1, part Ii, April 1918 (Issued November 1918). "The Tomb Of *Hepzefa*, Nomarch Of Siût," page 85, by Professor George A. Reisner

[73] Zeitschrift für ägyptische Sprache, vol. xx (1882) , pp . 159 ff.; Life in Ancient Egypt, pp. 145 ff.

[74] Breasted, *Ancient Records of Egypt*, vol. 1, pp. 258–271.

## THE CALENDAR

### Adolf Erman Version (1882)

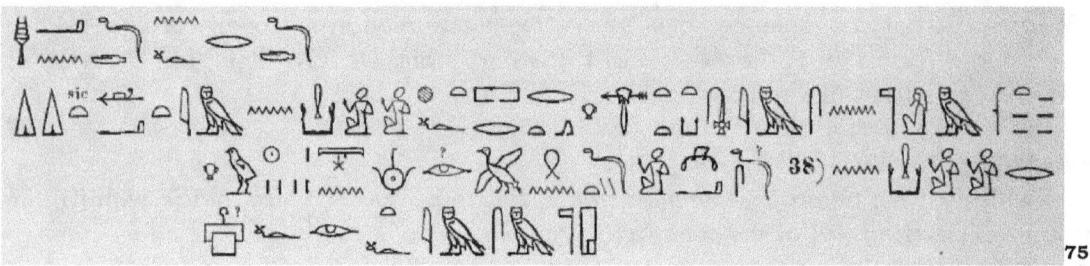

### Translation of text by Bunker-Pressler

| ahan | tchet | nef | ef | tchet [76] | tata |
|---|---|---|---|---|---|
| is | to say | by | him | to declare | gifts |

This is to say by him to declare gifts:

| ua | ta-t | em | en | hem ka | s | khefi | perr-t |
|---|---|---|---|---|---|---|---|
| one | portion | of | for | priest of ka | mine | with | appearance of a heavenly body |

One portion of gifts for the priests of my ka. With the appearance of a heavenly body

| her | sti | ames | en | neter | em | renp-t |
|---|---|---|---|---|---|---|
| above[77] | to kindle sacred fire | to conduct | before[78] | god | of | year |

above, to kindle a sacred fire, to conduct before the god of the year

| heriu | sepu [79] | gerh | en [80] | up-t renpit |
|---|---|---|---|---|
| who are over | five times | night | on | the opening of New Year |

<u>those who are over five times on the night of New Year's eve,</u>

---

[75] Erman, *Zeitschrift für Ägyptische Sprache*, page 176.
[76] Budge, *Egyptian Hieroglyphic Dictionary*, 913A, *tchet*.
[77] preposition
[78] preposition
[79] Refer to page 46 for comparison of *Heru* and *sepu*.
[80] Budge, *A Hieroglyphic vocabulary to the Book of the Dead*, p. 191

| maa | pa[81] | shen | tche-ti [82] |
|---|---|---|---|
| to see | to fly | to go round | the "two children,"[83] |

see *Shu* and *Tefnut* fly and go round.

| sa | aua | tches | en[84] | hem ha | s |
|---|---|---|---|---|---|
| my | offering | self | by | priest of the *ka* | mine |

My personal offering by the priest of my *ka*.

| er sa[85] | ef | maa | tef | am | sem | he-t neter |
|---|---|---|---|---|---|---|
| on the back of | it | see | this | with | priest | temple |

See this on the back of it with the temple priest.

---

[81] Budge, *Egyptian Language*, List of Signs, page 66. sign no. 73. **to fly**

[82] Budge, *Egyptian Hieroglyphic Dictionary*, 893A, *tche-ti*

[83] Naville, *Litanie du Soleil Inscriptions Recueillies*, page 61, i.e., *Shu* & *Tefnut* [Leo & Centaurus], Plates, 1875, *Seti I*.

[84] preposition

[85] Budge, *Egyptian Hieroglyphic Dictionary*, page 633B, *sa*.

# PART III – THE ZODIAC OF *DENDERA*

# THE ZODIAC OF DENDERA

# The Zodiac of *Dendera*

## The Zodiac Ceiling in the Temple of *Hathor*

The rectangular zodiac at *Dendera* is not entirely sequential. Even though it presents the goddesses of the hours of night from one to twelve in consecutive order; the positions of the constellations are from varying dates of solstices and equinoxes portrayed in a double panoramic view shown on the facing page. This non-sequential display of the zodiac was discovered by using Skyglobe planetary software and comparing the hours and dates with the positions of the stars. An interesting feature of the zodiac ceiling of the Temple of *Hathor* at *Dendera* is that, although it includes each hour of the night with zodiac characters, the positions of the accompanying zodiac characters are not from the same night. The following list shows the variation of dates.

| HOUR OF NIGHT | SEASON | DATE |
|---|---|---|
| 1st hour | summer solstice | June 21st, 2501 BC |
| 2nd and 3rd hours | autumnal equinox | September 21st, 2501 BC |
| 4th through 7th hours | spring equinox | March 21st, 2501 BC |
| 8th through 11th hours | autumnal equinox | September 21st, 2501 BC |
| 12th hour | winter solstice | December 21st, 2501 BC |

Norman Lockyer confirmed this variation of dates in an 1892 article entitled "The Astronomy and Mythology of the Ancient Egyptians": [86]

> In the southern half of the zodiac, the lower part is occupied by the southern stars, represented as different mythological personages, sailing along in boats; and above them we get the southern half of the zodiac with the signs of the Fish, the Ram, the Bull and the Twins. In the middle section the sun's course <u>in different parts of the day, and different parts of the year</u>, is given; whilst, outermost of all, we get the twelve solar positions, occupied by the sun each hour from rising to setting, represented by twelve boats.

---

[86] Lockyer, Norman. (1892). "The Astronomy and Mythology of the Ancient Egyptians." (*The Nineteenth Century*, Volume XXXII, July-December, Pages 29-51).

# THE ZODIAC OF *DENDERA*

## THE HOURS OF THE NIGHT

### The First Hour of Night
Summer Solstice June 21st, 2501 BC

In 1892 Norman Lockyer pointed out that *"The ancients, who had no telescopes, ... had to use their horizon as the only scientific instrument which they possessed."* [87]

On June 21st, the 1st hour of the night at *Dendera*, Capricorn was on the horizon with a small bull-headed bird. The name of the goddess of the first hour of the night was ⛉, *Neb-t heru*.

Jupiter
Bull-Headed Bird

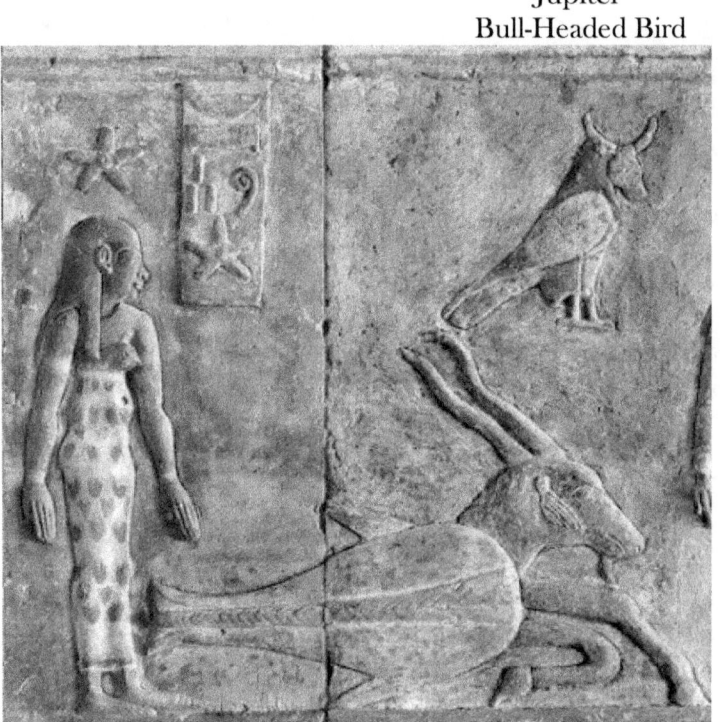

First hour goddess     Capricorn

---

[87] Lockyer, Norman. "The Astronomy and Mythology of the Ancient Egyptians." (*The Nineteenth Century*, vol. 32), page 34.

# The 1st Hour of the Night

Below is an illustration from Skyglobe for Windows showing Capricorn and Jupiter. They were just above the horizon during the first hour of the night on the summer solstice, June 21st, 2501 BC

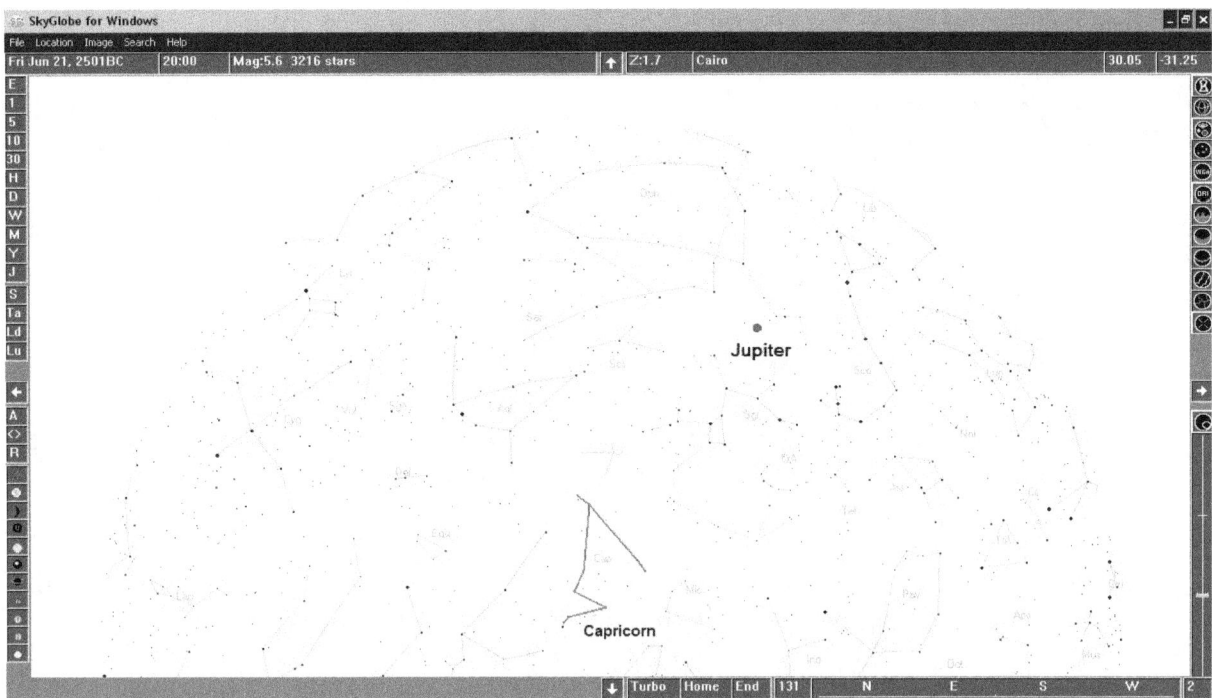

Below, we have overlayed the *Dendera* image with the matching constellations.

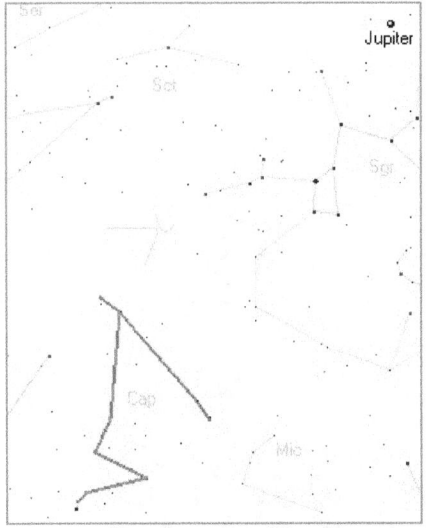

Capricorn and Jupiter
from Skyglobe

Capricorn and Jupiter
from *Dendera*

# THE ZODIAC OF *DENDERA*

## The Second and Third Hours of the Night
### Autumnal Equinox September 21st, 2501 BC

Next comes an illustration of the second and third hours of the night. The hours are in sequence, but here there is change in the date from the summer solstice on June 21st to the autumnal equinox on September 21st

During the 2nd and 3rd hour of the night Cetus, Taurus, and Sagittarius are on the horizon. A group of seven stars surrounding Taurus may represent the Pleiades star cluster. The goddess of the second hour of the night *Sar-nebs-s* and the goddess of the third hour *Seherit-tu* [88] are illustrated here, indicating this section of the zodiac applies to the hours of 8:00 through 10:00 p.m.

Written above the hawk-headed god holding a spear:

*Heru*   *s-heri*[89]   *khefti*
*Horus* drives away enemies

*Horus* drives away the stars with a shaft of sunlight.

---

[88] Budge, *Egyptian Hieroglyphic Dictionary*, 614A, *Seherit-tu*.
[89] Budge, *Egyptian Hieroglyphic Dictionary*, 684A, *s-heri*: to drive away, to repulse.
[90] http://www.egyptsearch.com/forums/ultimatebb.cgi?ubb=reply;f=8;t=005017;replyto=000007

# The 2ⁿᵈ & 3ʳᵈ Hours of the Night

Since all of these images are based in astronomy, this comment probably has a solar significance. The star gods were in opposition to the sun because they were images of the darkness and the darkness is in opposition to the light of day.

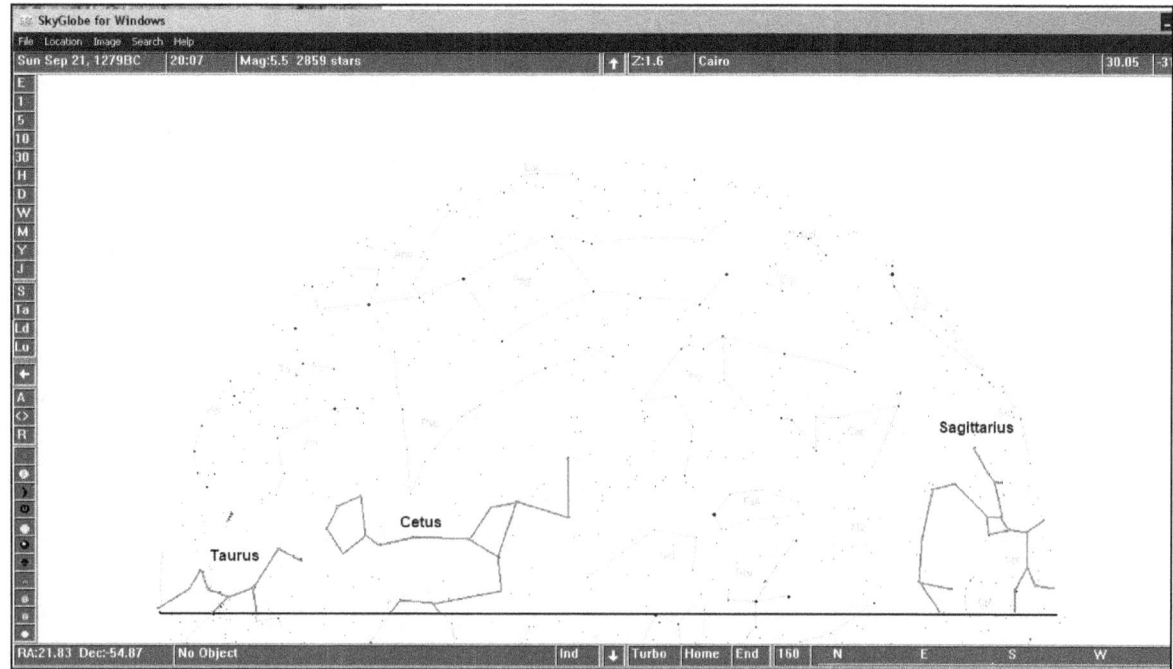

As on the ceiling of the temple of *Hathor* during the second hour of the night Taurus, Cetus, and Sagittarius are all on the horizon, but Taurus appears as if he has one leg. This reflects the fact that at this time of the night, the constellation of the bull is not completely visible above the horizon, and explains the appearance of a bull's haunch in the Egyptian astronomical art. The images of the hippopotamus and the one-legged bull became visible during the hours from 8:00 p.m. to 10:00 p.m. But where was the hawk-headed man with his spear? The answer is he was below the horizon during the second and third hour of night. However, by midnight the constellation of Eridanus was above the horizon. An alignment of two of the stars in Eridanus with the star in the horn of Taurus matches the idea presented in the image of the hawk-headed god holding a spear toward the horn of the bull, who is with the hippopotamus, in the rectangular zodiac ceiling of the temple of *Hathor* at *Dendera*. Therefore these images on the temple ceiling are associated with time 8:00 p.m. to 12:00 a.m.

## THE ZODIAC OF *DENDERA*

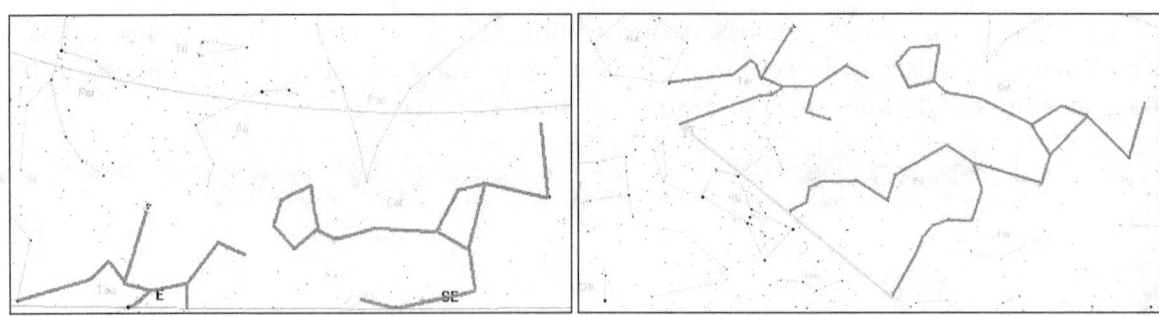

Taurus and Cetus
8:00 p.m.

Taurus, Eridanus and Cetus
12:00 a.m.

The image of the hawk-headed god with a spear from *Dendera*

Below the hawk-headed god and his spear overlay Eridanus.

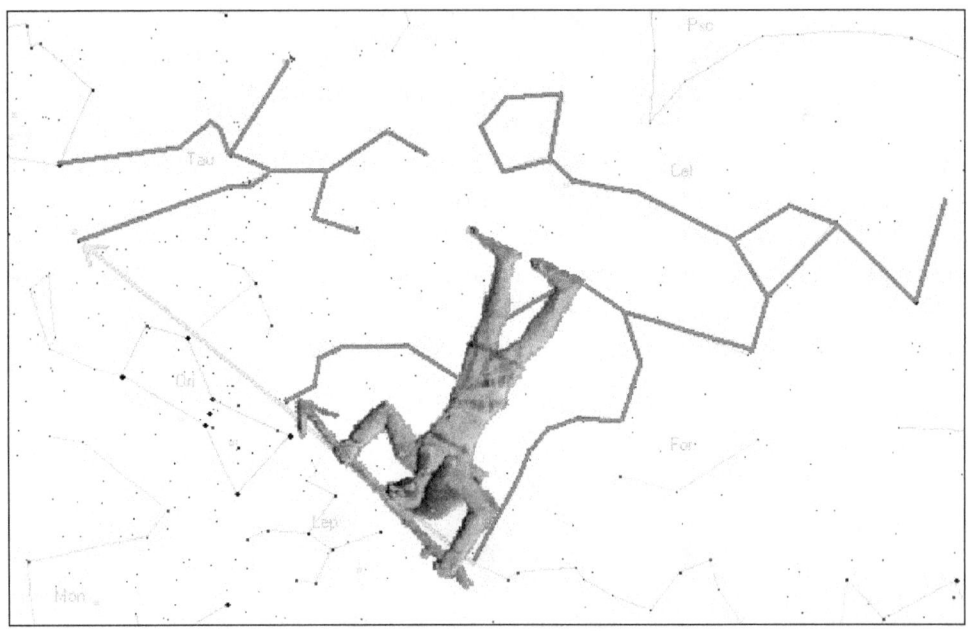

# THE 2ND & 3RD HOURS OF THE NIGHT

## Comparison with the Tomb of *Senmut*

The astronomical ceiling of *Senmut* includes star constellations similar to those found on the ceiling of *Seti I*'s tomb and the temple of *Hathor* at *Dendera*.

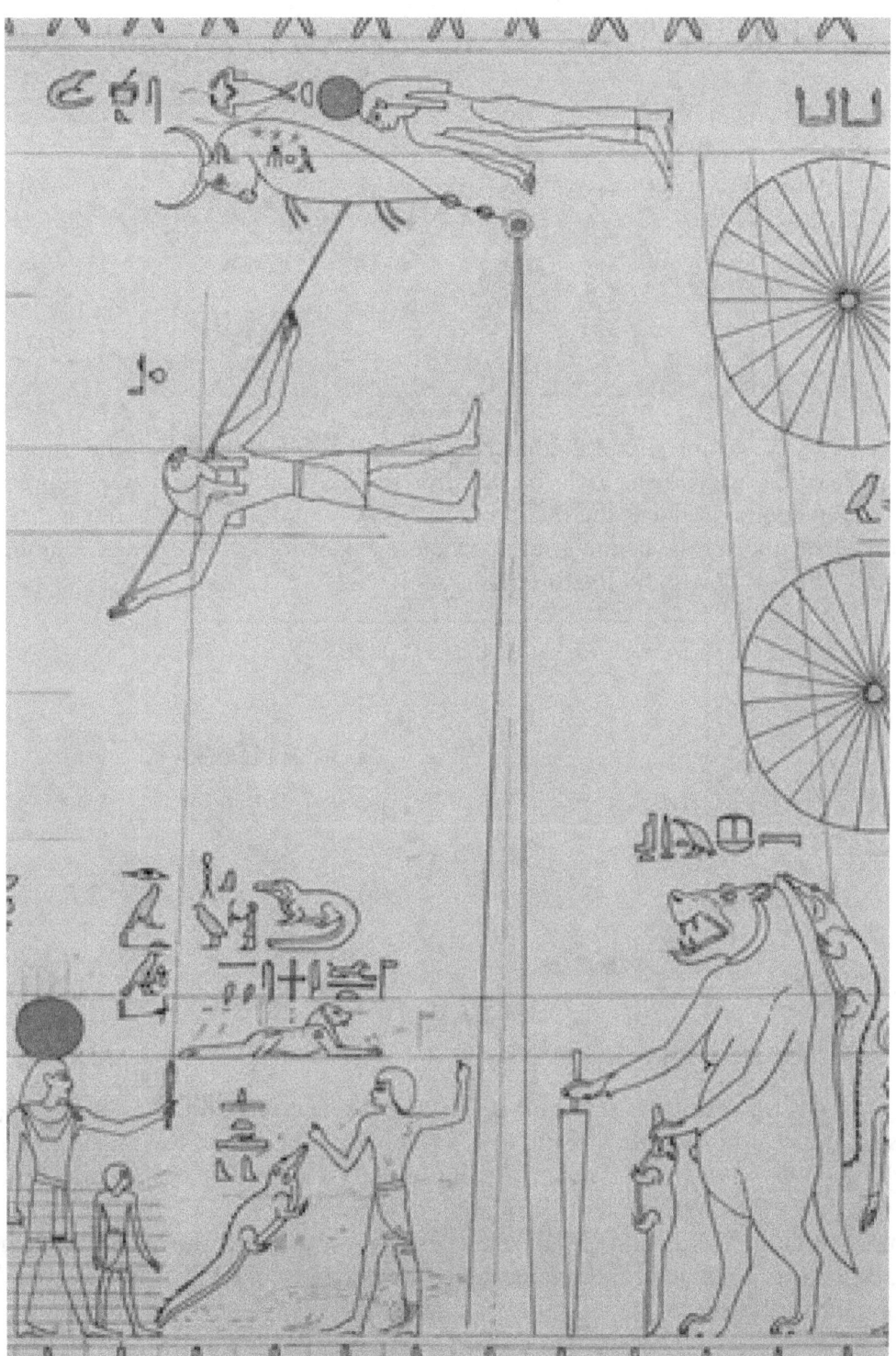

# THE ZODIAC OF *DENDERA*

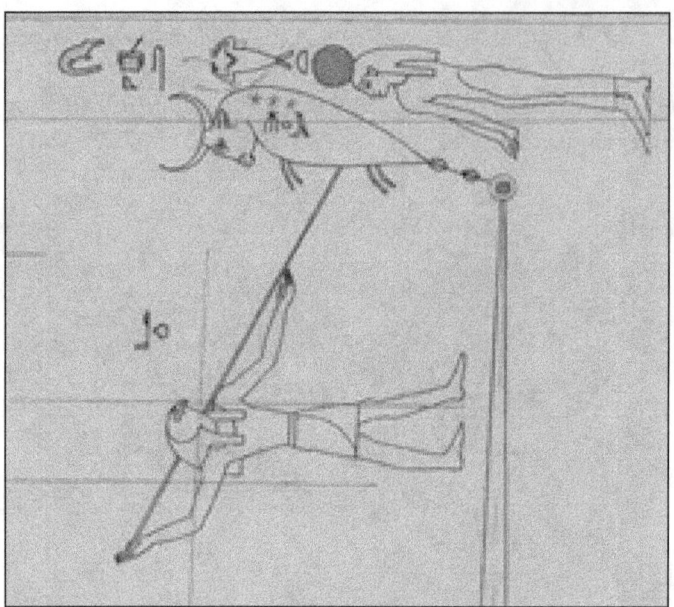

This section of the ceiling shows the hawk-headed god under the bull. The impression is that he is holding a balancing pole on the tips of his fingers, which may represent the balance of the equinox. (Near the bull there is a horizontal image of a goddess.) In fact, if we zoom in on the constellation Taurus to get a closer look, we can see why the artist emphasized the two horns and the three stars in the tail.

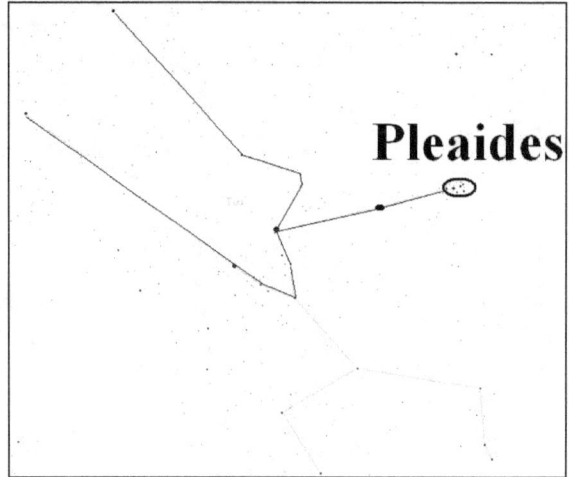

Below is an illustration of the positioning of star constellations on the autumnal equinox, 1463 B.C., the year of *Senmut's* death, at 1:48 a.m. Gemini is in a horizontal position like the goddess in *Senmut's* tomb, near the constellation Taurus the bull. Under Taurus in each tomb we see the constellation Eridanus, illustrated as a hawk headed god holding something with both hands (a spear, a balancing pole, or an unstrung bow). In each of the tombs the date is consistently the autumnal equinox and coincides with the year of the death of the tomb owner.

# The 2ⁿᵈ & 3ʳᵈ Hours of the Night

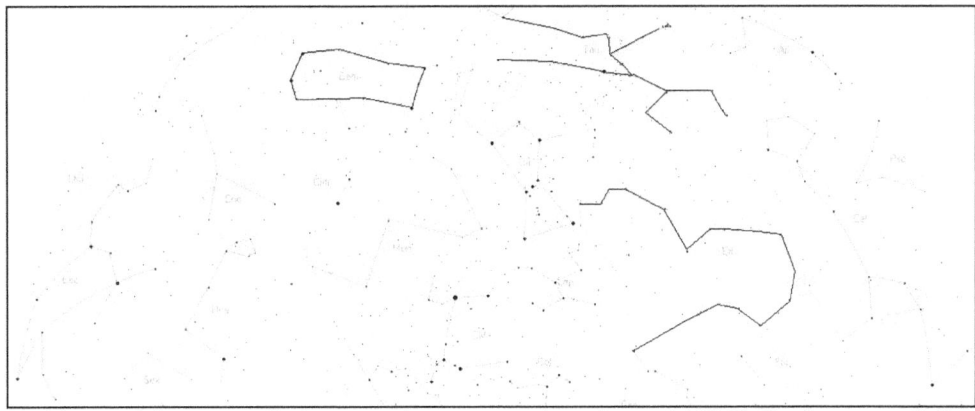

The positions of the constellations on the autumnal equinox, 1463 B.C., the year of *Senmut's* death, at 1:48 a.m.

The Tomb of *Seti I* shows these same constellations in similar positions:

*An* (Eridanus) the hawk headed man under *Meskh-ti* (Taurus) the bull

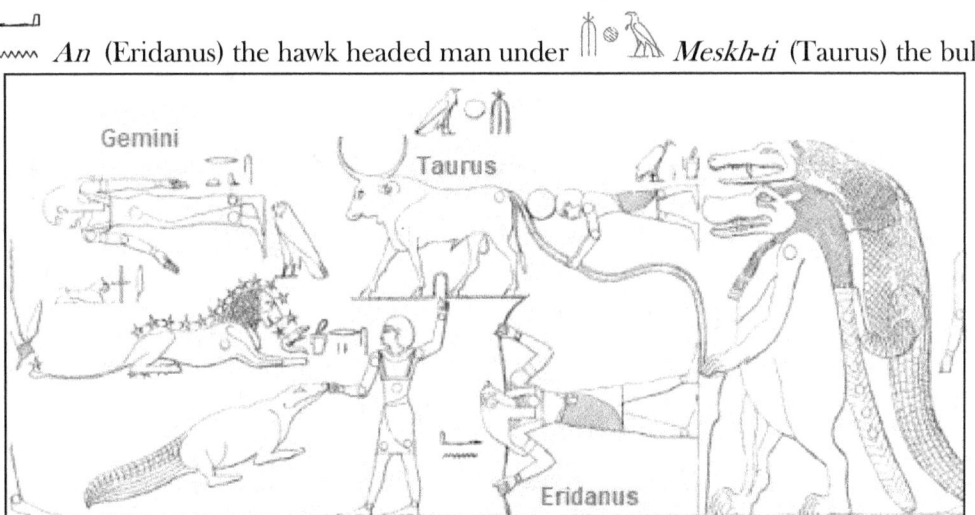

From the Tomb of *Seti I*

# THE ZODIAC OF DENDERA

Comparison with the Tomb of *Pedamenope*

Below, *An* is under Taurus in this drawing from the tomb of *Pedamenope*.

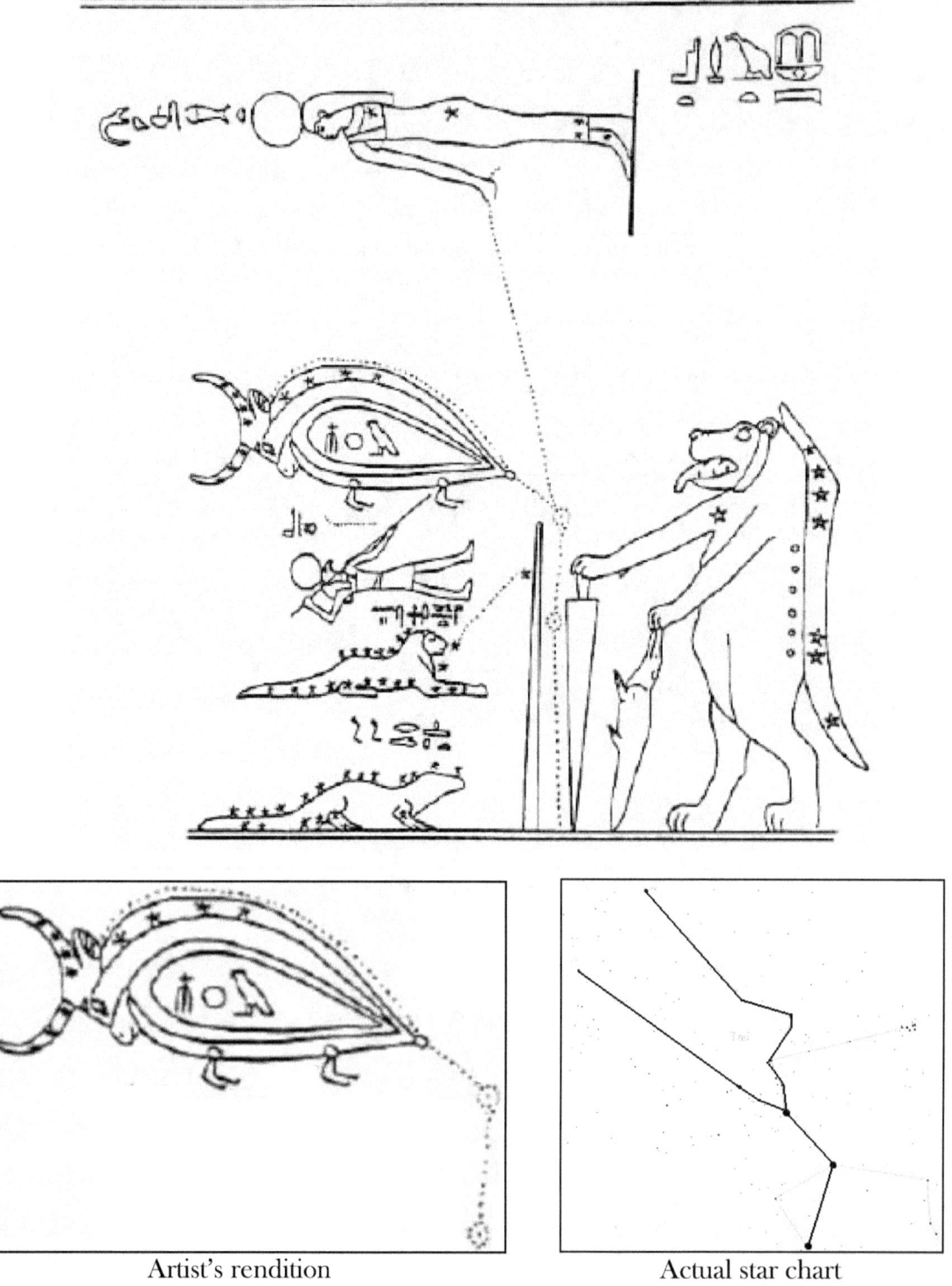

Artist's rendition          Actual star chart

Comparison of Taurus from *Pedamenope*'s tomb with the Skyglobe image of Taurus, it is easy to see the similarity to the constellation in the artist's rendition of the stars.

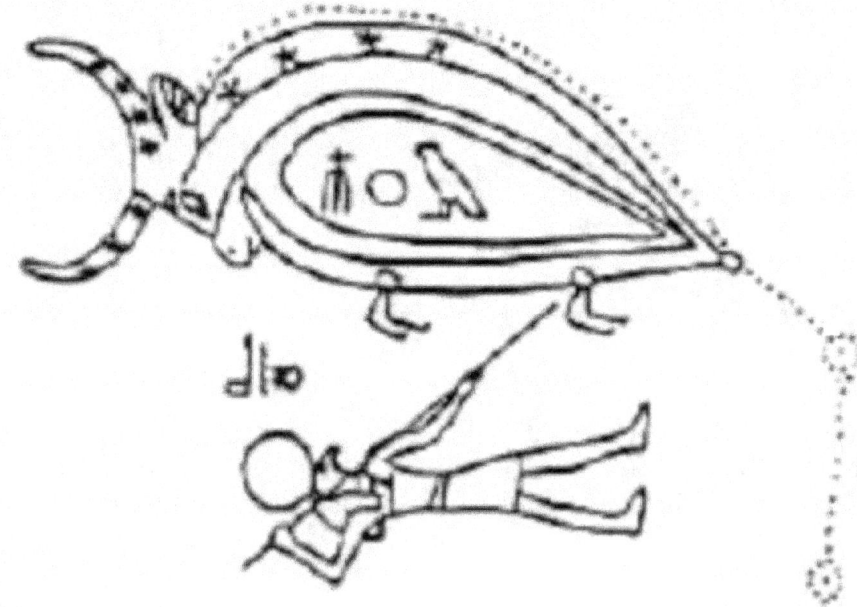

The pole held by *An* does not touch Taurus. It has no spear tip and probably is a balancing pole representing the balance of the autumnal equinox.

<u>The Fourth, Fifth, Sixth and Seventh Hours of the Night</u>
Spring Equinox March 21st 2501 BC

The next characters shown in sequence of hours on March 21, 2501 BC are the goddesses of the 4th, 5th, 6th and 7th hours of night with Cygnus, Aquila, Scorpio, and the goddess Serqet, with the moon in Libra.

Left half of previous illustration:

| *Aa-t- Shefit* | *Neb(t)-Ankh* | *Sab* | *Sep* | *Serqit* |
|---|---|---|---|---|
| Goddess of the 4th hour | Goddess of the 5th hour | Wolf god Vulpecula | a god Aquila | the scorpion goddess Scorpio |

Right half of previous illustration::

| *Neb-t-Shesta* | *Herit-tchatcha-aha-her-neb-set* | *aah* | *M'khaa-t* |
|---|---|---|---|
| Goddess of the 6th hour | Goddess of the 7th hour | the moon Moon god[92] | Great Scales of the Hall of Judgement[93] Libra |

---

[91] https://paulsmit.smugmug.com/Features/Africa/Egypt-Dendera-temple/
[92] Budge, *Egyptian Hieroglyphic Dictionary*, 29B, *aah*: the moon, Moon-god.
[93] Budge, *Egyptian Hieroglyphic Dictionary*, 285B, *M'khaa-t*: the Great Scales of the Hall of Judgement wherein souls were weighed.

# The 4th, 5th, 6th & 7th Hours of the Night

Just as before, the hours have remained in sequential order, but the date has changed to the Spring Equinox. So we see the 4th, 5th, 6th, and 7th hours of the night, 8:00 p.m. to 1:00 a.m. is the time for Cygnus, Vulpecula, Aquila, Scorpio and Libra on the spring equinox March 25, 2501 B.C. On a modern star chart we see Cygnus, Vulpecula and Aquila like this:

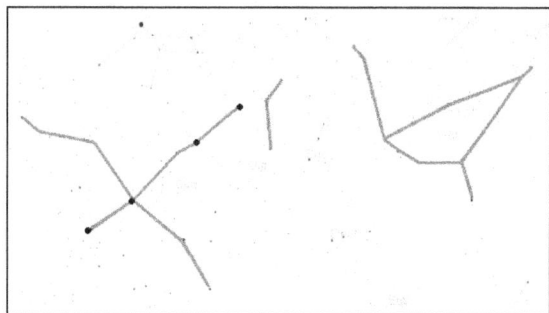

But to the ancient Egyptians they probably looked like this:

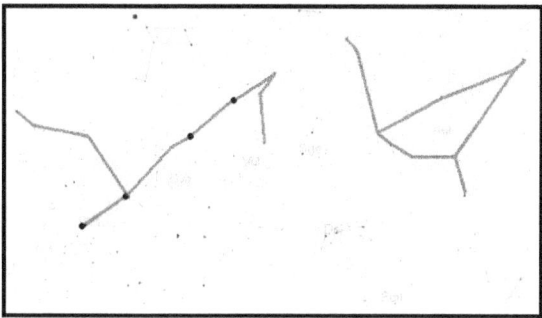

The positions of the feet of the fox match the four stars in Cygnus and the hook of the reaping tool matches the shape of Vulpecula.

The Fox, the Scythe and the Eagle

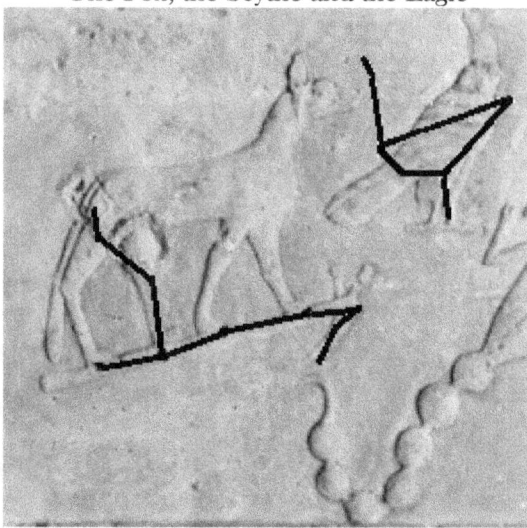

Cygnus    Vulpecula    Aquila

The constellation Aquila [94] takes its name from the Latin for "eagle", but in ancient Egypt this pattern was considered the falcon of *Horus*. [95]

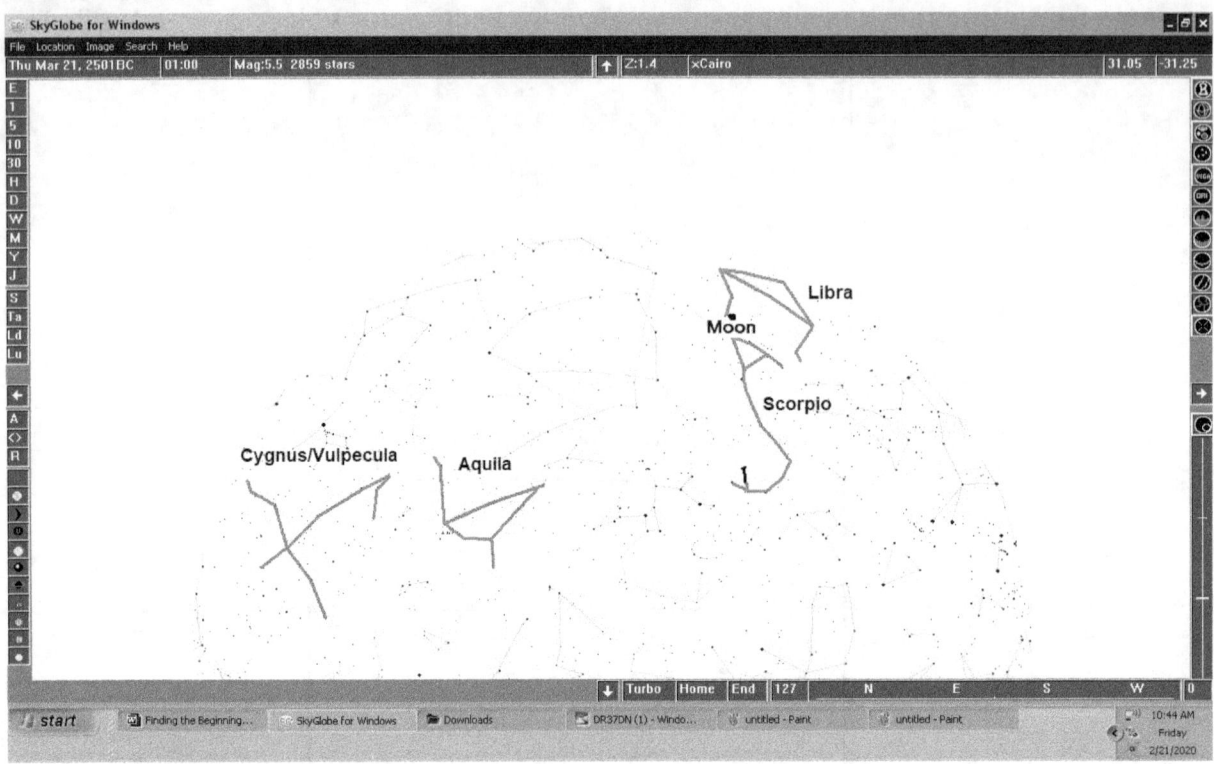

The Moon is between Scorpio and Libra 2501 BC 1:00 a.m., the 7th hour of the night.

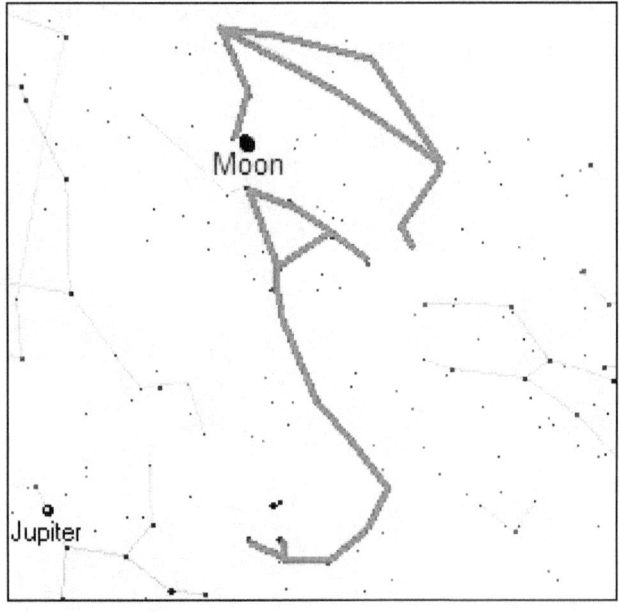

---

[94] http://sino-platonic.org/complete/spp253_ancient_egyptian_constellations.pdf, page 11
[95] http://megangafford.com/essays/2017/9/16/stories-under-the-stars-aquila

# The 4th, 5th, 6th & 7th Hours of the Night

Horus the Hawk is resting upon the moon, and the text in front of the hawk reads: *pi neter Heru-Tauti* "This god Horus of the Seventh hour."[96]

▢ // = *Pi* = "this."[97]

⌐ = *Neter* = "god"

🦅★ ☉ = *Heru-Tuati* = "Horus of the Seventh Hour."

The figure enclosed in the disk: 👤 to the left of it.
The priest magician with ram-headed staff,[98] or rod[99]

"*Ur-heka*," 🦅 ⏧ ⏧, i.e., "*Great one of words of power, or spells.*"
*Ur-heka* is the name usually given to the sinuous ram-headed staff or rod.

---

[96] Budge, *Egyptian Hieroglyphic Dictionary*, 506A.
[97] Budge, *Egyptian Hieroglyphic Dictionary*, 229A.
[98] Budge, *The Book of Opening the Mouth*, page xv, *Ur-heka* is the name usually given to the sinuous ram-headed staff, or rod, with which the mouth of the deceased was touched by the priest, as we see from the Vignettes in the papyri of the Book of the Dead.
[99] Budge, *Egyptian Hieroglyphic Dictionary*, page 171B. *ur-heka* or (*Ur-hekau*) "great words of power," a tool or instrument used in the performance of magical ceremonies.

# THE ZODIAC OF *DENDERA*

### The Eighth and Ninth Hours of the Night
Autumnal Equinox, September 21st, 2501 BC

Here the date shifts to the autumnal equinox once again and during the eighth hour of night the constellation of Leo and Hydra begin to rise. There is a bird, a bull headed god carrying a scythe, a tool used for cutting crops such as wheat, with a long blade at the end of a long pole attached to which are one or two short handles, and a goddess holding the head and stem of a grain plant.

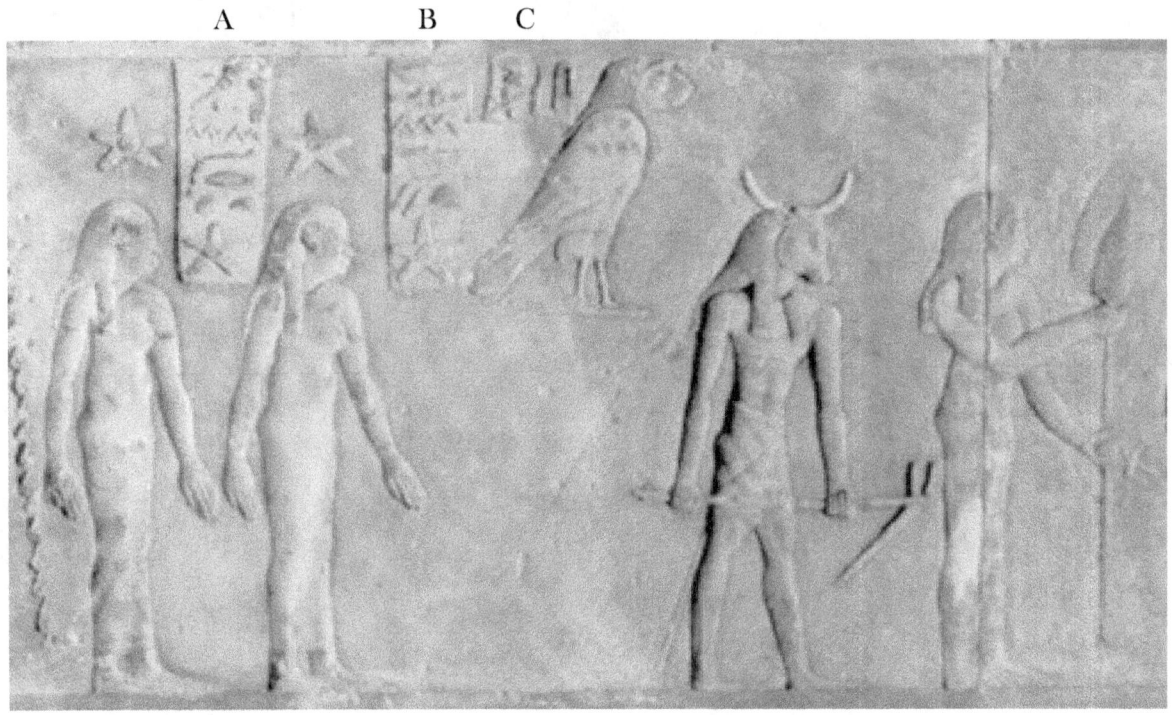

A.   *Smer nessert*   goddess of eighth hour

B.   *Neb-t sent-t* [100]   goddess of ninth hour

C.   *Sebit* [101]   the name of a goddess

When we got to these hours we were not sure of what was being represented. Eventually we understood that the maiden holding the plant is Virgo. Spica is the brightest star in this constellation. The name Spica comes from the Latin phrase *spīca virginis*, meaning "Virgo's ear of grain." The Latin word *spicum* refers to the ear of corn (or wheat or grain) Virgo holds.

---

[100] Budge, *Egyptian Hieroglyphic Dictionary*, 364A, *Neb-t sent-t*.
[101] Budge, *Egyptian Hieroglyphic Dictionary*, 654B, *Sebit*; see also 655A, *Sbatt*, a form of *Ament*.

# The 8th & 9th Hours of the Night

Having established that Virgo was represented in this image of the zodiac, we next wanted to understand the bull-headed god holding a tool and the identity of the bird near his shoulder. This was a good time to look at the actual positions of the stars using Skyglobe for Windows software. We set the date for September 21st, 2501 BC and set the clock for 2:30 a.m., the eighth hour of the night, and saw Virgo rising. We watched it rise until it was above the horizon during the eleventh hour of the night, just before sunrise. To the east of Virgo we saw Boötes and Corona Borealis. These we believed had to be the bull headed god holding a tool and the bird near his shoulder. But the positioning of Boötes and Corona Borealis looked perpendicular to Virgo. If we adjusted their position to a vertical one, they seemed to fit the positions of the other zodiac characters.

By the eleventh hour Virgo and Boötes and Corona Borealis are above the horizon.

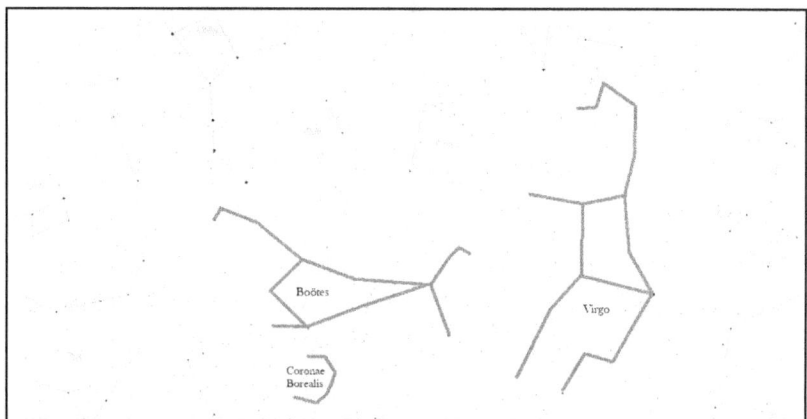

Boötes and Virgo - Ploughman and Maiden
September 21st, 2501 BC 5:34 a.m.

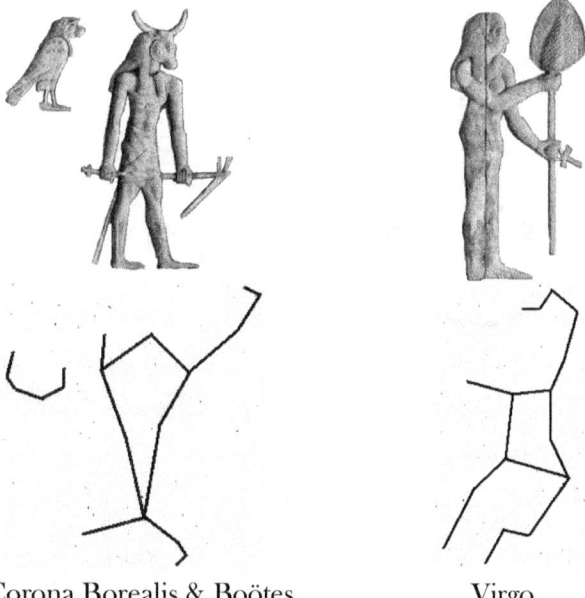

Corona Borealis & Boötes      Virgo

# THE ZODIAC OF *DENDERA*

This *frog headed bird* represents the star *Alpha Coronae Borealis*.

The text actually reads:  
sba kha  
star rising

On September 21ˢᵗ, 2501 B.C., at the end of the ninth hour of the night, *Alpha Coronae Borealis* was on the horizon beginning to rise.

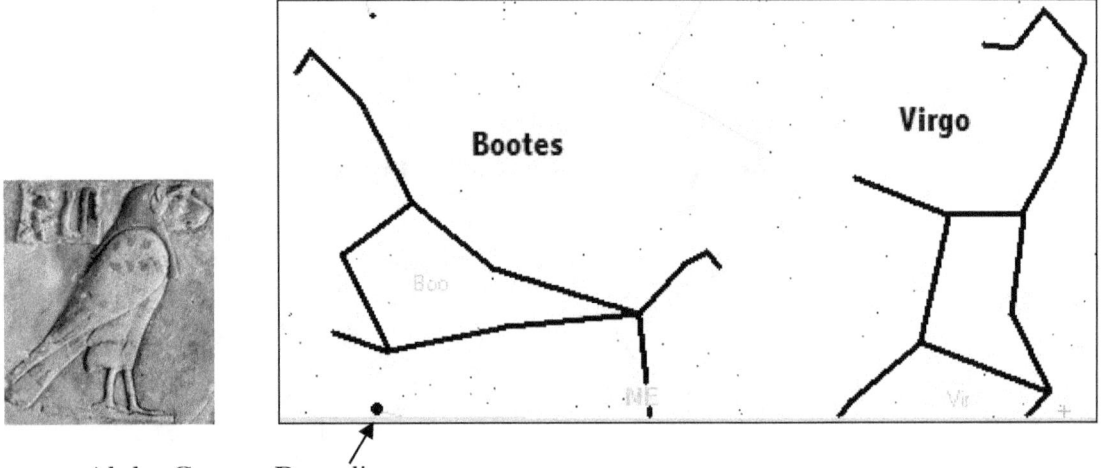

Alpha Corona Borealis
"star rising"

# The 8th & 9th Hours of the Night

In this drawing made in 1603, Boötes holds a sickle and a scythe. Boötes means "Ploughman" from the Greek word *boôtês*.[102]

The name Boötes comes from the Greek Βοώτης, Boōtēs, meaning "herdsman" or "plow-man" (literally, "ox-driver"; from βους bous "cow"). But in the temple of *Hathor* at *Dendera*, he carries a scythe, an agricultural tool used to harvest grain.

[103]

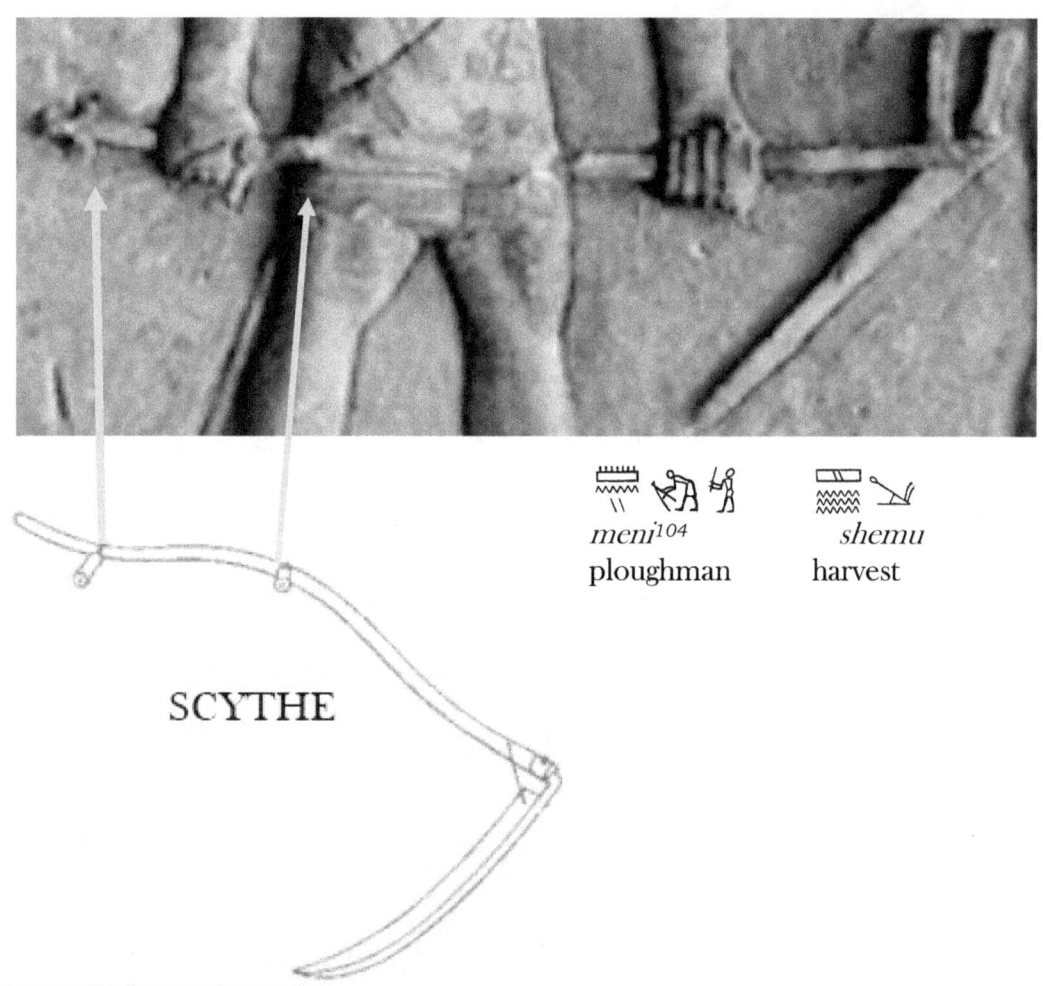

*meni*[104]
ploughman

*shemu*
harvest

SCYTHE

---

[102] https://www.theoi.com/Georgikos/Boötes.html
[103] *Uranometria* is a star atlas produced by Johann Bayer. It was published in Augsburg in 1603 by Christoph Mang under the full title *Uranometria: omnium asterismorum continens schemata, nova methodo delineata, aereis laminis expressa.* -- Wikipedia.
[104] Budge, *Egyptian Hieroglyphic Dictionary*, 302A, *meni*.

# THE ZODIAC OF DENDERA

## The Tenth and Eleventh Hours of the Night
Autumnal Equinox, September 21st, 2501 BC

The names of the goddesses are written above them. On the left is <u>M'k-neb-set</u>, the goddess of the tenth hour of the night. The other goddess is <u>Khesef-khemit</u>, goddess of the eleventh hour of the night. The square probably represents a body of water, i.e. *the celestial water*. Its body is here shown doubled back upon itself, which emphasizes the extreme length of this constellation. It is the biggest constellation in the sky, "Hydra stretches across this huge expanse, covering 102 degrees. Named after a mythical water snake, the constellation's head sits in the northern celestial sphere while its tail stretches into the southern one." [105]

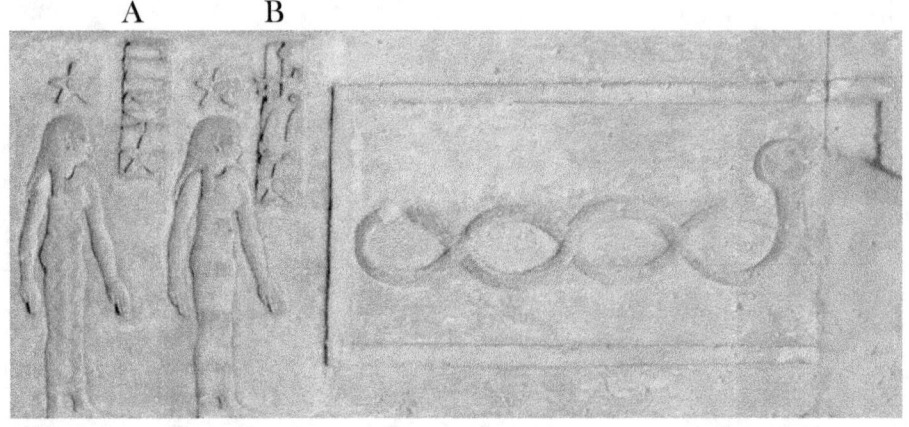

A. *M'k-neb-set* goddess of tenth hour

B. *Khesef-khemit* [106] goddess of eleventh hour

The square probably represents a body of water, i.e. *the celestial water.*

---

[105] https://www.newscientist.com/article/mg25033302-600-how-to-find-hydra-the-biggest-constellation-in-the-sky/

[106] Budge, *Egyptian Hieroglyphic Dictionary*, 565A, *Khesef-khemit.*

# THE 12ᵀᴴ HOUR OF THE NIGHT

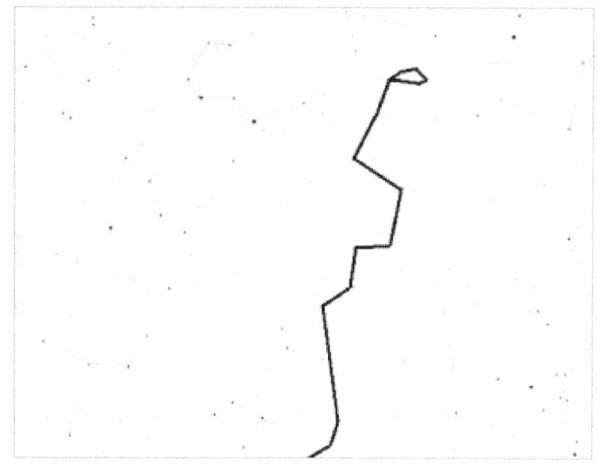

A star-chart of September 21ˢᵗ, 2501 BC shows Hydra is rising into a vertical position during the 10th and 11th hours of the night.

### Twelfth Hour of the Night
Winter Solstice December 21ˢᵗ, 2501 BC

Shifting back to the winter solstice, 2501 BC, during the 12th hour of night Virgo, Leo and Hydra.

The partially destroyed images are alternate illustrations of Virgo.

Leo and Hydra

*Per-neferu-en-neb-set*
Goddess of the 12th hour [107]

By comparing the round zodiac at *Dendera* with the square zodiac, we can recreate the outline of the missing image of a seated goddess holding an infant. The image below (left) is from the round zodiac at *Dendera*. Below (right) is the recreated image.

---

[107] Budge, *Egyptian Hieroglyphic Dictionary*, 243A, *Per-nefer-en-neb-set.*

## THE ZODIAC OF *DENDERA*

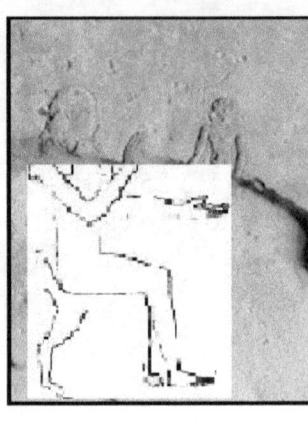

With reconstruction we can also see there is a bird perched upon the tail of the serpent.

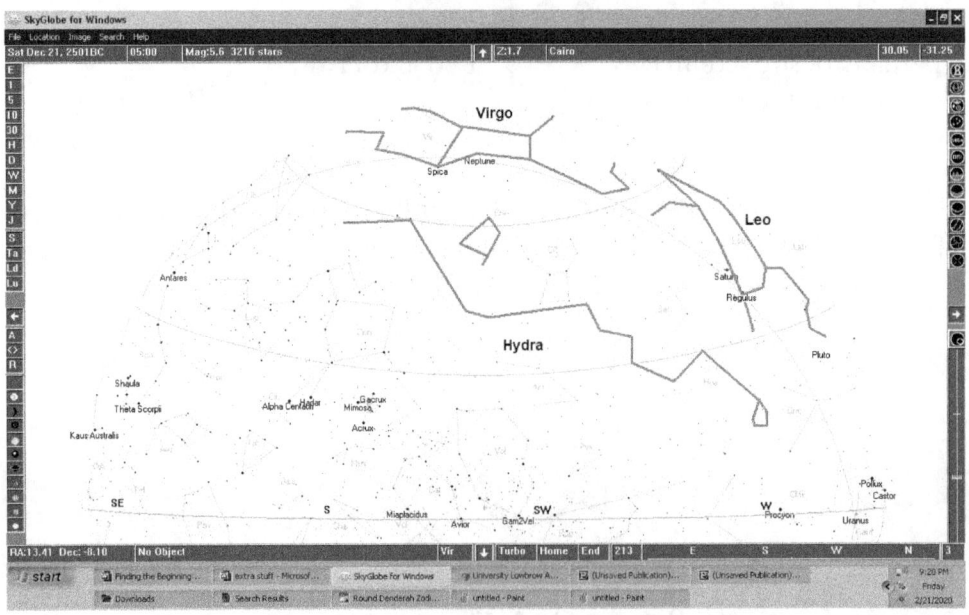

# PART IV – THE INVENTORY STELA

# THE INVENTORY STELA TEXT

The Inventory Stela

Ruins of the Temple of *Isis*

# The Inventory Stela

## Description of the Inventory Stela

What is the Inventory Stela? It is a stone tablet which was kept in the temple of *Isis*, and was discovered by Auguste Mariette in 1858 at Giza. It contains a list of sacred statues and a description of their size and the material from which they were constructed, hence its name "Inventory" Stela.

The main part of the panel is occupied with various representations of sacred statues and emblems, arranged in four superposed registers, and accompanied by explanatory inscriptions. This stone tablet also contains an account of the story of *Khufu* around the outside edge written in hieroglyphic characters. It is stated that *Khufu* (4th dynasty) made a journey to Giza to restore the temple of *Isis* and repair the Sphinx.

Since the discovery of this stela there has been ongoing controversy over its age and authenticity. This may be because of repair and reconstruction that took place during the 18th dynasty, the 21st dynasty, and again during the 26th dynasty when the Inventory Stela was re-copied. As told by Salim Hassan: *"The stela claims that the temple was found (apparently in ruins) by Khufu, and was rebuilt by him. In which case, it must at the very latest, have been built in the beginning of the third dynasty."* Hassan goes on to say, *"Most probably this temple was built during the eighteenth dynasty."* [108] Hassan makes this statement concerning the text of the Inventory Stela, *"the whole stela, in its form, method of inscription, decoration, and similarity of writing to that of the graffiti in the temple, all point to it being entirely the work of the twenty-sixth dynasty."*[109] The copying of the original story of *Khufu* may have been influenced by the contemporary language and orthography common to the time of the 26th dynasty. This knowledge helps quell the thoughts of deception and fraud connected with this artifact.

When Mariette discovered the stela in 1858, it was believed to contain a genuine account of an event that took place during the 4th dynasty. In 1886 Gaston Maspero resumed the work begun by Mariette. Maspero stated that in his opinion the Inventory Stela was not an original document dedicated by *Khufu*, but was a later copy. He said the temple of *Isis* was re-built where it was found during the 21st dynasty by the Tanite king, *Pasebekhanu*, and the stela must have been made or restored under this King, or perhaps under one of the Ethiopian pharaohs. If it is a copy of a decayed monument, it probably preserves the arrangement of the original.

Salim Hassan agreed that it was, as Maspero said, quite possible that this stela was, in actual fact, a copy of an older document, such occurrences having been known. A good example of such a restoration is the black granite stela of King *Shabaka* (25th dynasty), which states that the king had found the original document being eaten by worms (a papyrus or perhaps a wooden tablet) and *"illegible from beginning to end"*, and he ordered the writing to be made anew *"more beautiful than the one that was before"*. Therefore, we have no reason to doubt that the Inventory Stela is a copy of an older text, like that of *Shabaka*.[110]

---

[108] Hassan, *The Great Sphinx and Its Secrets, Excavations at Giza, 1936-7,* Vol. 8, page 111 (published 1953).

[109] Hassan, *The Great Sphinx and Its Secrets, Excavations at Giza, 1936-7,* Vol. 8, page 116.

[110] Hassan, *The Great Sphinx and Its Secrets, Excavations at Giza, 1936-7,* Vol. 8, page 116-117.

# THE INVENTORY STELA TEXT

111 Mariette, *Monuments Divers*, plate 27.

# THE FOUR REGISTERS

## TEXT OF THE INVENTORY STELA

### Translation of the Four Registers by Selim Hassan

Below are Hassan's translations of the four registers of the Inventory Stela. His complete translation can be found in Appendix B of this book.

#### The Top Register[112]
(1) A statue of the God Min, standing upon a pedestal provided with carrying-poles. It is inscribed: "*Min*, acacia wood, height 1 ell, 1 hand (60 cm.)."
(2) A figure of a jackal standing upon a support, the front of which ends in a spiral. Before its front legs is a uraeus; inscribed: "*Wep-wat*, gilded acacia wood."
(3) The same as the preceding.
(4) A hawk, crowned with the disk and plumes[113], perching upon a papyrus-headed standard, to which is attached a *menat*; inscribed: "Gilded wood ".
(5) An ibis on a perch; inscribed: "Gilded wood".

#### The Second Register
(1) A portable barque of *Isis*, on the prow and stern of which are aegises of that Goddess. There is a veiled *naos* amidships; it is inscribed: "Support for the splendors of *Isis*; gilded wood, inlaid with stones."
(2) A statue of *Isis*, crowned with the disk and horns, and seated within a *naos*; it is inscribed: "*Isis* the Great, the Divine Mother, Mistress of the Pyramid. *Hathor* in her barque; nen-stone, plated with gold; head-dress and uraeus of silver. Height: 3 hands, 2 fingers (26'4 cm.) "
(3) *Nepthys*, seated upon a low-backed throne; inscribed: "*Nepthys*, gilded nen-stone, head-dress of gold; height: 3 hands."
(4) *Isis* suckling *Horus*; it is inscribed: "*Isis*, Mother, nen-stone, head-dress of black bronze; height: 2 hands, 2 fingers (19 cm.)"
(5) The Goddess *Selkt*, seated and wearing a scorpion upon her head; inscribed: "*Isis-Selkt*, nen-stone, scorpion of gold; height: 2 hands, 2 fingers (19 cm.)"

#### The Third Register
(1) *Horus* the Child, seated, and inscribed: "*Horus* the Protector of His Father, ebony, eyes of inlaid stone; height: 2 hands, 2 fingers (19 cm.)"
(2) *Horus* the Child, seated, but without a throne, inscribed: "*Horus* the Child, gilded wood, eyes of inlaid stone; height: 4 hands, 2 fingers (32 cm.)"
(3) The God *Ptah*, standing in a *naos*; inscribed: "*Ptah*, gilded wood."
(4) *Sekhmet*, standing and holding a papyrus scepter; inscribed: "*Sekhmet*, black bronze; height: 3 hands, 2 fingers (26'4 cm.)"
(5) *Osiris*, standing in a *naos*; inscribed: "*Osiris*, gilded wood, eyes of inlaid stone."
(6) Isis, Seated and suckling *Horus*; inscribed: "*Isis*, Superior of the Great Place; black bronze; height: 3 hands (22'6 cm.)"
(7) *Isis* suckling *Horus* ; inscribed: "*Isis*, gilded wood; height: 5 hands" (37' 7 cm.).

---

[112] Hassan, *The Great Sphinx and Its Secrets,* Excavations at Giza, 1936-7, Vol. 8, page 114-116.

[113] The hawk image is described as crowned with a disk and plumes, however the illustration on the facing page by Mariette (1872) does not include the disk.

# THE INVENTORY STELA TEXT

(8) *Horus*, wearing the Double Crown[114], seated, but without a throne; inscribed "*Horus*, who Takes Possession of the Two Lands, gilded wood, eyes of inlaid stone; height: 3 hands, 1 finger (24'5 cm.)"

## The Fourth Register

(1) At the top of the space "F" is a figure of the *Apis* bull, standing on a low pedestal. It has a disk between its horns, and its special distinguishing marks are engraved upon its body. It is inscribed: "*Apis*."

(2) Below the bull is a curious object, consisting of two plumes springing out of a lotus flower, which is set horizontally upon a rectangular pedestal. It is the emblem of the God *Nefer-tum*, and is inscribed: "*Nefer-tum*, gilded wood; height: 3 ells (1'58 meters)".

(3) Behind the two preceding figures, and occupying the full height of the register, is the figure of a uraeus having the head of a woman, and crowned with the head-dress of the Goddess *Hathor* -- a disk between two long horns, and surmounted by two plumes. It is inscribed: "Uraeus of gilded wood; height: 1 ell (52'8 cm.)."

(4) In space "G" is the representation of a sphinx, couchant upon a high pedestal, and evidently intended to represent the Great Sphinx of Giza ; above it is inscribed: which seems to be a corruption of "*seshep*": apparently the first mention of this word as a name for the Sphinx in this district and also "*Hor-em-akhet*." [115]

There is a discrepancy in register four as compared with the statues of the gods listed before it, all of which provide size and material from which they were made. This indicates that this image is not of a statue found within the temple of *Isis*. So why is it listed here? Perhaps because this stela is a combination of several different things: it is an inventory listing the statues of the temple of *Isis*, it is also the story of *Khufu*'s restoration of the temple and the statue of the Great Sphinx, and it is the retelling of a dream that *Khufu* had of the goddesses *Isis* cutting new limestone blocks for the repair of the statue of the Great Sphinx. It was this dream that motivated *Khufu* to make a journey to Giza to rebuild the temple of *Isis* and repair the Sphinx.

---

[114] There is a discrepancy in the illustration of the crown of Horus in register 3. He is depicted with a single crown of upper Egypt, but the description says he wears a double crown, representing both upper and lower Egypt.

[115] Hassan, *The Great Sphinx and Its Secrets,* Excavations at Giza, 1936-7, Vol. 8, page 114-116.

# THE OUTSIDE EDGE AND BASE

### The Outside Edge and Base of the Inventory Stela

This is the hieroglyphic text from outside edge of the Inventory Stela.

Center top of stela:

Left Side:

Right side:

The outlined text has been previously believed to contain the name of *Khufu's* daughter *Hent-sen*. However, we translate *hent sen* as two distinct words. We will be discussing this at length in this section.

In 1908 an article written by Georges Daressy was printed in a French Publication: *Collection of Works Relating to Egyptian and Assyrian*. The title of his article was "The Stela of the Daughter of *Cheops*,"[116] also known as the Inventory Stela. In it he translated the complete hieroglyphic text from the stela into French. Below is a summary of his translation in English. The complete translation is available in Appendix B.

Center top of stela:
   Long live *Horus* slaughterer, King of the South and North, *Khufu*, given life!

Left Side:
   He did for his mother *Isis*, the divine mother, *Hathor*, Queen of the West,[117] an ordinance consigned to a stela and gave her again sacred offerings. He built his temple in stone, renewing what he had found.

Right Side:
   The residence of *Isis*, regent of the Pyramid, is close to the sphinx of...[118], which is northwest of the home of *Osiris*, lord of *Ro-satu*. He built his pyramid near the

---

[116] Daressy, *Recueil de Travaux Relatifs à la Philologie et à l'Archéologie Égyptiennes et Aassyriennes*, "La Stèle de la Fille de Chèops"

[117] ⵔⵔⵔ is a fault for ⵔⵔⵔ ⵎ the funerary mountain, the west.

[118] The engraver has skipped the name of *Harmakhis*.

# THE INVENTORY STELA TEXT

temple of this goddess, and he built the pyramid of the royal daughter *Hent-sen* to the side.

## Translation by Bunker-Pressler

Translation of the outlined text on the previous page:

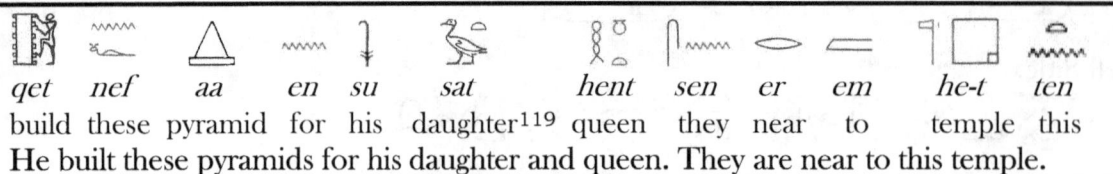

| qet | nef | aa | en | su | sat | hent | sen | er | em | he-t | ten |
|---|---|---|---|---|---|---|---|---|---|---|---|
| build | these | pyramid | for | his | daughter[119] | queen | they | near | to | temple | this |

He built these pyramids for his daughter and queen. They are near to this temple.

Center top of stela:
Living *Horus*, King of the South and North *Khufu* given life.

Left Side:
*Khufu* made this for his mother *Isis*[120], the mother of the god, *Hathor* queen of Celestial waters, a gift of writing inscribed upon a stone tablet. This belonging to the god he was happy to make anew, and he rebuilt the temple to the original condition. He found these gods at this her place.

Right side:
He discovered this house of *Isis,* the pyramid queen near the house of the Sphinx, upon the northwest of the house of *Osiris*, the lord of the abode of the dead community. He built this, his pyramid, near to the divine temple of this goddess, and <u>he built these pyramids for his daughter, and the queen. They are near to this temple.</u>

## The Egyptian word *Hent*

The word *hent* is written in the text of the Inventory Stela. It is used five times: thrice written ⌒ and twice written 𓎛⌒.

---

[119] Breasted, *Ancient Records of Egypt*, volume 1, page 85, footnote i: "According to Herodotus, the middle of the three small pyramids east of the Great Pyramid, belonged to *Khufu's* daughter (Herodotus II, 126)." [*The History of Herodotus,* Book II, Chapter 126, page 203.])

[120] Her name translates to "Queen of the Throne" which is reflected in her headdress, which is typically a throne. Sometimes she is also depicted with the vulture headdress of the goddess *Mut,* and other times with a disk with horns on the sides, attributed to the goddess *Hathor.*

## The Outside Edge and Base

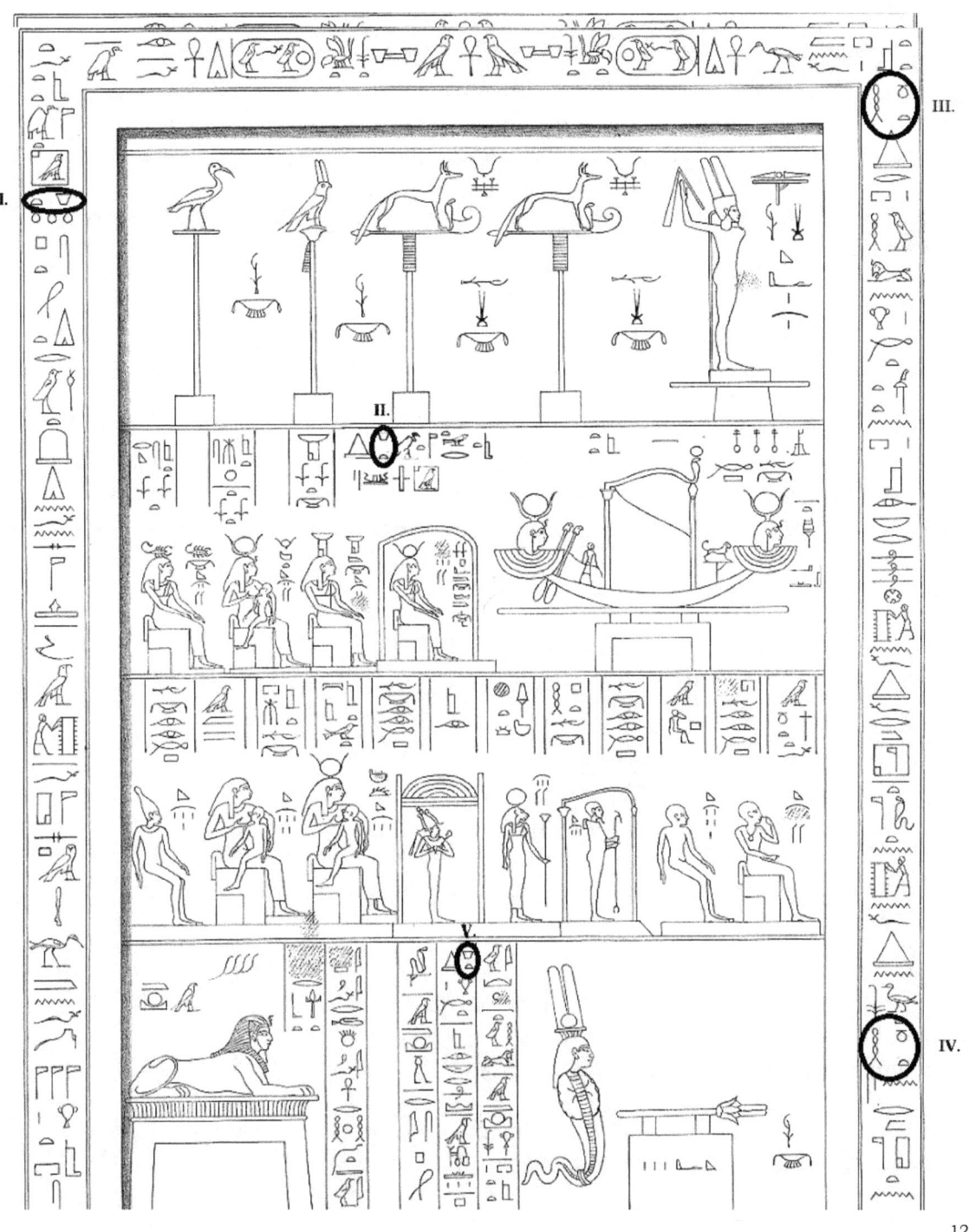

121

What does *hent* mean? It means mistress, lady, or queen.[122] Let us begin by looking at the text incised upon the upper left side of the Inventory Stela.

---

[121] Mariette, *Monuments Divers*, plate 27.
[122] Budge, *Egyptian Hieroglyphic Dictionary*, 486A, *hen-t*.

# THE INVENTORY STELA TEXT

I.  
    *mut*    *ef*    *Ast*     *mu-t neter*[123]    *He-t-Hor*    <u>*hen-t*</u>      *Nu*  
    mother his   *Isis*   mother of the god   *Hathor*    <u>queen</u>    Celestial waters  
    his mother *Isis* the mother of the god, *Hathor*, queen of heaven.

II. The second register shows the word *hent* used in the same group of hieroglyphs as shown above.

    *mut*    *ef*    *Ast*     *mu-t neter*[124]    *He-t-Hor*    <u>*hen-t*</u>      *Nu*  
    mother his   *Isis*   mother of the god   *Hathor*    <u>queen</u>    Celestial waters  
    his mother *Isis* the mother of the god, *Hathor*, queen of heaven.

In Egyptian mythology *Isis* was the sister goddess of *Nephthys* and together they were the twin goddesses; the twin stars of the constellation Gemini, which was the last constellation in the sky on the western horizon before sunrise on September 21$^{st}$ 10,390 BC, when the calendar began.[125] This is the basis of the legend that *Isis* was the mother of the Sun god.

III. In the third example of the word *hent,* at the upper right side of the Inventory Stela, we read:

    *keme*    *nef*    *per*    *Ast*    <u>*hen-t*</u>    *aa*  
    find      this house   *Isis*   <u>queen</u>    pyramid  
    He found this house [of] *Isis*, pyramid queen,

IV. In the fourth example of the word *hent,* at the lower right side of the Inventory stela, we read:

    *qet*    *nef*    *aa*    *en*    *su*    *sat*    <u>*hent*</u>  
    to build these pyramid for his daughter <u>queen</u>  
    He built these pyramids for his daughter [and] queen.

V. In the fifth example of the word *hent,,* in the top center of the lower register of the Inventory Stela, we read:

    *au*   *aa-t*   *neth*   *Hu*    *en*    *Hor em akhet*    *her*   *su*   *en*   *per*   *Ast*  
    is   tomb   of   Sphinx of Giza   of   *Horus* in the horizon   upon south of   house   *Isis*  
    The tomb of the Sphinx of *Horus* is upon the south of the house of *Isis*,

---

[123] Budge, *Egyptian Hieroglyphic Dictionary*, 295A, *mu-t neter*.  
[124] Budge, *Egyptian Hieroglyphic Dictionary*, 295A, *mu-t neter*.  
[125] See more information about the beginning of the calendar in *The Coffin Texts Resurrected*.

# THE OUTSIDE EDGE AND BASE

<u>hen-t</u>   aa-t   her   meh-t
<u>queen</u>  pyramid upon north
the queen's pyramid is upon the north

Since the beginning of attempts to understand and translate the hieroglyphic text of this artifact, these two words *hent* and *sen* have been considered and translated as one word, thought to be the name of the daughter of king *Khufu*.

Below are two consecutive lines of text from the Inventory Stela, that include the words *hent* and *sen*. The Egyptian language has no special word for the coordinating conjunction "and". The coordination of the noun is often through direct juxtaposition.[126] Also, there is no definite article "the" or "a" in ancient Egyptian.[127]

*qet*  *nef*  *aa*  *ef*  *er*  *em*  *he-t*  *net*  *netri-t*  *ten*
build this pyramid his near to temple of goddess this
He built this his pyramid near to the temple of this goddess.

*qet*  *nef*  *aa*  *en*  *su*  *sat*  <u>*hent*</u>[128]  *sen*[129]  *er*  *em*  *neter he-t*
build these pyramid for his daughter[130] <u>queen</u> <u>they</u> near to divine temple
He built these pyramids for his daughter [and] queen; they [are] near to the divine temple.

These two lines of text refer to three pyramids that *Khufu* built close to the temple of the goddess *Isis* near the Great Pyramid.

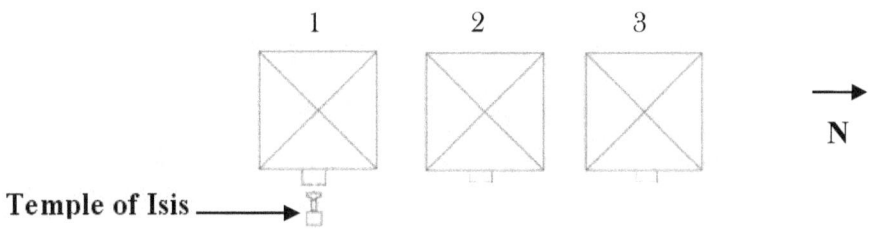

---

[126] https://www.bibalex.org/learnhieroglyphs/lesson/LessonDetails_En.aspx?l=72

[127] http://www.ardownes.com/myEgyptianpage.html

[128] Budge, *Egyptian Hieroglyphic Dictionary*, 486, *Ahen-t*; lady, mistress, queen

[129] Budge, *Egyptian Hieroglyphic Dictionary*, 673B, *sen*: they, them, their;

[130] Rawlinson, George, *Herodotus*, Book II, 1862, page 174, #126. The pyramid of *Khufu's* daughter stands midmost of the three pyramids that are in front of the Great Pyramid.

# THE INVENTORY STELA TEXT

Most likely, the stela was originally embedded in a wall of the temple of Isis that abutted against the southernmost of the three pyramids (1) built near the Great Pyramid to the east. *Khufu* built his own pyramid (1) near the temple of this goddess[131] and he built the middle of the three small pyramids for his daughter (2)[132] However neither the name of *Khufu*'s daughter, nor the name of his queen (3) is recorded upon the stela, probably due to the lack of adequate space that would be required to include their names.

How did the idea develop that *Khufu* had a daughter named *Hent-Sen*, which has been written in various forms such as *Hentwsen, Hennutsen,* and *Henoutsen*? There is no clue from the 4th dynasty of the Old Kingdom period that sheds light on the existence of a princess of this name.[133] We decided to see if we could find out how the words *hent sen* came to be interpreted as the name of *Khufu*'s daughter.

The idea that *Khufu* had a daughter named *Hent-sen* may have begun in 1858 when Mariette found the Inventory Stela in the Temple of *Isis* at Giza. Before that discovery, the history of Giza had been firmly established and it was believed that *Khufu* was responsible for the construction of the Great Pyramid. The Inventory Stela contained information that might pose an encroachment upon this established hypothesis. The issue was with two of the words found on the stela:

1. *hent* - lady, mistress, queen, goddess
2. *sen* - they, them, their

If these words had been interpreted by their literal definitions they would have conflicted with the established belief, so the text *hent sen* was interpreted as the name of the daughter of *Khufu*, thus circumventing the obstacle it otherwise presented. The earliest record of this may be the book *Recherches Sur Les Monuments,* resulting from a trip to Egypt by Emmanuel de Rouge in 1863-1864.[134]

Over time attempts were made to support the theory that *Khufu* had a daughter named *Hent-sen.* Heinrich Brugsch provided two references in this regard in his book *Thesaurus,* volume V, printed in 1891. We looked at his original statements of this claim and the basis given for it.

At the top of the illustration on page 1231 in his book, he wrote, "*Aus der sogenannten Sphinx-Stele in Museum von Kairo,*" being translated means "*From the so-called Sphinx stela in the Cairo Museum.*"

---

[131] Mariette, *Monuments divers rcueillis en Egypte et en Nubie*, page 17.
[132] Rawlinson, George, *Herodotus*, Book II, 1862, page 174, #126.
[133] Zivie-Coche, *Giza au premier millénaire,* page 224.
[134] Rouge, *Recherches Sur Les Monuments*, page 47.

# The Outside Edge and Base

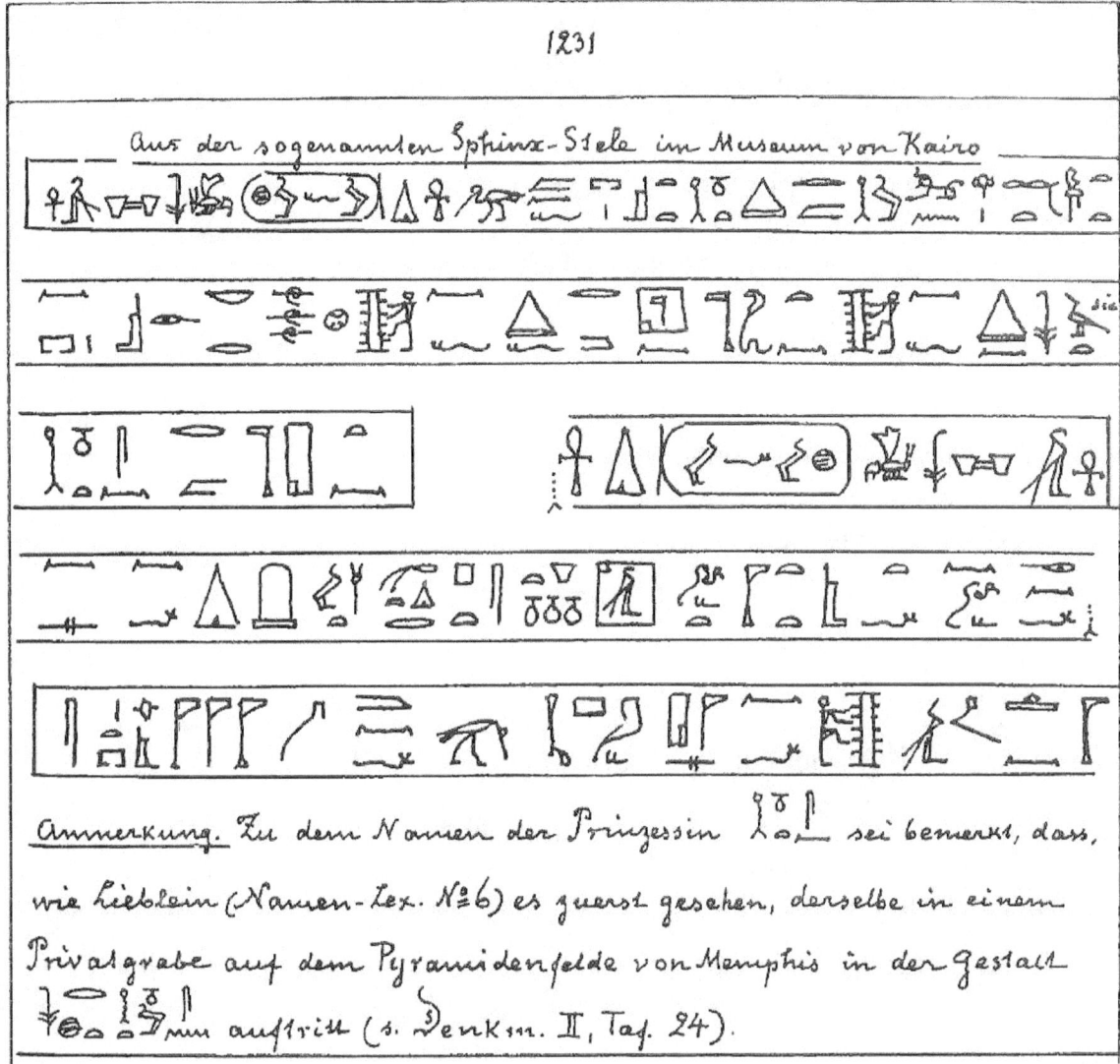

At the bottom of the illustration he has written:

"<u>Anmerkung</u>. Zu dem namen der prinzessin [glyph] sei bemerkt, dass, wie Lieblein (Namen-Lex. No.6) es zuerst gesehen, derselbe in einem privatgrabe auf dem pyramidenfelde von Memphis in der gestalt [glyph] auf schritt (s. Denkm. II, Taf. 24).'

---

[135] Brusch, *Thesaurus*, vol. 5, page 1231.

# THE INVENTORY STELA TEXT

Translation:

"**Note**. *The name of the princess* [hieroglyphs] *it should be noted, as in Lieblein (Names*[136] *Lex. No. 6) is similarly seen on a private grave in the pyramid field of Memphis in the form of* [hieroglyphs] *on step (see Denkm. II, plate 24)."* [137]

## Brugsch's References

Brugsch refers to both Lieblein's *Dictionary of Names* (1871) and Lepius' *Denkmaler aus Aegypten und Aethiopen Text* (1897) as evidence that the daughter of *Khufu* was named *Hent-sen* [hieroglyphs]. Lieblein also gives a reference for his lists of names at the bottom of section six, which we shall also examine in due course.

### Brugsch's first reference

(Hieroglyphic text is from Lieblein's *Dictionary of Names*)[138]

The first of Brugsch's references for [hieroglyphs] *hent-sen* was *Names*, Lex. No. 6, published in 1871 and written by Jens Lieblein.[139] Here, the hieroglyphic text was written [hieroglyphs], slightly different than the form given by Brugsch.

Lieblein's list has certain characteristics that distinguish these terms as names. One is the title before each name, designating who this person was, such as "his son," or "His daughter," or "royal kinsman." Another is the use of a determinative for man or woman [hieroglyph] at the end of each name. This can be seen in the following page from his book.

---

[136] Lieblein. *Hieroglyphisches Namen-Wörterbuch, genealogisch und alphabetisch geordnet*, 1871, page 2.

[137] Original text in German: "Anmerkung. Zu dem namen der prinzessin [hieroglyphs] sei bemerkt, dass, wie Lieblein (Namen-Lex. No.6) es guerst gesehen, derselbe en ei nem privatgrabe auf dem pyramidenfelde von Memphis in der gestalt [hieroglyphs] auf schritt (s. Denkm. II, Taf. 24)" [Author note: This reference is incorrect and should be *Denkmaeler*, Volume I, 34a.]

[138] Lieblein. *Hieroglyphisches Namen-Wörterbuch, genealogisch und alphabetisch geordnet*, 1871, page 2.

[139] https://en.wikipedia.org/wiki/Jens_Lieblein - Lieblein was appointed professor of Egyptology at the Royal Frederick University in 1876, the first professor of Egyptology in Norway.

# The Outside Edge and Base

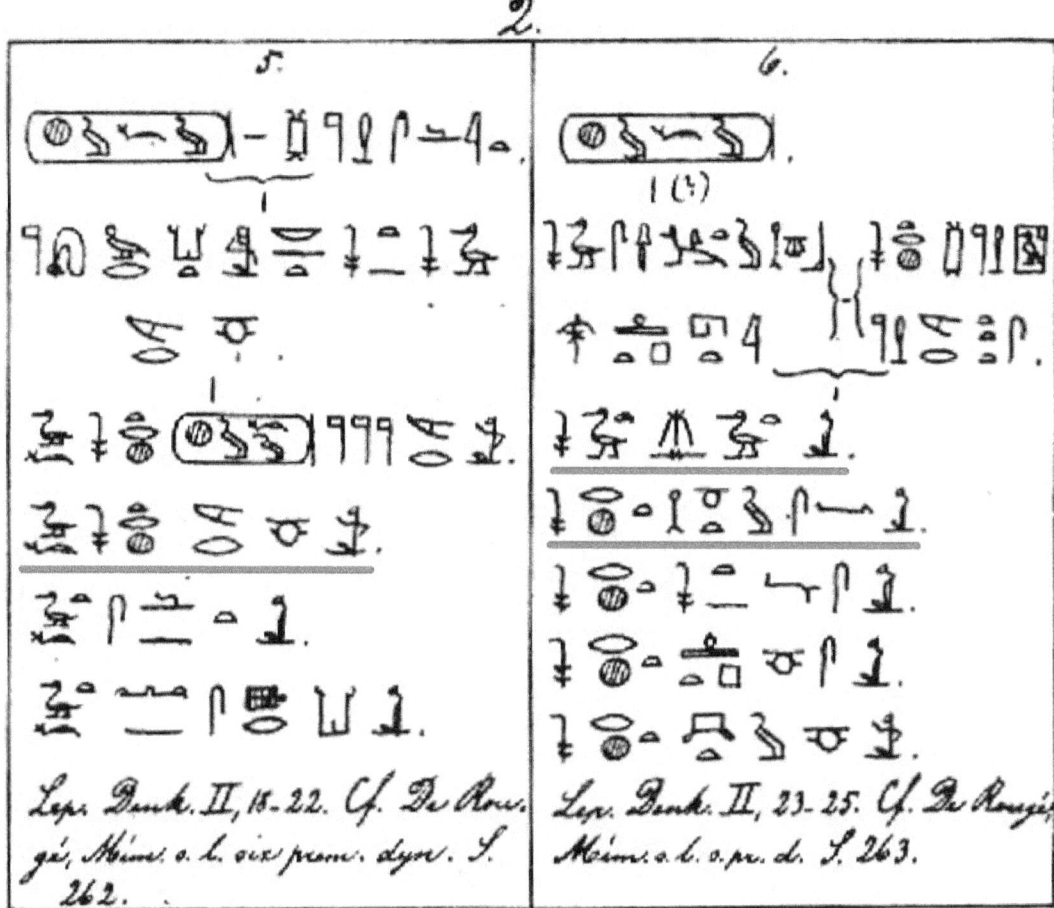

- This text ![glyph] has a male determinative.

  ![glyphs]
  *ef   sa   rekh nesu   Mer- ab*

  It reads: his  son  royal kinsman  *Mer-ab*

- This text ![glyph] has a female determinative.

  ![glyphs]
  *ef   sat   Mes-sat*

  It reads:  his daughter  *Mes-sat*

- This text ![glyph] has a female determinative.

  ![glyphs]
  *rekh nesu   Hent  u  sen*

  It reads:  royal kinsman  *Hent - u - sen*

# THE INVENTORY STELA TEXT

## Comparison of Hieroglyphic Texts

| Hieroglyphic Dictionary of Names | Inventory Stela Text |
|---|---|
| *rekh nesu*[140]   *Hent-nu-sen* | *su   sat   hent   sen* |
| royal kinsman   *Hent-nu-sen* | ...his daughter and queen. They... |

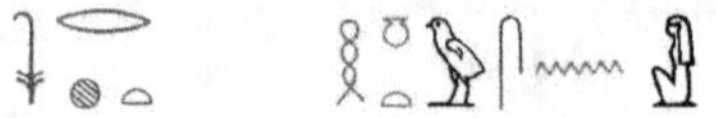

### Brugsch's second reference

The second reference was Denkmaeler II, plate 24,[141] from Grave 69 at Giza.[142] The text from the grave in the pyramid field was ⌇. It was written on a ruined tomb, the remaining fragment of original text. Lepsius wrote he had discovered the text on the broken wall of a tomb. The next image is a copy of the section about Grave 69 from Lepsius.

---

[140] Budge, *Egyptian Hieroglyphic Dictionary*, 430B, *rekh nesu*.

[141] located on the internet at http://giza.fas.harvard.edu/pubdocs/315/full/ and http://gizamedia.rc.fas.harvard.edu/images/MFA-images/Giza/GizaImage/full/library/LD_pOlates_II_3_giza.pdf

[142] We also found this reference to ⌇ in Denkmaeler, Volume I, 1897, page 89, grave 69.

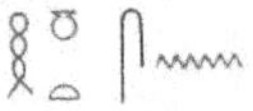

## The Outside Edge and Base

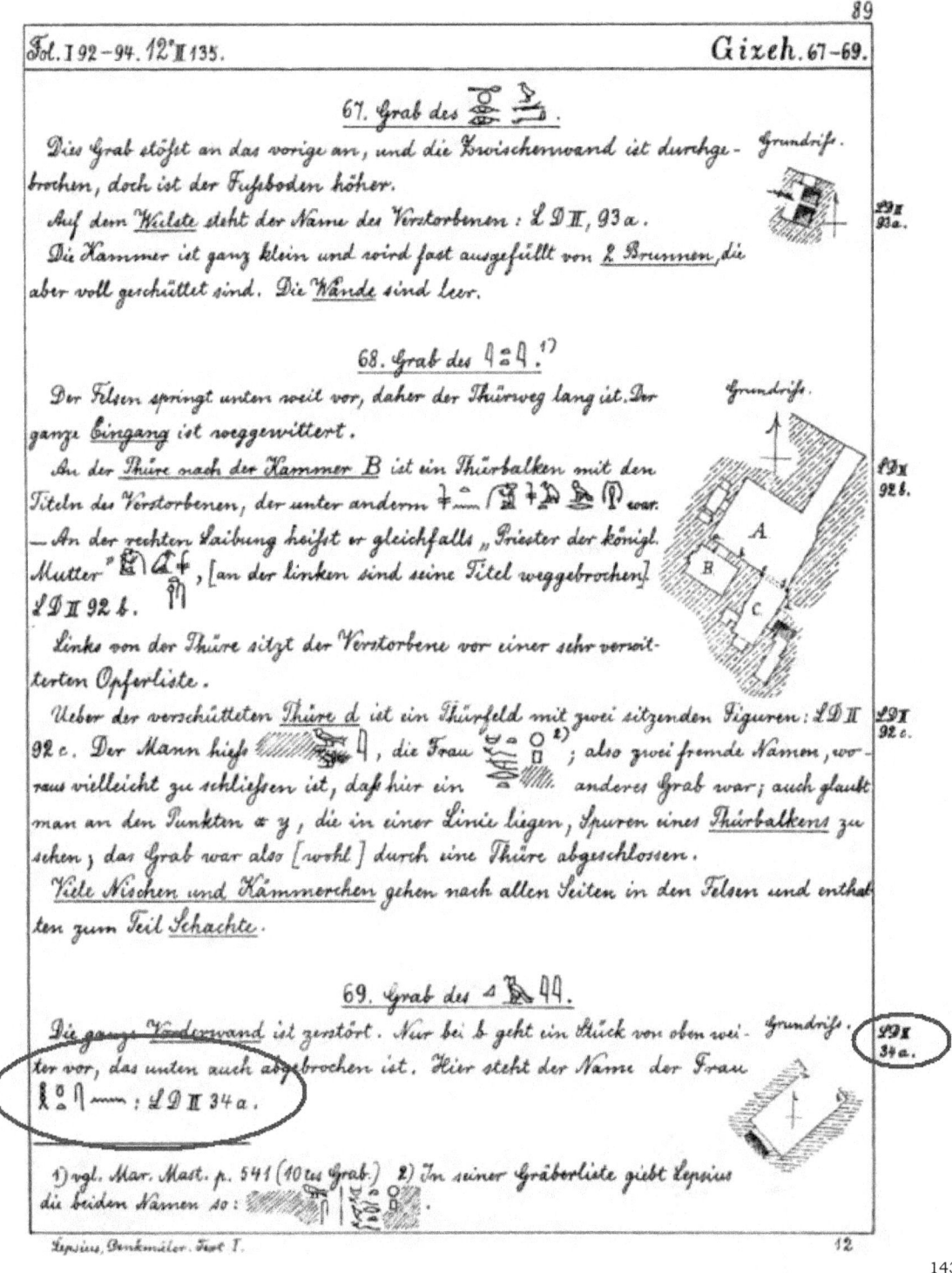

"*LD II 34 a*" is written just after the hieroglyphic text and on the right border. We have circled both.

---

143 Lepsius, *Denkmaler aus Aegypten und Aethiopen Text*, Volume I, 1849, page 89.

# THE INVENTORY STELA TEXT

Next we will zoom in on text from grave 69 and translate it.

Original Text in German:

69. Grab des 🪶🐦 ⵊⵊ

"Die ganze Vorderwand ist zerstört. Nur bei b geht ein Stuck von oben weiter vor, das unten auch abgebrochen ist. Hier steht der Name der Frau ⵊⵊ ⵊⵊ :L D II 34a."

English translation:

69. Grave of 🪶🐦 ⵊⵊ

"The whole front wall is destroyed. Only at b. does a piece continue from above, which is also broken off below. Here is the woman's name ⵊⵊ ⵊⵊ :L D II 34a"

[NOTE: LD II 34a and 34b refers to the images from plate 34 of Lepsius' book, shown on the next pages.]

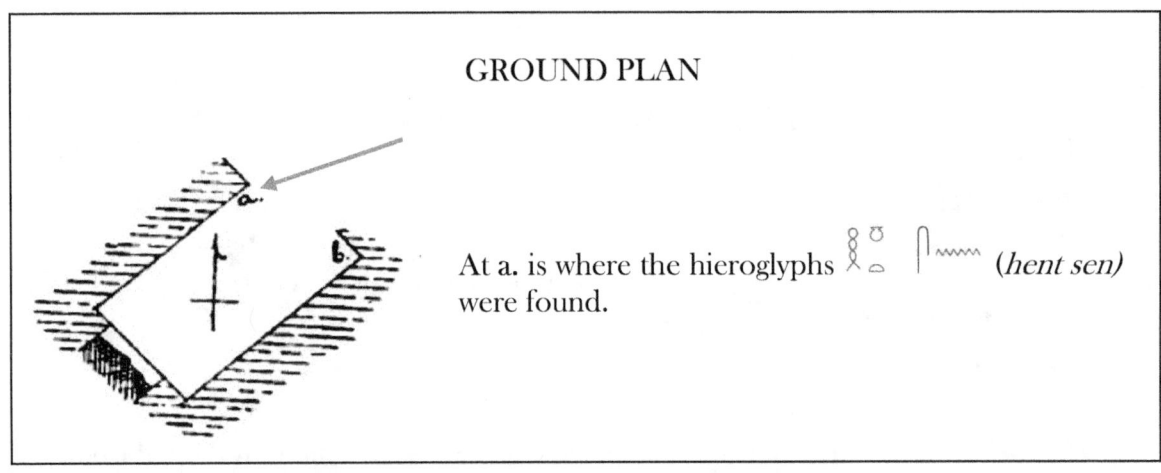

## The Outside Edge and Base

Surviving text from Grave 69 (Plate 34 of Lepsius' *Denkmaeler*)

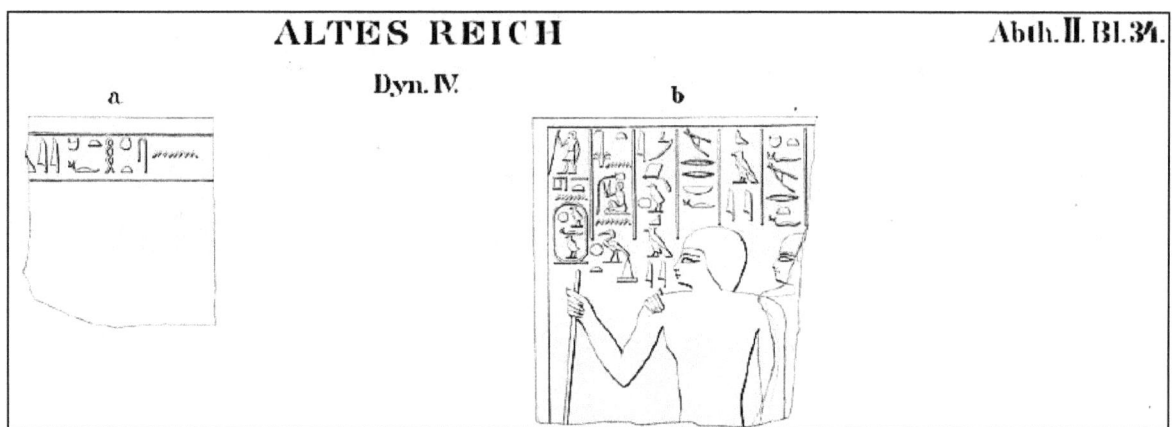

Note that the only name included here is *Qaii*, his wife, their queen:

a.

qai       hemt   ef   <u>hent</u>   <u>sen</u>
Qaii       wife   his   <u>queen</u>   <u>their</u>
Qaii his wife, <u>their queen</u>.

---

[144] Lepsius, *Denkmäler aus Aegypten und Aethiopien*, plates2, band 3, page 30.
http://gizamedia.rc.fas.harvard.edu/images/MFA-images/Giza/GizaImage/full/library/LD_plates_II_3_giza.pdf

# THE INVENTORY STELA TEXT

b.

| ser | h | aakhut | en | Khufu | suten | seth | en | aakhut | aa |
|---|---|---|---|---|---|---|---|---|---|
| noble | gift | horizon | of | Khufu | king | pour out a libation | for | horizon | pyramid |

Noble gift for horizon King *Khufu*. Pour out a libation for the horizon pyramid.

| amakhu[148] | | Qaii | merr | neb-t | ef | Qaii | hemt | ef |
|---|---|---|---|---|---|---|---|---|
| one who is worthy to be honored | | Qaii | love | lady | his | Qaii | wife | his |

One who is to be honored Qaii, his lady love, Qaii his wife,

| hent | sen | hem | ef | mer | tef... |
|---|---|---|---|---|---|
| queen | their | wife | his | love | this |

their queen. His wife loved this...

---

[145] Budge, *Egyptian Hieroglyphic Dictionary*, 680A, *ser*

[146] Budge, *Egyptian Hieroglyphic Dictionary*, 438A, *h*

[147] Budge, *Egyptian Hieroglyphic Dictionary*, 25A, *aakhut*,: horizon

[148] Budge, *Egyptian Hieroglyphic Dictionary*, 50A, *amakhu*: One who is worthy to be honored, revered, or worshiped.

# The Outside Edge and Base

## Lieblein's Reference

Lieblein's reference for *Khufu*'s daughter being named *Hent-sen* is on page 263 of Emmanuel de Rouge's *Monuments Qu'on Peut Attribuer Aux Six Premieres Dynasties*.[149] This reference is in error, since the book has only 228 pages, however we found ⟨hieroglyphs⟩ *hent sen* on page 47 of the same book.

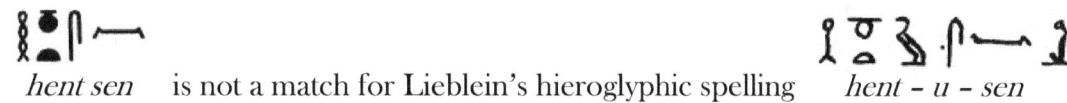

*hent sen* is not a match for Lieblein's hieroglyphic spelling *hent - u - sen*

\* \* \*

The result of checking all of these references has been that we found none of them supported the theory that ⟨hieroglyphs⟩ was the name of a princess.

---

[149] Rouge, *Recherches sur les Monuments qu'on peut Attribuer aux Six Premières Dynasties de Manéthon*, 1866. (English: *Research on the Monuments that can be Attributed to the First Six Dynasties*), page 47.

# THE INVENTORY STELA TEXT

Below is additional text of the Inventory Stela. Some of the text was damaged, but Daressy said there were faint traces of the missing text, so he attempted to restore as much as he could.

Additional text from the stela before restoration`

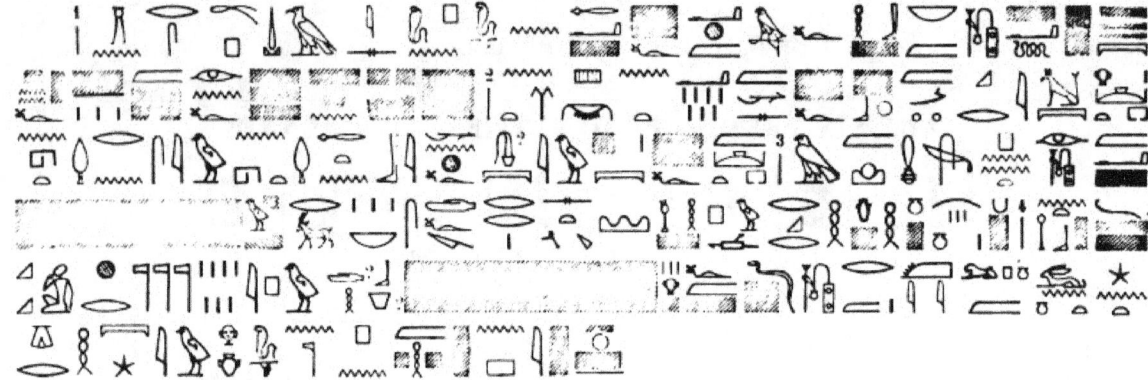

Additional text from the stela including restored text

## Translation of text by Bunker-Pressler (2021)

Center top of stela:
Living *Horus*, King of the South and North *Khufu* given life.

Left Side:
*Khufu* made this for his mother *Isis*[150], the mother of the god, *Hathor* queen of Celestial waters, a gift of writing inscribed upon a stone tablet. This belonging to the god he was happy to make anew, and he rebuilt the temple to the original condition. He found these gods at this her place.

---

[150] Her name translates to "Queen of the Throne" which is reflected in her headdress, which is typically a throne. Sometimes she is also depicted with the vulture headdress of the goddess *Mut*, and other times with a disk with horns on the sides, attributed to the goddess *Hathor*.

## The Outside Edge and Base

Right side:
> He discovered this house of *Isis*, the pyramid queen near the house of the Sphinx, upon the northwest of the house of *Osiris*, the lord of the abode of the dead community. He built this, his pyramid, near to the divine temple of this goddess, and he built these pyramids for his daughter, and the queen. They are near to this temple.

Additional text from the stela:
> The tomb of the Sphinx of *Horus* is upon the south of the house of *Isis*, and the queen's pyramid is upon the north in the writings of *Osiris* lord of this land of the dead, writings of this goddess of *Horus* - he brought this book about her. The Sphinx receives the Sun, the stone body of hard sandstone, the body to live until eternity, everlastingly to come over in front of it in the east - *Khufu* brought this book with him. He made the journey to see this goddess, the goddess of great power. He gave hard limestone. He covered over all the image of the god as it was designed, to exalt the Sun God *Ra* in this sky. He makes the wind in the place below. See, he made this carved back head covering to have the splendor of stone with the gold of seven cubits behind him. He came to wander about in this place and saw Qera, a storm god, in the sky over the tomb and a sycamore tree. He named this *Sau*'s Great Sycamore Tree Place of Wood. He who is over rises in the eastern sky. Follow him unto the tomb, *Horus* of the horizon, together with this likeness, which is seen in the great book {damaged portion of text} with gazelles all cut in pieces. Near the entrance ground of the hill cemetery this inscribed memorial stone. One circle in the Tuat, the width of eternity of bodies without life, thou swallow the Tusk of Ivory and the Thigh, to eat before the Seven Gods and consider them as a cup of grain {damaged portion of text} to see fly over. According to his written decree concerning the protection of this lion, the goddess[151] of this god[152] came in the hour of midnight to cut stones for the stone flesh, hard limestone.

It is interesting to note that the oldest known papyri with text is the diary of Merer,[153] discovered in 2013. It records stone transportation of 200 blocks per month from the Tura limestone quarry to Giza during five months in the 26th year of the reign of Pharaoh *Khufu*. The diary does not specify where the stones were to be used or for what purpose.

---

[151] *Isis*
[152] Sphinx
[153] https://en.wikipedia.org/wiki/Diary_of_Merer

# THE INVENTORY STELA TEXT

This diagram, created by Selim Hassan, is intended to show the flow of the text and the order in which it should be read.

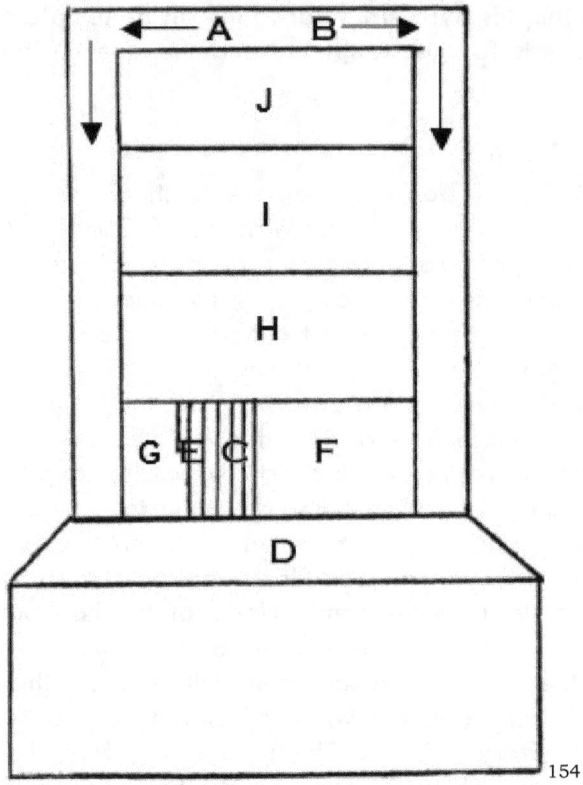

Translation of text by Bunker-Pressler

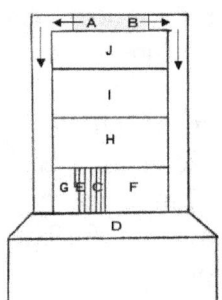

At the top center is the name and title of *Khufu*:

ankh   Hor   metchet-t          bati         Khu-fu   tu   ankh
living *Horus* strength   king South and North *Khufu* given life
Living *Horus*, strong king of the South and North, *Khufu*, given life

---

[154] Hassan, *The Great Sphinx and Its Secrets,* Excavations at Giza, 1936-7, Vol. 8, page 113.
[155] Budge, *Egyptian Hieroglyphic Dictionary,* page 919, *Horus,* Names of the Kings of Dynasty IV.

SECTION A

## Translation of the Text

### Section A

<u>Translation by Bunker-Pressler:</u>

Reading toward the left across the top of the stela then down the left side:

| ar | nef | en | mut | ef | Ast | mu-t neter[156] |
|---|---|---|---|---|---|---|
| make | this | for | mother | his | Isis | mother of the god |

made this for his mother *Isis*, mother of the god,[157]

| He-t-Hor | hen-t | | Nu |
|---|---|---|---|
| Hathor | queen | | Celestial waters |

*Hathor* queen of Celestial waters,

| sep-t[158] | ta-t | er | utch |
|---|---|---|---|
| writing | gift | upon | inscribed stela |

a gift of writing inscribed upon a stone tablet

| nef | nes | neter | hetep | en | ma [159] |
|---|---|---|---|---|---|
| that | belonging to | god | happy | to | make new |

that belonged to the god. [He was] happy to make a new [copy].

| qet | nef | neter[161] | sep | unem |
|---|---|---|---|---|
| build | this | temple | condition | renew |

[He] rebuilt the temple to its original condition.

---

[156] Budge, *Egyptian Hieroglyphic Dictionary*, 295A, *mu-t neter*.

[157] *Isis* was the mother of Horus

[158] Budge, *Egyptian Hieroglyphic Dictionary*, 661A, list, writing, document, ordinance.

[159] Budge, *Egyptian Hieroglyphic Dictionary*, 269A, *ma:* to be new, to make new, freshness, young, fresh

[160] 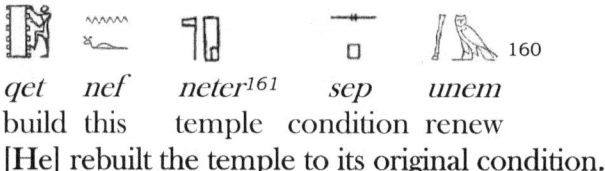 This image is from page 1232 of Brugsch's *Thesaurus*, number V, 1891. It is a portion of the text from a copy of the Inventory Stela made by Brugsch.

[161] Budge, *Egyptian Hieroglyphic Dictionary*, 455B, *neter*.

# THE INVENTORY STELA TEXT

| gem | nef | nu | neteru | her | s-t | s | ten[162] |
|---|---|---|---|---|---|---|---|
| find | this | these | gods | at | place | her | this |

[He] found this these gods at her place [the temple of *Isis*

## Section B

<u>Translation by Bunker-Pressler:</u>

Reading toward the right across the top of the stela then down the right side:

| ankh | Hor | metchet-t [163] | | bati |
|---|---|---|---|---|
| Living | *Horus* | strength | | King South and North |

Living *Horus*, strong king of the South and North,

| Khu-fu [164] | | tu | ankh | gem | nef | per | Ast |
|---|---|---|---|---|---|---|---|
| *Khufu* | | given | life | discover | this | house | *Isis* |

*Khufu*, given life, discovered this house of *Isis*,

| hent | aa | er | em | per | Hu | en[165] | her |
|---|---|---|---|---|---|---|---|
| queen | pyramid | near | to | house | Sphinx | of | upon |

the pyramid queen, near to the house of the Sphinx upon

| meh-t | ament | en | per | Asar | neb | Re-stau | nu-t |
|---|---|---|---|---|---|---|---|
| north | west | of | house | *Osiris* | lord | abode of the dead | community |

the northwest of the House of *Osiris* lord of the abode of the dead community.

| qet | nef | aa | ef | er | em | he-t | net | netrit | ten |
|---|---|---|---|---|---|---|---|---|---|
| build | this | pyramid | his | near | to | temple | of | goddess | this |

[He] built this his pyramid near to the temple of this goddess

---

[162] Brackets indicate missing text.
[163] Budge, *Egyptian Hieroglyphic Dictionary*, 338B, *metchet-t:* violent, strength, zealous, strenuous
[164] Budge, *Egyptian Hieroglyphic Dictionary*, page 919, *Horus*, Names of the Kings of Dynasty IV.
[165] Budge, *Egyptian Language*, see page 134, page 119, page 113, where ⌇⌇⌇ is translated "of."

## Sections C, D & F

| qet | nef | aa | en | su | sat | hent | they | er | em | he-t |
|---|---|---|---|---|---|---|---|---|---|---|
| build | these | pyramid | for | his | daughter[166] | queen | they | near | to | temple |

[He] built these pyramid[s] for his daughter [and] queen. They are near to [the] temple.

### Sections C, D & F

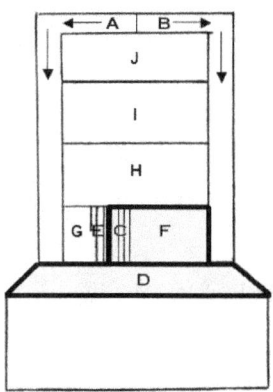

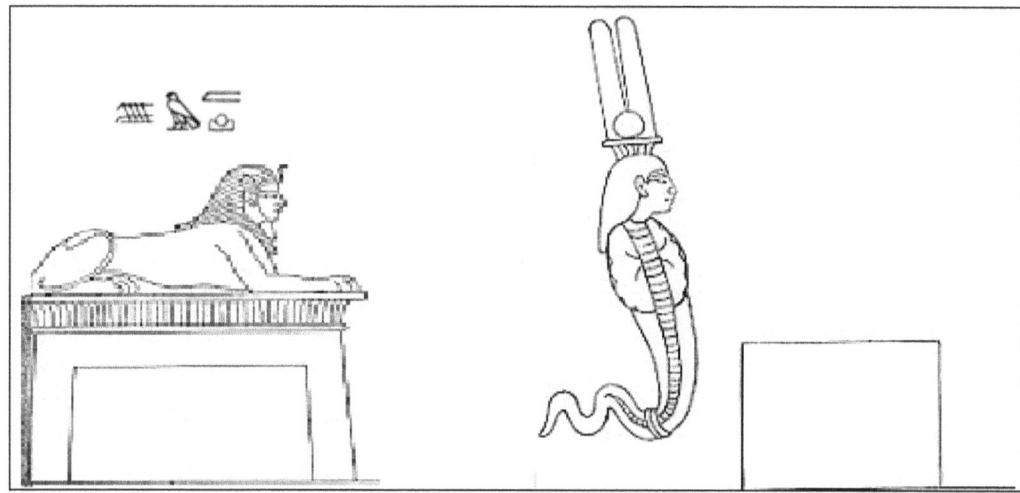

Images from *Khufu*'s Dream

The images above, engraved upon the stela, portray *Khufu*'s dream! The dream was the reason *Khufu* came to repair the temple of *Isis* and the Sphinx.

---

[166] Breasted, *Ancient Records of Egypt*, volume 1, page 85, footnote 1. "According to Herodotus, the middle of the three small pyramids east of the Great Pyramid, belonged to *Khufu's* daughter (Herodotus II, 126)." [The *History of Herodotus*, Book II, page 203, chapter 126.]

# THE INVENTORY STELA TEXT

The stela reads:

| ef | em | utch | sesh | er | maki ¹⁶⁷ | ru | pu | nu |
|---|---|---|---|---|---|---|---|---|
| his | according to | decree | to write | concerning | to protect | lion | this | of |

According to his written decree concerning the protection of this lion

| em | unnut | net | gerh | au | heri ab | netrit | en | neter | pen | em |
|---|---|---|---|---|---|---|---|---|---|---|
| in | hour | of | night | to come | the middle | goddess | of | god | this | in |

the goddess of this god came in the midnight hour

| qah¹⁶⁸ | aner | auf | rut-t |
|---|---|---|---|
| to cut stones | stone | flesh | hard sandstone |

to cut stones for the stone flesh of hard sandstone.

There is another inscription written above and in front of the Sphinx. It is separated from the first inscription that is written behind *Isis* by an empty column.

| seshep | Hor em akhet |
|---|---|
| receive | *Horus* in the horizon |

receive *Horus*¹⁶⁹ in the horizon,

| aner | auf | rut-t | nut | auf | ankh | er | heh | tche-t | au |
|---|---|---|---|---|---|---|---|---|---|
| stone | body | hard sandstone¹⁷⁰ | of | body | live | until | eternity | everlasting | to come |

the stone body of hard sandstone the body to live until eternity, everlastingly to come

| her | meter | aabtt |
|---|---|---|
| over | in front of | the east |

over in front of [it in the] east.

---

¹⁶⁷ Budge, *Egyptian Hieroglyphic Dictionary*, 288B, *m'ki*.
¹⁶⁸ Budge, *Egyptian Hieroglyphic Dictionary*, 764B, *qah*.
¹⁶⁹ the sun
¹⁷⁰ Budge, *Egyptian Hieroglyphic Dictionary*, 421B, *rut-t*, quartzite sandstone.
¹⁷¹ Daressy, *La Stele De La Fille De Cheops*, 1908. This group is not very distinct, the stone being worn and chipped.

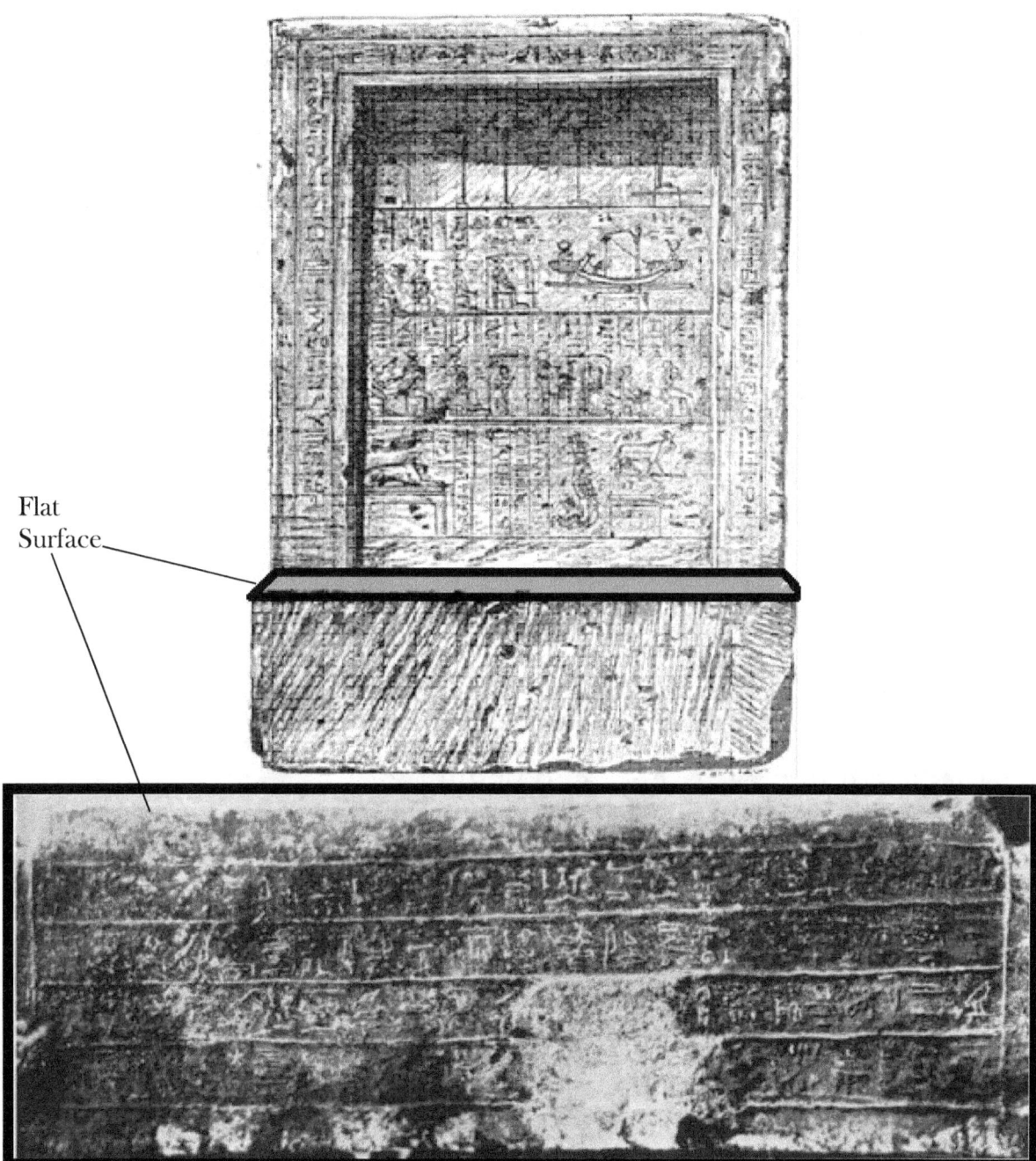

The flat horizontal surface of pedestal of the Inventory Stela[172]

Four lines of text were cut into the pedestal of the Inventory Stela which Daressy called an "offering table." The journal *Recueil de Travaux Relatifs a la Philologie* contains the only edition ever made of the text engraved on the horizontal part of the stela and its translation.[173]

---

[172] Hassan, *The Great Sphinx and Its Secrets,* Excavations at Giza, 1936-7, Vol. 8, page 140, Plate LVI.
[173] Daressy, *La Stele de la Fille de Cheops.*

## THE INVENTORY STELA TEXT

Below is the text from the base of the Inventory Stela. Some of the text was damaged, but Daressy said there were faint traces of the missing text, so he attempted to restore as much as he could.

Additional text from the stela before restoration

Additional text from the stela including Daressy's restored text

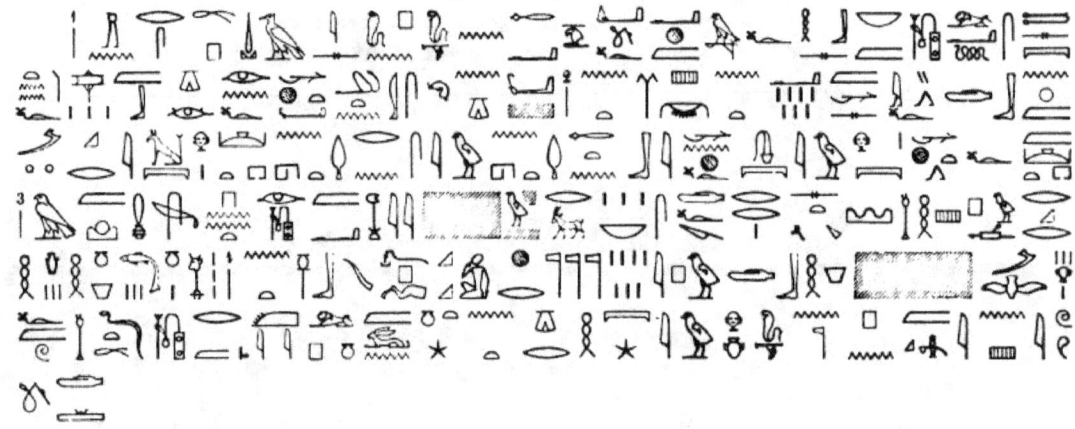

Summary of the translation of the base by G Daressy (1908):

The place of the sphinx of *Harmakhis* is south of the residence of *Isis*, regent of the Pyramid, and north of O*siris* (sic) [174], lord of Ro-satu. The chosen of the gods being in his house, the drawings of the image of *Harmakhis* were brought for the restoration of this colossus, portrait of the very (formidable). He has restored the statue covered with paint (the guardian of the atmosphere, which guides the winds of the gaze.[175] "He cut the back of the nemes[176] which was missing in a gilded stone which has seven cubits in its length. (He came to take a turn) to see "the storm on the place of sycamore[177], so named because of a large sycamore with the

---

[174] The word ▭ was jumped on the stele
[175] In *Makrizi's* time, the sphinx was regarded as a talisman charged with preventing the invasion of the Gizéh lands by the sands.
[176] One can still see on the Sphinx that the back of the hairstyle was made of a separate stone.
[177] Of course, there are sycamores in the nearby Sphinx Valley, 220 meters to the south. The offspring of these trees still succeed each other and currently house Bedouin tombs. Here is a

## SECTIONS C, D & F

thunder branch when the master of the sky (?) Went down on the place of *Harmakhis*, and also this image retracing the fire (?) ... of all the animals killed at *Ro-satu*. It is a table for the vases full of the remains of the animals that, (except the thigh?), Are eaten near these seven gods (?), Asking. .. (the rays of his face on the stela) traced near this colossus at the time of the darkness. The figure of this god being (cut in) stone, is solid and will subsist for eternity, forever, the face looking east. "

Summary of the translation of the base by Bunker-Pressler (2021):

The tomb of the Sphinx of *Horus* is upon the south of the house of *Isis*, and the queen's pyramid is upon the north in the writings of *Osiris* lord of this land of the dead, writings of this goddess of *Horus* - he brought this book about her. The Sphinx receives the Sun, the stone body of hard sandstone, the body to live until eternity, everlastingly to come over in front of it in the east - *Khufu* brought this book with him. He made the journey to see this goddess, the goddess of great power. He gave hard limestone. He covered over all the image of the god as it was designed, to exalt the Sun God *Ra* in this sky. He makes the wind in the place below. See, he made this carved back head covering to have the splendor of stone with the gold of seven cubits behind him. He came to wander about in this place and saw Qera, a storm god, in the sky over the tomb and a sycamore tree. He named this *Sau's* Great Sycamore Tree Place of Wood. He who is over rises in the eastern sky. Follow him unto the tomb, *Horus* of the horizon, together with this likeness, which is seen in the great book {damaged portion of text} with gazelles all cut in pieces. Near the entrance ground of the hill cemetery this inscribed memorial stone. One circle in the *Tuat*, the width of eternity of bodies without life, thou swallow the Tusk of Ivory and the Thigh, to eat before the Seven Gods and consider them as a cup of grain {damaged portion of text} to see fly over. According to his written decree concerning the protection of this lion, the goddess[178] of this god[179] came in the hour of midnight to cut stones for the stone flesh, hard limestone.

It is interesting to note that the oldest known papyri with text is the diary of Merer,[180] discovered in 2013. It records stone transportation of 200 blocks per month from the Tura limestone quarry to Giza during five months in the 26th year of the reign of Pharaoh *Khufu*. The diary does not specify where the stones were to be used or for what purpose.

---

bouquet of sycamores that has survived for more than 2,400 years and has a mention several centuries earlier than that of the tree of the Virgin of Matarieh.

[178] *Isis*
[179] Sphinx
[180] https://en.wikipedia.org/wiki/Diary_of_Merer

# THE INVENTORY STELA TEXT

Full translation of the base by **Bunker-Pressler:**

Text from the horizontal surface of the base of the stela:

| ani | er | si | pu | sheftu | ta | as | netrit | pen |
|---|---|---|---|---|---|---|---|---|
| bring | with him | this | book | make journey | to behold | | goddess | this |

*Khufu* brought this book with him. He made the journey to see this goddess,

| netrit | en | aa | shefit |
|---|---|---|---|
| goddess | of | great | power |

the goddess of great power.

| ta | rut-t | ef | akhm | ef | hebs | neb | em | sesh |
|---|---|---|---|---|---|---|---|---|
| give | hard sandstone | he | image of a god | he | cover over | all | as | design |

He gave hard limestone to the image of the god. He covered over all as designed

| Ra | sethes | pet | ten | en | ef | qema | as | em | bu | kher |
|---|---|---|---|---|---|---|---|---|---|---|
| Sungod | to exalt | sky | this | in | he | make | wind | in | place | under |

to exalt the Sun-god *Ra* in this sky. He makes the wind in the place below.

| maa | ar | nef | khefti | peh | nemes | en | kher | shesp |
|---|---|---|---|---|---|---|---|---|
| see | make | this | carve | the back | head covering | to | having something | splendor |

See, he made this carved back head covering to have the splendor

| neth | em | aner | sau | meh | neth | sefekh | m khet | s |
|---|---|---|---|---|---|---|---|---|
| of | with | stone | gold | cubit | of | seven | behind | him |

of stone with gold of seven cubits behind him.

| ai | ef | teben | em |
|---|---|---|---|
| come | he | to wander around a place | in |

He came to wander about in this place

---

181 Budge, *Egyptian Hieroglyphic Dictionary*, page cxxxix, List of tools and agricultural implements, no. 2.

maa    Qera¹⁸²    her    aa    nuhati
to see    a storm god    over    tomb    sycamore tree
and saw a storm cloud over the tomb and a sycamore tree

ren    Sau    nuhati    aa ten    bu    akhet en
name    mythological serpent    sycamore tree    great this    place    wood    of
and named this Sau's great sycamore tree place of wood.

kh¹⁸³ ef    aab pet    au em    heri    khet ef    em    aa
to rise he    east sky    come in    he who is over    follow him    to    tomb
He who is over rises in the eastern sky; follow him to the tomb.

Hor-em-akhet    ma    seshem    pen    net    maa    sesh    em    aa
Horus of the Horizon    together with    likeness    this    which    see    book    in    great
Horus of the horizon together with this likeness, which is seen in the great book.

Recall this image from an ancient book painted in the tomb of *Ramesses VI,* which seems to embody the idea of *Horus* of the horizon (the sun) in front of his likeness, the Sphinx.

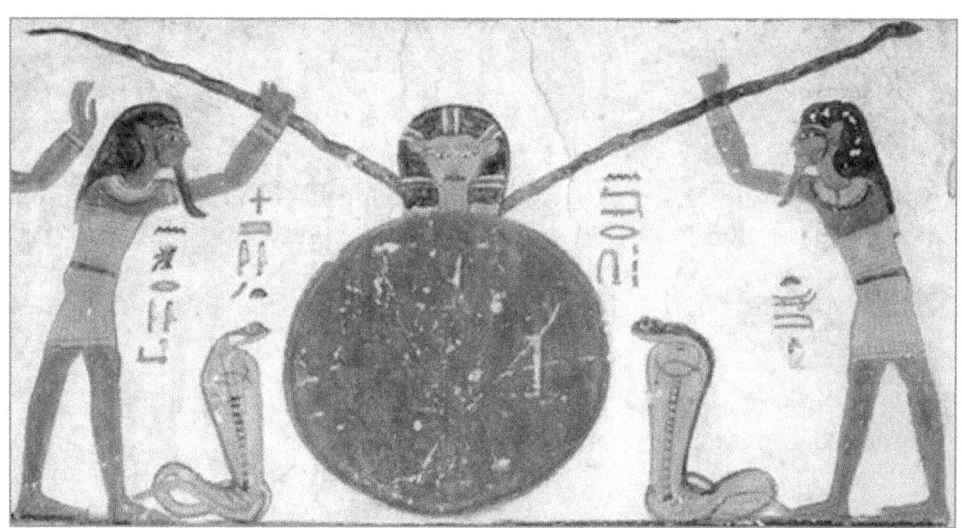

---

¹⁸² Budge, *Egyptian Hieroglyphic Dictionary,* 775B, *Qera.*
¹⁸³ Budge, *Egyptian Hieroglyphic Dictionary,* 525A, *Khr.* to rise (of the Nile)

112

## Sections G & E

On the left of the last register, a sphinx is lying on a high pedestal, adorned with a cornice:

The Great Sphinx

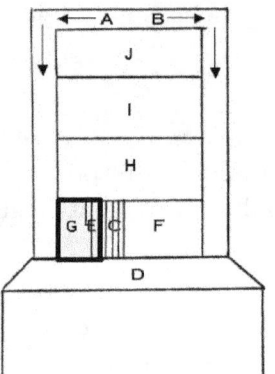

<u>Translation by Bunker-Pressler:</u>

The text above the Sphinx reads:

*seshep    Hor em akhet*
receive    *Horus* in the horizon
To receive the sun in the horizon

The two columns in front of the Sphinx read:

*aner    auf    rut-t         nut    auf    ankh    er    heh    tche-t*
stone body hard sandstone[184] of body live until eternity everlasting
the stone body of hard sandstone, the body to live until eternity everlastingly,

*au    her    meter[185]    aabtt*
to come over in front of the east
to come over in front of it in the east.

---

[184] Budge, *Egyptian Hieroglyphic Dictionary*, 421B, quartzite sandstone.
[185] Daressy, *La Stele De La Fille De Cheops*, 1908. This group is not very distinct, the stone being worn and chipped.

# SECTIONS G & E

Continuing with the text of the base of the stela:

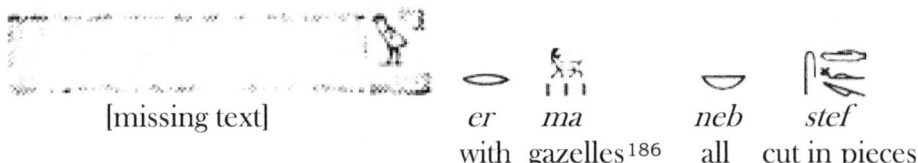

| [missing text] | er | ma | neb | stef |
|---|---|---|---|---|
| | with | gazelles[186] | all | cut in pieces |

...with gazelles all cut in pieces

| er | re | set | semi-t | utch | pu |
|---|---|---|---|---|---|
| near | entrance | ground | hill cemetery | inscribed stela | this |

near the entrance ground of the hill cemetery this inscribed Memorial Tablet.

| ua | qerr | heh | nu | usekh | khat [188] | nu |
|---|---|---|---|---|---|---|
| one | circle in the Tuat | eternity | of | width | bodies without life | of |

One circle in the Tuat the width of eternity of bodies without life.

| am | net | ab | khepesh | kek | kher | neteru | sefekh |
|---|---|---|---|---|---|---|---|
| swallow thou | tusk of ivory[189] | thigh[190] | | to eat | before | gods | seven |

Thou swallow the tusks of ivory and the thigh to eat before the seven gods,

| apu | ta | tebh | missing text | maa | pa | her |
|---|---|---|---|---|---|---|
| count | them | a grain measure | (missing text) | see | fly | over |

considering them as a cup of grain...seen to fly over.

The context is in reference to the great size of the Tuat. Its enormity swallows the ivory tusks of the hippopotamus constellation (Cetus) and the Egyptian thigh constellation (Ursa Major), and engulfs the seven stars of Pleiades (near Taurus).

---

[186] Budge, *Egyptian Hieroglyphic Dictionary*, 268A, *ma*.

[187] Budge, *Egyptian Hieroglyphic Dictionary*, 627B, *set*: , earth, ground.

[188] *Khat* has been translated as corpse, but a corpse is a body without life and this idea more accurately describes star constellations in my opinion.

[189] Budge, *Egyptian Hieroglyphic Dictionary*, page 4A, *ab*.

[190] great bear constellation

## The Tuat

### "One circle in the Tuat the width of eternity"

The Tuat was so big it swallowed the star constellations. The images below from left to right are the constellations Ursa Major (*the Egyptian thigh constellation with the stars of the gazelle footprints*), Taurus (*the bull with the Pleiades star cluster at the tip of its vertical appendage*) and Cetus.

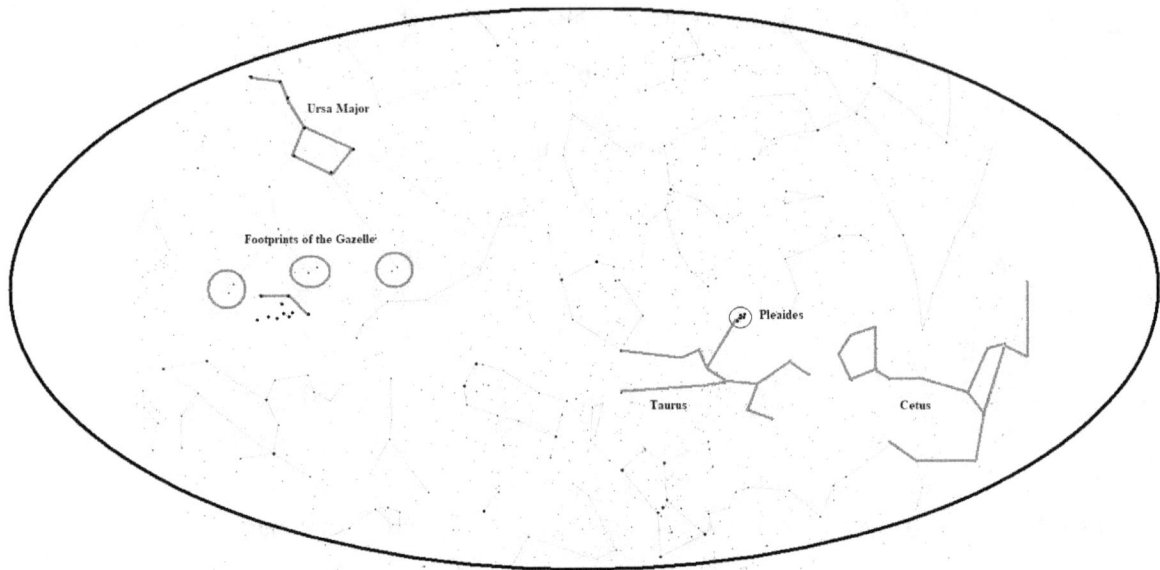

The circle of the Tuat

Salim Hassan stated, "If we consider the evidence afforded by the meaning of its name during the Old Kingdom, we shall see that originally the *Tuat*, the future Underworld, was localized in the sky..."[191]

---

[191] Hassan, *Excavations at Giza*, vol. VI, part I, 1934-1935, page 277.
http://gizamedia.rc.fas.harvard.edu/images/MFA-images/Giza/GizaImage/full/library/hassan_giza_6_1.pdf

# The Tuat

The enormity of the *Tuat* swallows the hippopotamus.

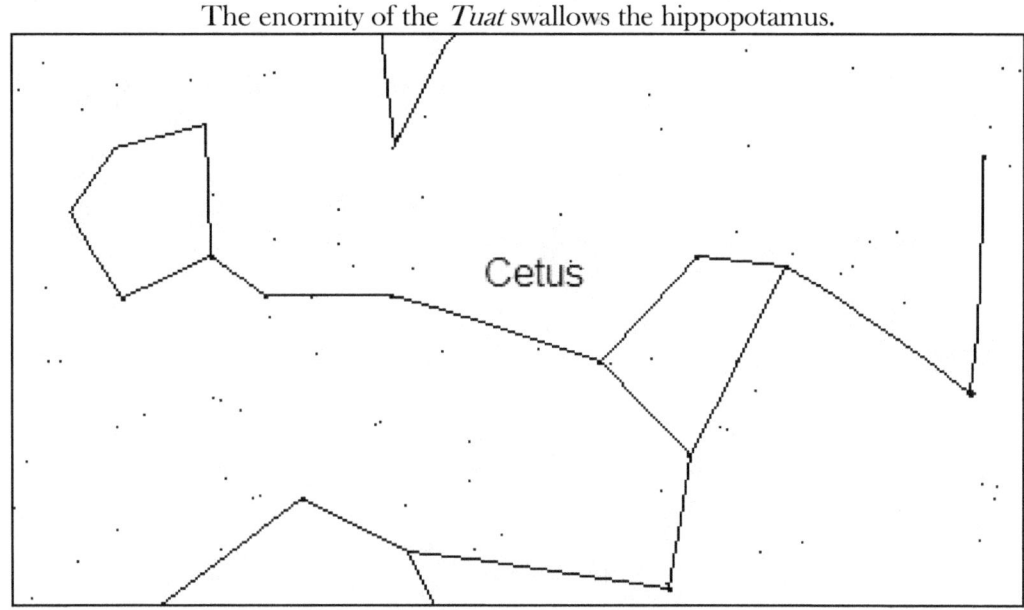

The *Tuat* swallows the constellation of the Thigh (the Ursa Major)

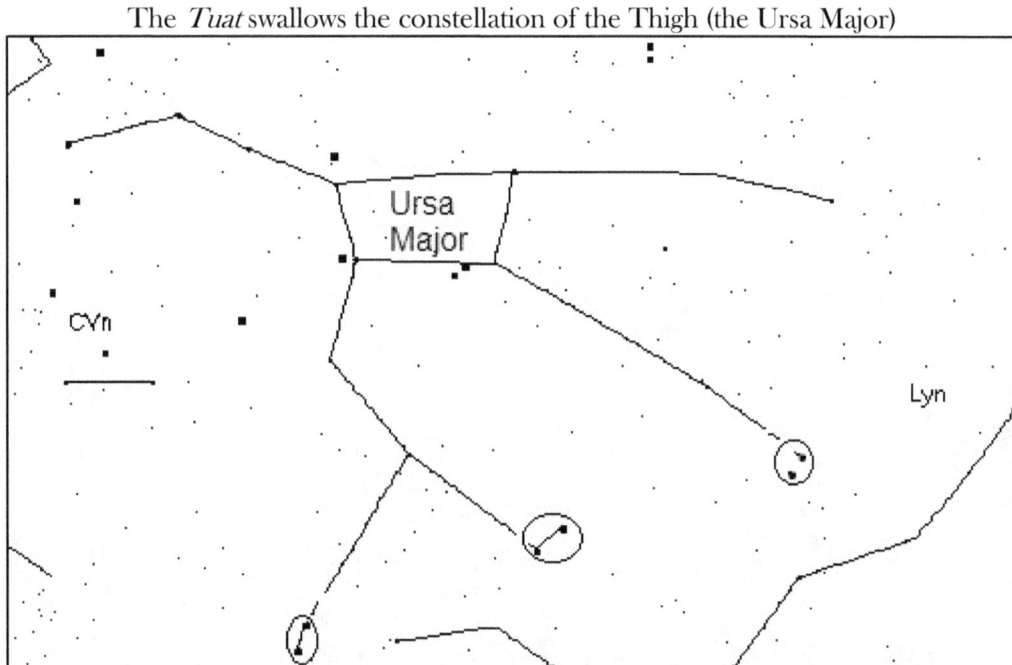

The three gazelle footprint stars of Ursa Major constellation

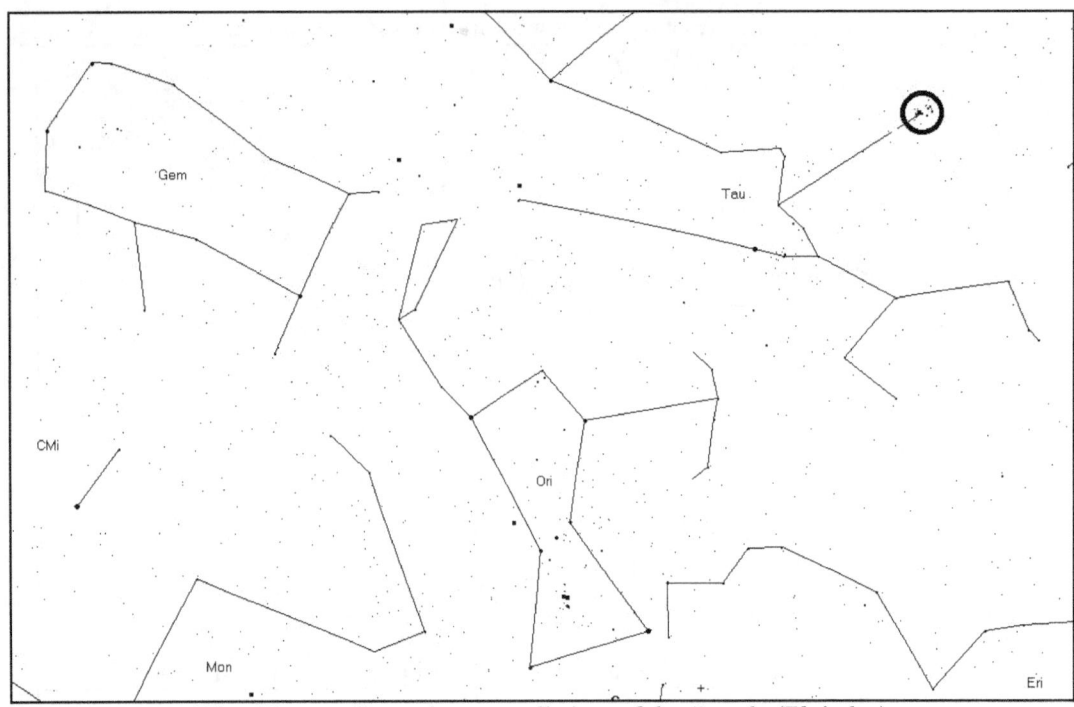

The *Tuat* swallows the constellation of the 7 gods (Pleiades)
The circle surrounds the 7 stars of the Pleiades star cluster of Taurus.

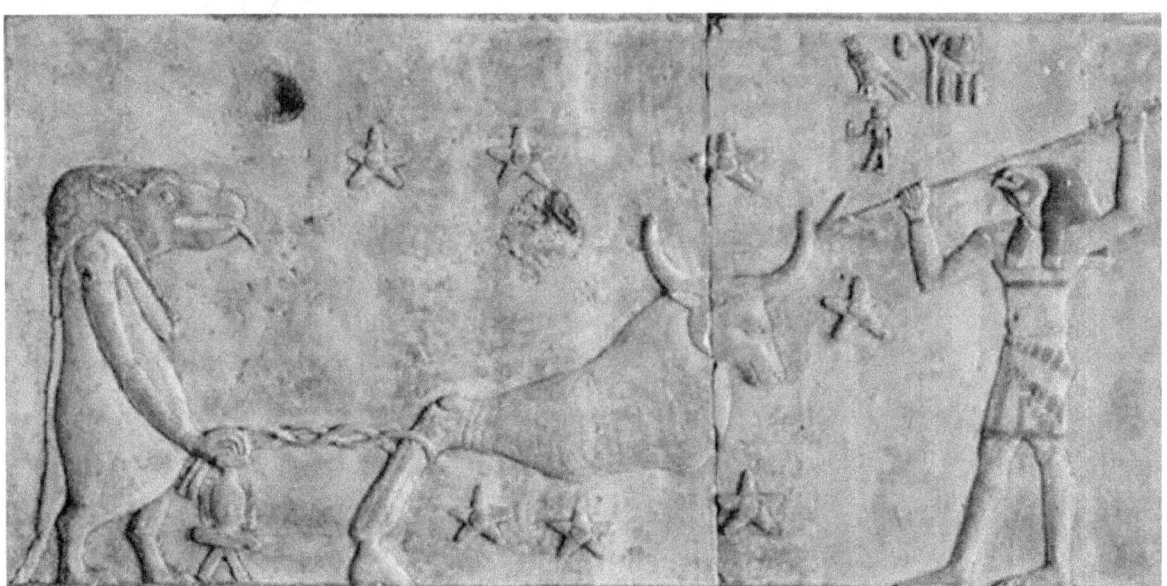

At *Dendera* the Pleiades were illustrated as seven stars surrounding Taurus.

# THE INVENTORY STELA

## ANALYSIS OF THE INVENTORY STELA

There is no substantial evidence that *Khufu* constructed the Great pyramid. Early researchers of Egyptian history relied heavily upon Greek historians, like Herodotus (c.460 BC) and Menetho (c.280 BC). Herodotus lived about as far removed from the time of *Khufu* (c.2500 BC) as we are removed from the time of Christ. Herodotus provided stories that he had heard repeated from others. He did not specialize in Egyptian history, but wrote about many places he had visited and presented ideas he had heard from stories shared with him by people he met during his extended travels to many countries. Two other Greek writers who influenced our ideas about Egypt, Diodorus and Plutarch, lived during the first century A.D. It should be noted that together all of these writers of the history of ancient Egypt, lacking empirical evidence, provided the basis for modern belief.

Although it has never been proven who built the Great Pyramid, the idea has continued to be expressed that it was *Khufu*. When the Inventory Stela was discovered in 1858, the text of the Inventory Stela was translated and interpreted in such a way so as not to conflict with pre-existing beliefs.

Taken simply at face value, the text of the Inventory Stela provides a basis in fact for the existence of the three smaller pyramids just east of the Great Pyramid, pyramids (it states) *Khufu* constructed for himself, his daughter, and his queen. Other details about Giza can be understood by gleaning information the stela provides; like the presence of the Sphinx in a ruined condition, and the presence of the Great Pyramid near which *Khufu* found the temple of *Isis* in a ruined condition.

The real question is what do you choose to believe?

---

**FOOD FOR THOUGHT**

From a 1932 psychic "reading" of prophet, Edgar Cayce:[192]

(Q) What was the date of the actual beginning and ending of the construction of the Great Pyramid?
(A) 10,490 to 10,390 BC

---

[192] Edgar Cayce Reading 5748-006 TEXT
Date Reading Given 07/01/32
   7. (Q) What was the date of the actual beginning and ending of the construction of the Great Pyramid?
     (A) Was one hundred years in construction. Begun and completed in the period of Araaraart's time, with Hermes and Ra.
   8. (Q) What was the date B.C. of that period?
     (A) 10,490 to 10,390 before the Prince entered into Egypt.

# THE INVENTORY STELA

There seems to be more information to be gleaned by a closer examination of the Inventory Stela than has been recognized before. To begin, why does the stela make the statements that it does, and what are the implications of the reasoning behind the thoughts of its creator? Let's look at the statements of the Inventory Stela and then examine them more closely

Statements of the Inventory Stela:

1. *Khufu* made this for his mother *Isis*[193], the mother of the god, *Hathor* queen of Celestial waters.
2. A gift of writing inscribed upon a stone tablet. This belonging to the god he was happy to make anew, he rebuilt the temple to the original condition.
3. He found these gods at this her place.
4. He discovered this house of *Isis*, pyramid queen,[194] near the house of the Sphinx, upon the northwest of the House of *Osiris*, the lord of the abode of the dead community.
5. He built this, his pyramid, near to the divine temple of this goddess and he built these pyramids for his daughter and queen. They are near to the divine temple.
6. The tomb of the Sphinx of *Horus* is upon the south of the house of *Isis* and the queen's pyramid is upon the north
7. In the writings of *Osiris* lord of this land of the dead, and the writings of this goddess of *Horus*; he brought this book about her.
8. The Sphinx receives the Sun, (the stone body of hard sandstone, the body to live until eternity), everlastingly to come over in front of it in the east; *Khufu* brought this book with him.
9. He made the journey to see this goddess, the goddess of great power. He gave hard limestone to the image of the god. He covered over all as designed to exalt the Sun God *Ra* in this sky, he makes the wind in the place below.
10. He made this carved back of the head covering having the splendor of stone with gold, of seven cubits behind him.
11. He came to wander about in this place and saw *Qera*, a storm god, in the sky over the tomb and a sycamore tree, and he named this great sycamore tree *Sau's* Dwelling Place of Wood.
12. He who is over rises in the eastern sky. Follow him unto the tomb, *Horus* of the horizon, together with this likeness, which is seen in the great book.
13. {damaged portion of "text} with gazelles all cut in pieces.

---

[193] Her name translates to "Queen of the Throne" which is reflected in her headdress, which is typically a throne. Sometimes she is also depicted with the vulture headdress of the goddess Mut, and other times with a disk with horns on the sides, attributed to the goddess *Hathor*.

[194] https://penelope.uchicago.edu/Thayer/E/Roman/Texts/Diodorus_Siculus/1A*.html
This webpage reproduces a portion of The Library of History of Diodorus Siculus published in Vol. I of the Loeb Classical Library edition, 1933. Section 27:

> 3. Now I am not unaware that some historians give the following account of Isis and Osiris: The tombs of these gods lie in Nysa in Arabia, and for this reason Dionysus is also called Nysaeus. And in that place there stands also a stele of each of the gods bearing an inscription in hieroglyphs. 4 On the stele of Isis it runs: "I am Isis, the queen of every land...."

# ANALYSIS OF THE INVENTORY STELA

14. Near the entrance ground of the hill cemetery this inscribed memorial stone.
15. One circle in the Tuat, the width of eternity of bodies without life; thou swallow the tusk of ivory (*Hippopotamus constellation*) and the thigh (*Canis Major*) to eat before the seven gods (*Pleiades star cluster*) and consider them as a cup of grain {*damaged portion of text*} see fly over.
15. According to his written decree concerning the protection of this lion, the goddess of this god (*Isis*) came in the hour of midnight to cut stones for the stone flesh hard limestone.

Let's take a look at each of these lines and what they mean.

## Line 1. The mother of the god

1. *Khufu* made this for his mother *Isis*[195], the mother of the god. *Hathor* queen of Celestial waters.

*Why was Isis called the mother of the god? How was Hathor involved? Who was the god that Isis was the mother of? Was Isis also identified as Hathor the queen of Celestial Waters?*

Egyptian mythology explains that *Isis* gave birth to *Horus* the sun god, but it does not openly explain the facts surrounding this event, because it was forgotten that it was a story that had its roots in astronomy. *Isis* was the twin goddess of *Nephthys*, and together they were the goddesses of Truth, the twin stars in the constellation Gemini, which was on the western horizon just before the sun rose up in the east. Because of this fact, the mythology was created that made *Isis* the mother of *Horus* the newly risen sun. The Lamentations of *Isis* and *Nephthys* read: **Thy son, the youth Horus, the child of (thy) two sisters.**[196] A further study of the astronomical basis for the legend of *Isis* and *Horus* and the death of *Osiris* can be found in Part V of this book.

Besides *Isis*, *Hathor* was also mentioned as the mother of *Horus* in the Pyramid Texts, "**You are Horus, the son of Osiris; you, Unis, are the senior god, the son of Hathor; you are the seed of Geb.**" There seems to have been a fusion of the identity of the goddesses *Isis* and *Hathor*, with *Isis* being dominant in this instance. [197]

---

[195] Her name translates to "Queen of the Throne" which is reflected in her headdress, which is typically a throne. Sometimes she is also depicted with the vulture headdress of the goddess *Mut*, and other times with a disk with horns on the sides, attributed to the goddess *Hathor*.

[196] McCarthy, *The World's Greatest Literature*, "Lamentations of *Isis* and Nephthys," page 364.

[197] Mercer, *The Pyramid Texts*, page 160, "Utterance 303, 466a. Art thou Horus, son of Osiris? Art thou, O N., the god, the eldest, son of Hathor?"; Also see Yoo, Sung Hwan, *Patterns of Ancient Egyptian Child Deities*, pages 151, 152, "*3.3.1 Mother goddesses of Horus. Besides Isis, Hathor and Nut are also mentioned as the mother of Horus (Kurth 1977: 1001). Hathor as the mother of Horus is mentioned in Pyramid Texts Spell 303 (Pyr. §§ 466a-b): Twt Hrw zA wsjr, Twt (wnjs)| nTr smsw zA Hwt-Hrw, Twt mtwt gbb "You are Horus, the son of Osiris; you, Unis, are the senior god, the son of Hathor; you are the seed of Geb." Some Egyptologists believe that Hathor was the original mother of Horus and later she was replaced by Isis when a genealogical adjustment was made in order to fit Horus in to the Osirian cycle (Sethe 1930: 54-55; Griffiths 1960: 13; Tassie 2005: 67). Others hold the view that Hathor, who personalizes the concept of heavenly motherhood, was regarded as the mother of Horus the Elder (or the*

# THE INVENTORY STELA

## Line 2. The house, temple & the pyramid

2. A gift of writing inscribed upon a stone tablet. This belonging to the god he was happy to make anew, he rebuilt the temple to the original condition.

The temple of *Isis* was also referred to as her house. These two terms were interchangeable. Here *Isis* is referred to as *Isis* the pyramid queen. Reading toward the right across the top of the stela then down the right side:

| gen | nef | per | Ast | hent | aa |
|---|---|---|---|---|---|
| discover | this | house | *Isis* | queen | pyramid |

discovered this house of *Isis* the pyramid queen

This implies there was already a pyramid near the temple of *Isis* when *Khufu* got there.

According to Professor Selim Hassan, Ph.D., the Inventory Stela claimed that the temple of *Isis* was found in ruins by *Khufu*, and was re-built by him. In this case it must, at the very latest, have been built in the beginning of the 3rd dynasty.[198] What other evidence is there that suggests such an early date for the temple of *Isis*? If one is willing to accept information provided by Edgar Cayce, the famous twentieth century clairvoyant, he indicated that the temple of *Isis* predated the creation of the Sphinx. **"We see this sphinx was builded as this: The excavations were made for same in the plains above where the temple of Isis had stood."**[199]

NOTE: We often wondered why Cayce, when referring to the position of the sphinx in reference to the temple of *Isis*, said excavations were made for the sphinx *above* where the temple of *Isis* had stood. It was because of the ancient Egyptian perspective of the country and the Nile. Upper Egypt was to the south, because it was up river. The Nile flowed from south to north. Excavations for the Sphinx were made in land situated above (*up river*), or south from the temple of *Isis*.

---

*sun-god) and as the wet nurse or foster mother of Horus the Younger (Barta 1973: 163; Bleeker 1973: 25; Pinch 2002: 80). Barta claims that Hathor in this role represents a localized part of the sky (Pyr. § 1327b). Hathor as the foster mother has to do with the depiction of kings on temple walls as the Horus child being washed or suckled by a cow in the marshes. Hathor in this role has a great significance in that royal children were usually raised by foster mothers. For the suckling of the royal child by Hathor, see Bleeker 1973: 51-52. For the prominent position of royal wet-nurses, see Janssen 1990: 17-18. Also, a parallel is noted by many scholars between the motif of the Horus child and the biblical tradition of Moses who was hidden in a floating basket among rushes and then given to his own mother to be nursed]"*

[198] Hassan, *The Great Sphinx and Its Secrets,* Excavations at Giza, 1936-7, Vol. 8, page 111.
[199] Edgar Cayce Reading 195-14, given on 7/8/1925, paragraph 29

## ANALYSIS OF THE INVENTORY STELA

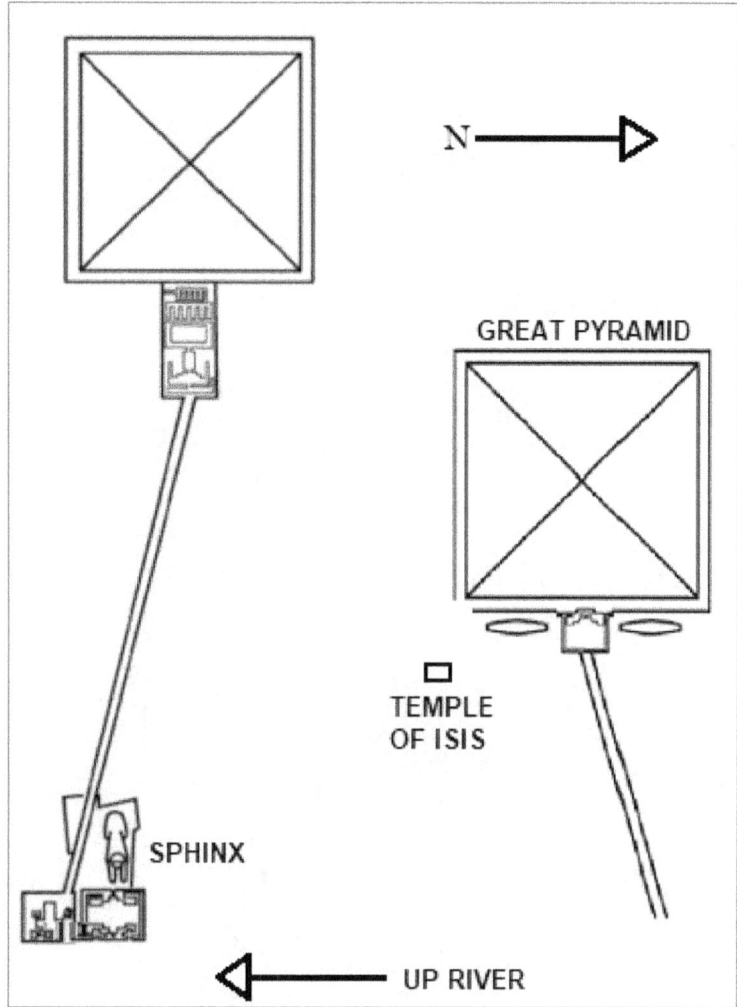

The structures in this image all existed at the time Khufu made his journey to Giza. The Sphinx and the Temple of Isis were in ruins.

# THE INVENTORY STELA

Though a modern image, this picture illustrates the idea that "The base of the Sphinx was laid out in channels."[201]

---

[200] http://www.griffith.ox.ac.uk/gri/heathcote/image.php?i=90
[201] Edgar Cayce Reading 195-14, para. 29.

## Line 3. The gods

3. He found these gods at this her place.

The stela reveals that *Khufu* "found these gods" at the ruined temple of *Isis*. The Stele contains a list of the statues of gods, their sizes, and the material from which they were constructed.

## Line 4 & 5. The pyramids that *Khufu* built

4. He discovered this house of *Isis* the pyramid queen near the house of the Sphinx, upon the northwest of the House of *Osiris*, the lord of the abode of the dead community.
5. He built this, his pyramid, near to the divine temple of this goddess and he built these pyramids for his daughter and queen. They are near to the temple.

This stela appears to be stating that Khufu built the three smaller pyramids that are between the Temple of Isis and the Great Pyramid.

After *Khufu* reconstructed the temple of *Isis*, he built three pyramids:
1. His (adjoining the temple of *Isis*),
2. one for his daughter,
3. and one for his queen.

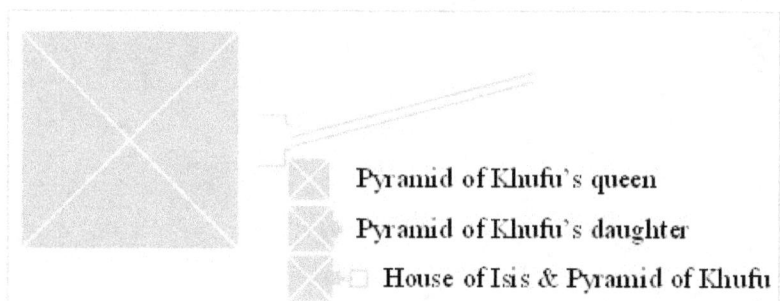

The Inventory Stela explains that *Khufu* built his pyramid near to the temple of *Isis*.

| qet | nef | aa | ef | er | em | he-t | net | netrit | ten |
|---|---|---|---|---|---|---|---|---|---|
| build | this | pyramid | his | near | to | temple | of | goddess | this |

He built this his pyramid near to the temple of this goddess

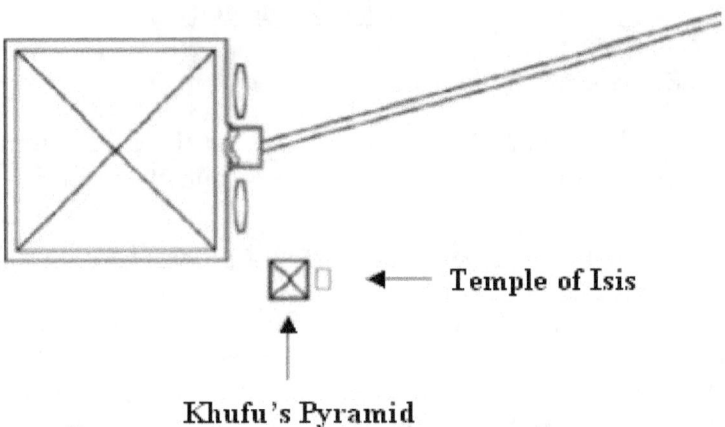

This pyramid (referred to as G-1c) was built by *Khufu* next to the temple of *Isis* (in the foreground). The Great Pyramid is in the distance behind it, toward the right.

---

[202] By Francesco Gasparetti - originally posted to Flickr as *Giza: piramidi di Henutsen e Cheope, CC BY 2.0*, https://commons.wikimedia.org/w/index.php?curid=5297097

## Line 6. The positioning of other buildings

**6. The tomb of the Sphinx of *Horus* is upon the south of the house of *Isis* and the queen's pyramid is upon the north**

There were several comments referencing buildings and locations on the Inventory Stela. These have been labeled for reference in the illustration below.

- house of *Isis* near the house of the Sphinx upon the northwest of the House of *Osiris*.
- he built his pyramid, near to the divine temple of this goddess.
- he built these pyramids for his daughter and queen...near to the divine temple.
- tomb of the Sphinx of *Horus* is upon the south of the house of *Isis*.

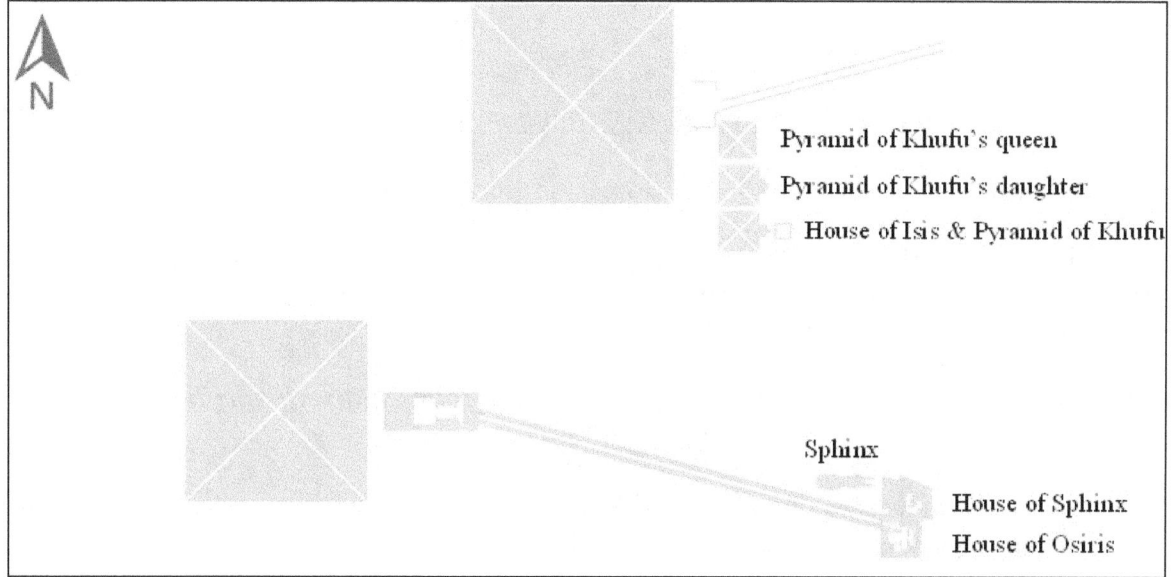

| qet | nef | aa | ef | er | em | neter he-t | net | netrit | ten |
|---|---|---|---|---|---|---|---|---|---|
| build | this | pyramid | his | near | to | divine temple | of | goddess | this |

He built this his pyramid near to the divine temple of this goddess.

| qet | nef | aa | en | su | sat | hent | they | er | em | he-t |
|---|---|---|---|---|---|---|---|---|---|---|
| build | these | pyramid | for | his | daughter[203] | queen | they | near | to | temple |

He built these pyramids for his daughter and queen; they are near to the temple.

---

[203] Breasted, *Ancient Records of Egypt*, Volume 1, page 85, footnote 1: According to Herodotus, the middle of the three small pyramids east of the Great Pyramid, belonged to *Khufu's* daughter (*Herodotus* II, 126). [*The History of Herodotus*, Book II, page 203, Chapter 126.]

# THE INVENTORY STELA

### Line 7 & 8.  The books

7. In the writings of *Osiris* lord of this land of the dead, and the writings of this goddess of *Horus*; he brought this book about her.
8. The Sphinx receives the Sun, (the stone body of hard sandstone, the body to live until eternity), everlastingly to come over in front of it in the east; *Khufu* brought this book with him.

Apparently *Khufu* brought more than one book with him when he made the trip to Giza. There may have been four:

A. Writings of *Osiris* Lord of the Land of the Dead (line 7)
B. Writings of *Isis* the Goddess of *Horus* (line 7)
C. Book of the Sphinx (line 8)
D. Great Book (line 12)

### Line 9 & 10.  The purpose of *Khufu*'s trip to the Giza Plateau

9. He made the journey to see this goddess, the goddess of great power. He gave hard limestone to the image of the god. He covered over all as designed to exalt the Sun God *Ra* in this sky, he makes the wind in the place below.
10. He made this carved back of the head covering having the splendor of stone with gold, of seven cubits behind him.

*Did Khufu come to the Giza Plateau upon a mission to repair the Sphinx because he had a dream about the Goddess Isis?* (line 16)

Apparently *Khufu* had two ideas in mind when he came to Giza, because he had a dream about the goddess *Isis* involving the repair of the Sphinx.

A. He came to see the temple of the *Isis*.
B. He came to repair the monument of the Sphinx.

ANALYSIS OF THE INVENTORY STELA

## Line 11. Naming the Sycamore Tree

11. He came to wander about in this place and saw Qera, a storm god, in the sky over the tomb and a sycamore tree, and he named this great sycamore tree *Sau's* Dwelling Place of Wood.

*Was there fire from heaven (lightning) that damaged the sphinx and a Sycamore tree, as Daressy concluded?* (see page 166)

Perhaps the intended meaning of the text was that while *Khufu* was visiting the Giza plateau, he saw a storm cloud[204] over a sycamore tree near the tomb of the Sphinx, and named it *Sau's* Great Sycamore Tree, the Dwelling Place of Wood. *Sau* was the name of a mythological serpent god.

## Line 12. The great book, *Horus*, and his likeness

12. He who is over rises in the eastern sky. Follow him unto the tomb, *Horus* of the horizon, together with this likeness, which is seen in **the great book.**

*Was the Great Book painted in the tomb of the king??*

Below is an illustration from an ancient Egyptian book painted in the tomb of *Ramesses VI* of the 20th Egyptian dynasty. This illustrates *Horus* of the Horizon, together with this likeness, the Sphinx. It is as if the Sphinx receives the Sun as it rises.

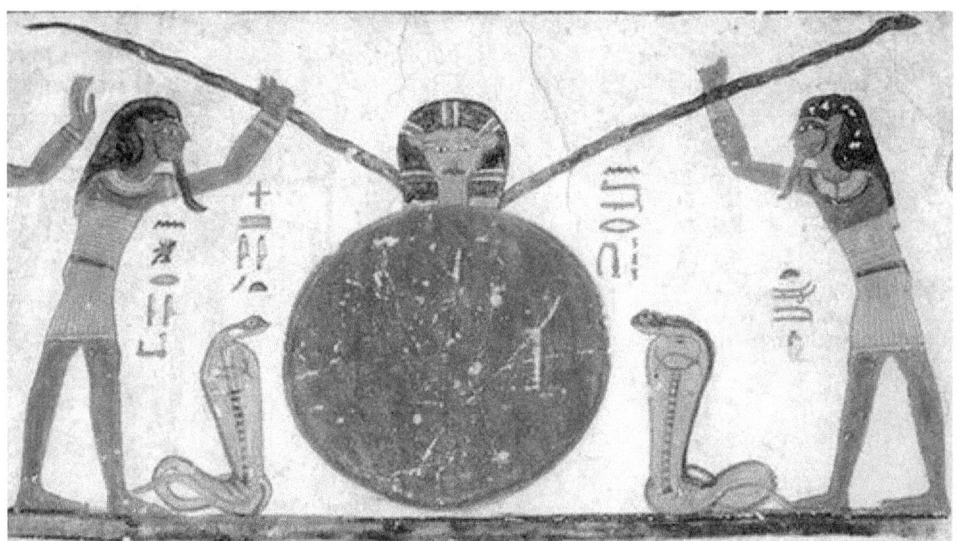

---

[204] *Qera* and *Sau* were words associated with *Apep* the god of storms, chaos, and corruption. See Budge, *Egyptian Hieroglyphic Dictionary*, pages 642A (*Sau*) and 775B (*Qera, qera*); also see Budge, *Gods of the Egyptians*, volume I, page 326 (number 28. *Sau*); also see Budge, *Hieroglyphic Vocabulary to the Theban Recension to the Book of the Dead*, 1911, page 325 (*Sau*) and page 417 (*Qera*).

## THE INVENTORY STELA

### Line 13. The gazelles

13. {*damaged portion of text*} with gazelles all cut in pieces.

*Do the gazelles all cut in pieces; the tusks; the thigh; the seven gods - all refer to star constellations?*

In *An Eleventh-Century Egyptian Guide to the Universe*, five stars in the constellation Ursa Major were viewed as forming gazelles. Sometimes three additional stars in the area were included, depicted as gazelles running before a lion. Twin stars in each of the three prominently depicted feet of Ursa Major were identified as representing the leaps of the gazelles. The offspring of gazelles are small stars between the gazelles themselves and their 'leaps',[205] and the stars of Leo Minor were termed the Gazelle with her young.[206] The ancient Egyptians recognized the small group of stars as the hoof prints left by a herd of gazelles as they fled from the pursuit of Leo.[207] The Inventory Stela may be indicating the stars in these constellations by its reference: *"... with gazelles all cut in pieces."*

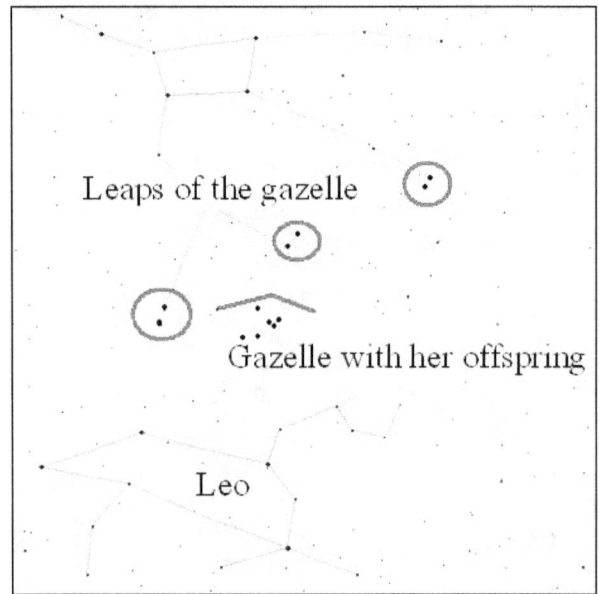

The circles contain marks of the leaps of gazelles

gazelle cloven hoof prints

---

[205] Rapoport, *An Eleventh-Century Egyptian Guide to the Universe: The Book of Curiosities*, page 360, book one, chapter 5.

[206] German astronomer Christian Ludwig Ideler posited that the stars of Leo Minor had been termed *Al Thibā' wa-Aulāduhā*", "Gazelle with her Young," on a 13th-century Arabic celestial globe recovered by Cardinal Stefano Borgia and housed in the prelate's museum at Velletri. Ideler, 1766–1846, was the translator of *Kazwini*, an Arabian astronomy book). See also: Allen, *Star names(reprint ed.)*, page 42. See also: Chartrand, *Skyguide*, page 158.

[207] https://osr.org/constellations/leo-minor/

## ANALYSIS OF THE INVENTORY STELA

### Line 14. Entrance ground of the hill cemetery and inscribed memorial stela

**14. Near the entrance ground of the hill cemetery this inscribed memorial stone.**

*Was the entrance to the hill cemetery the Wall of the Crow?*

The Giza Necropolis sits upon a sloping hillside. The ancient entrance to the cemetery of Giza was through the Wall of the Crow. *Khufu's* Inventory stela was found inside the temple of *Isis*, beyond the entrance to the Giza necropolis.

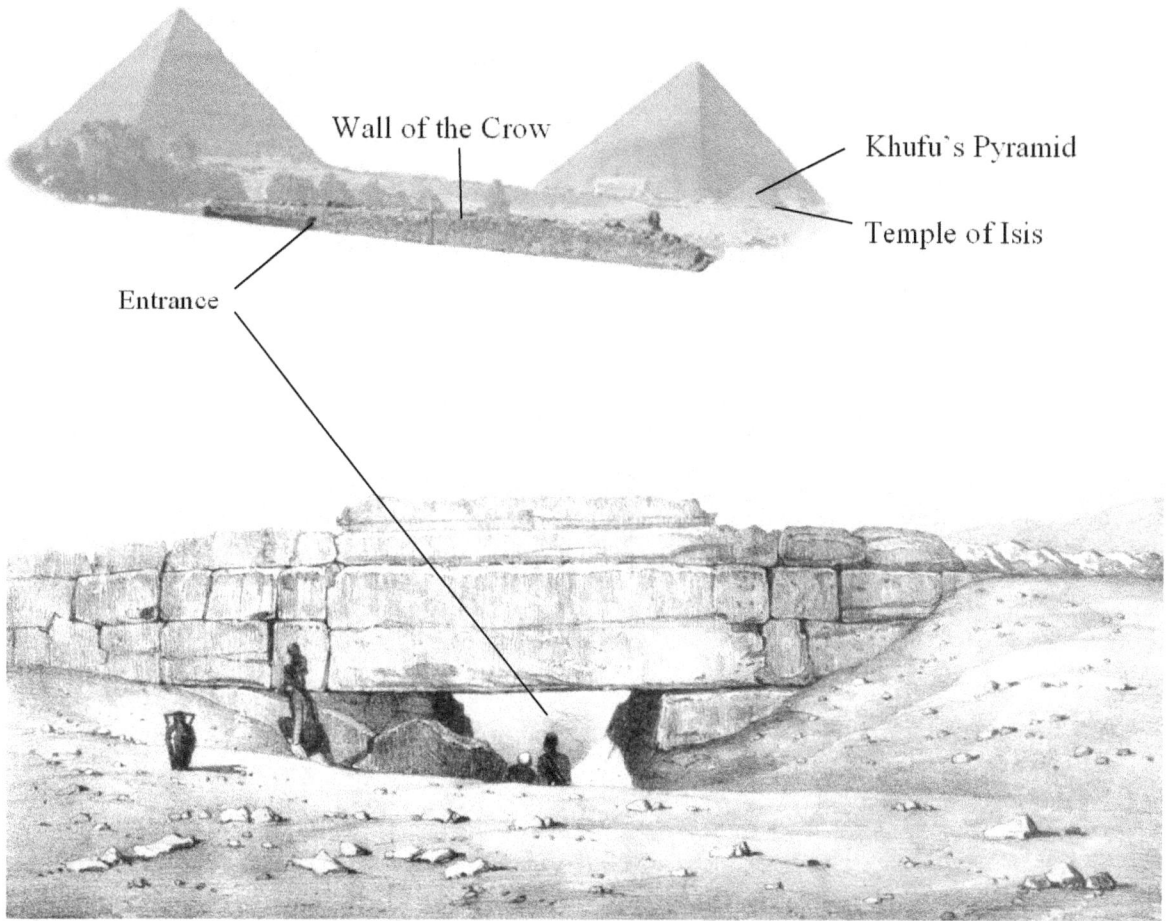

The entrance to Giza in the Wall of the Crow [208]

---

[208] Vyse, *Operations Carried on at the Pyramids*, Vol. I, 1837, page 166.

# THE INVENTORY STELA

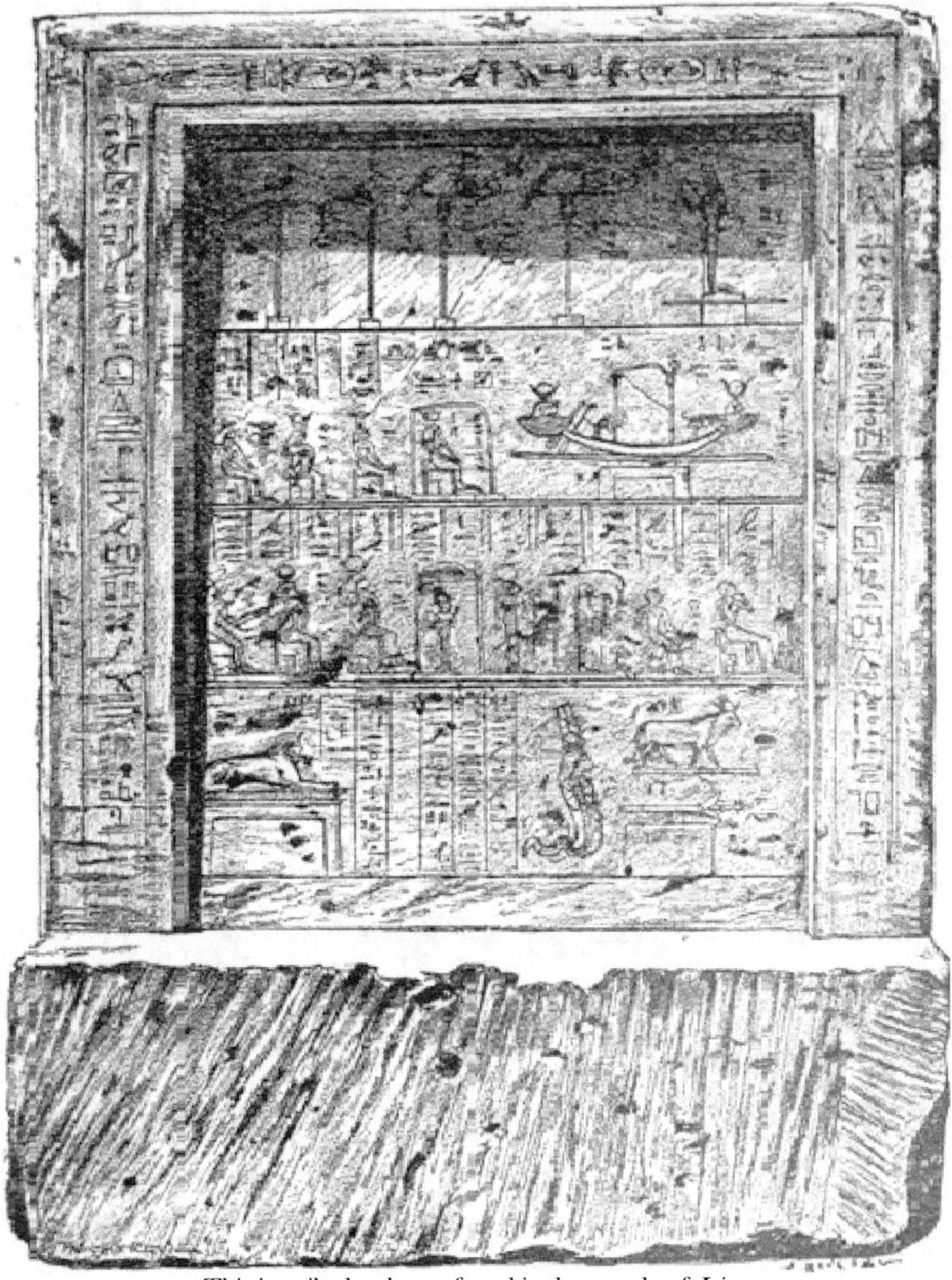

This inscribed stela was found in the temple of *Isis*.

## Line 15. The circle of eternity in the Tuat

15. One circle in the Tuat, the width of eternity of bodies without life; thou swallow the tusk of ivory (*Hippopotamus constellation*)[209] and the thigh (*Canis Major*) to eat before the seven gods (*Pleiades star cluster*) and consider them as a cup of grain {*damaged portion of text*} see fly over.

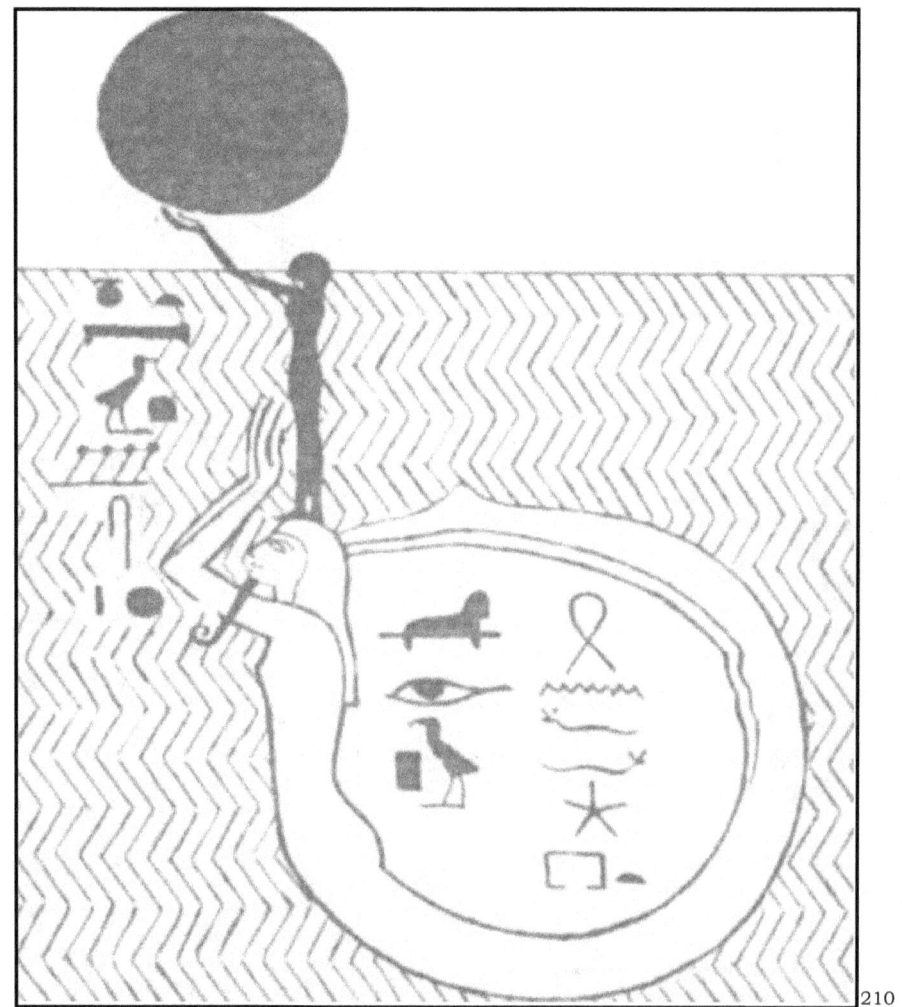

The sarcophagus of *Seti I* contains this illustration of the Tuat.

Translation of text from the tomb of *Seti I*:

*Nut    pu    seshep    si    Re*
Sky goddess this    receive    her    sun
This sky goddess she receives her sun.

*Asar    pu    shen    ef    ef    Tuat*
Osiris this    encircle    he    his    Tuat
This *Osiris* he encircles his *Tuat*.

---

[209] The constellation Cetus.
[210] Sharpe, *The Alabaster Sarcophagus of Oimeneptah I., King of Egypt*, plate 14, 1864.

# THE INVENTORY STELA

The bodies without life may refer to star constellations, which fly over in the sky. The Thigh was Ursa Major. The ancient Egyptians used the ivory tusks of hippopotami for carving because it was a dense, fine-grained material. The tusks referred to in the Inventory Stela may have been an allusion to the ancient Egyptian hippopotamus goddess *Hesamut*[211] and was perhaps the constellation Cetus. The seven gods were almost certainly the stars of Pleiades.

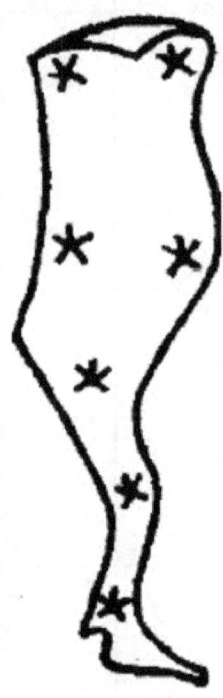

The Thigh
Ursa Major

The Hippopotamus
Cetus

---

[211] Budge, *Egyptian Hieroglyphic Dictionary*, 510B, *Hesamut* , Tomb of *Seti I*, the goddess of a constellation in the northern sky who appears in the form of a hippopotamus.

## ANALYSIS OF THE INVENTORY STELA

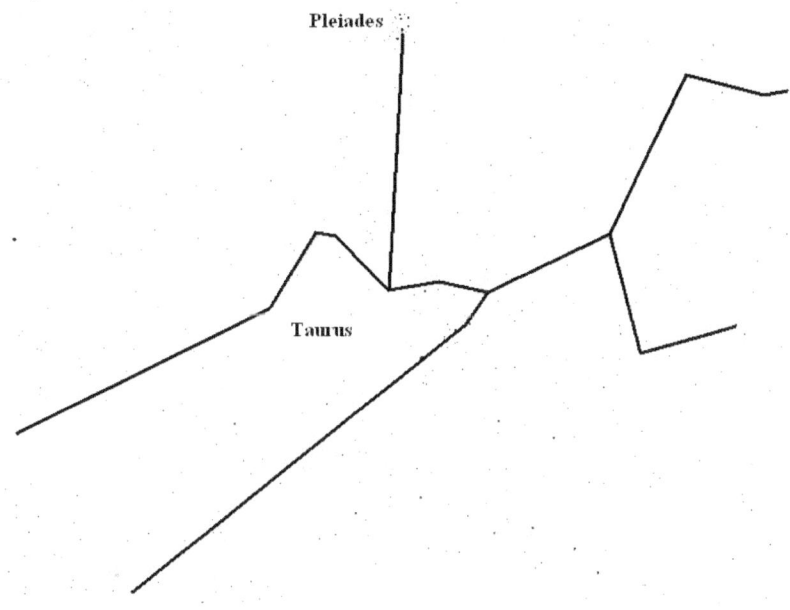

The seven stars of Pleiades near Taurus

### Line 16. The protection of the lion and the goddess

16. According to his written decree concerning the protection of this lion, the goddess of this god (Isis) came in the hour of midnight to cut stones for the stone flesh hard limestone.

# THE INVENTORY STELA

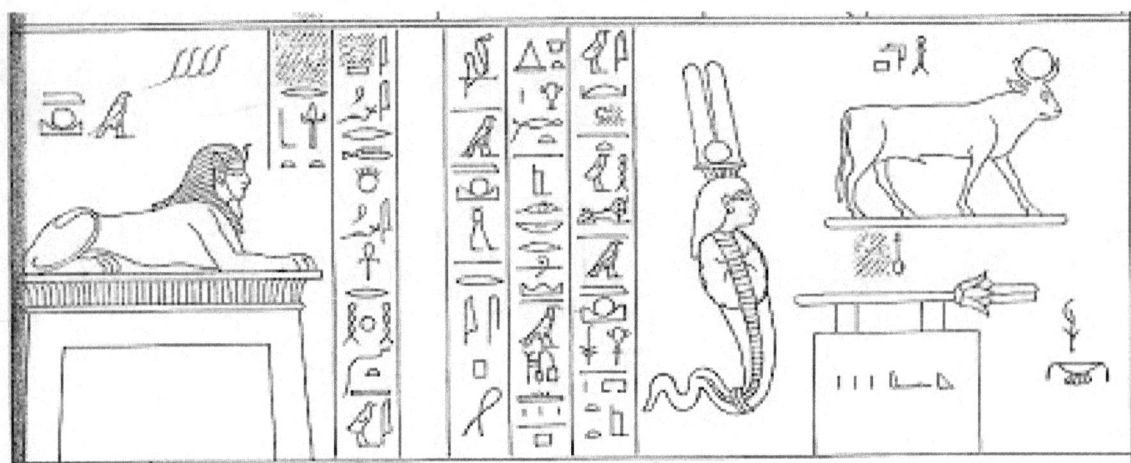

The lower register of the Inventory Stela[212]

The standing serpent goddess is a form of *Isis*.[213] The image of an upright serpent was sometimes used to represent a goddess. In this instance, she is wearing a royal Egyptian crown known as *Shuti* (two-feather crown[214]). Double ostrich feathers were the symbol for the twin goddesses of truth, *Isis* and *Nephthys*. In the middle of this register, two inscriptions are engraved in columns.

The first inscription written in three columns behind reads:

1. *au  aa-t  neth  Hu  en  Hor em akhet  her  su  en  per  Ast*
   is  tomb  of  Sphinx of Giza  of  *Horus* in the horizon  upon  south  of  house  *Isis*
   The tomb of the Sphinx of *Horus* is upon the south of the house of *Isis*,

2. *hen-t*[215]  *aa-t  her  meh-t  en  sesh  Asar  neb  Re-stau  na*
   queen  pyramid  upon  north  in  writings  *Osiris*  lord  dead land  this
   the queen's pyramid is upon the north in the writings of *Osiris*, Lord of this land of dead

3. *sesh  en  pu  netri  en  Hor em akhet  ani  er  sa  art  pu*
   writings  of  this  goddess  of  *Horus* in the horizon  bring  concerning  her  book  this
   writings of this goddess of *Horus*, bring this book concerning her

---

[212] https://scholarship.rice.edu/bitstream/handle/1911/9181/MusBo1872_121.jpg?sequence=243 and https://scholarship.rice.edu/jsp/xml/1911/9181/1/MusBo1872.tei-timea.html and https://scholarship.rice.edu/handle/1911/9181  TIMEA Travelers in the Middle East Archives.

[213] Zivie-Coche, Christiane M., *Giza au premier millénaire*, 1991, The last goddess of the register is a particular form of *Isis*-scorpion found also on the naos of *Saft el-Henneh* page 236, with footnote 737.

[214] Budge, *Egyptian Hieroglyphic Dictionary*, 733B, *shuti*.

[215] Budge, *Egyptian Hieroglyphic Dictionary*, 486A, *hen-t*.

# Analysis of the Inventory Stela

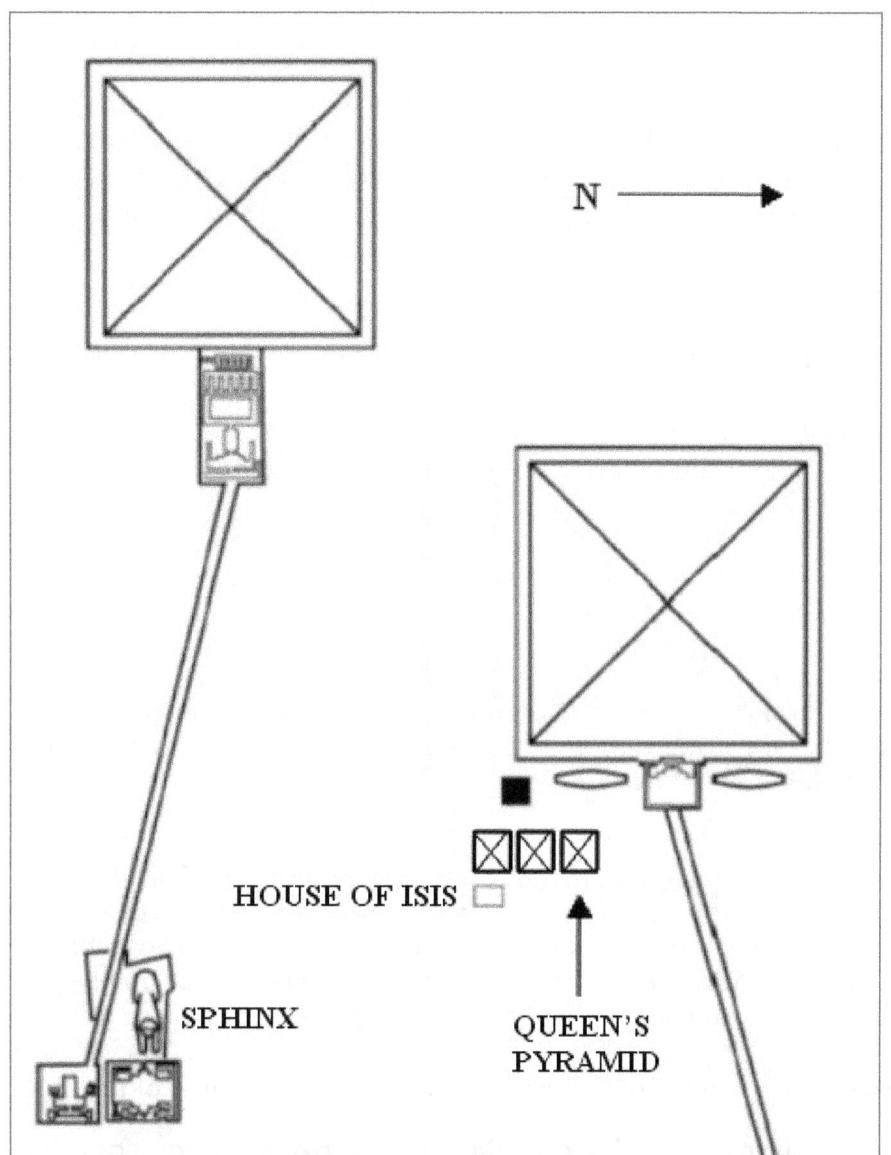

The tomb of the Sphinx of *Horus* is on the south of the House of *Isis* and the Queen's pyramid is upon the north.

# THE INVENTORY STELA

## CHANGING HISTORY

It is difficult to understand why there has been such reluctance to believe the text of the Inventory Stela. It is probably more difficult for some because they have preconceived ideas which conflict with the text of the Inventory Stela. It may also be that not many have studied the text, but go by what they have been told, with no firsthand knowledge of the text. Another confusing aspect is history itself, because it is generally accepted as a fact that *Khufu* was responsible for the construction of the Great Pyramid. And it has been generally assumed that the Temple of *Isis* was constructed some time anterior to that of the Great Pyramid.

It was Auguste Mariette who discovered the Inventory Stela in the temple of *Isis* at Giza in 1858. In 1872, he published it in *Album du Musée de Boulaq*, commenting that the Great Sphinx of Giza and the Temple of *Isis* already existed in the time of *Khufu*.[216] The Inventory Stella makes this statement about *Khufu*: "*He built his pyramid beside the temple of this goddess.*"

After Auguste Mariette died in 1881, Gaston Maspero became head of Egyptian Antiquities. In 1882, he wrote regarding the Temple of Isis:

> "This temple is so placed that it must have been sanded up at the same time as the Sphinx; I believe, therefore, that the restoration effected by *Khufu*, according to the inscription, was merely a clearing away of the sand from the Sphinx analogous to that accomplished by Khafra."[217]

In 1906, James Breasted wrote,

> "According to this statement, the little *Isis*-temple east of the Great Pyramid was standing on the Gizeh plateau before any of the pyramids were built! If Maspero accepts this statement, he should add this *Isis*-temple to the buildings which he believes were the predecessors of the pyramids on the Gizeh plateau."[218]

Cayce stated that the Temple of *Isis* existed before the construction of the Sphinx of Giza:

> "We see this sphinx was builded as this: The excavations were made for same in the plains above where the temple of Isis had stood." [219]

---

[216] Mariette, *Album du Musée de Boulaq,* 1872, plate 27, Monuments Historiques.
https://scholarship.rice.edu/jsp/xml/1911/9181/1/MusBo1872.tei-timea.html

[217] Mariette identifies the temple which he discovered to the south of the Sphinx with that of Osiris, lord of the Necropolis, which is mentioned in the inscription of the daughter of Cheops (*Le Se'rapéum De Memphis,* Maspero's edition, vol. I, pp. 99, 100)

[218] Breasted, *Ancient Records of Egypt,* Vol. 1, 1906, page 85, footnote j.

[219] The Complete Edgar Cayce Readings, reading 195-14, Page 5, paragraph 29.

## ANALYSIS OF THE INVENTORY STELA

The history of the Monuments of Giza according to Edgar Cayce:

> In remote antiquity, in a time far distant from the beginning of recorded history, there was another long-lived civilization whose inhabitants migrated to the Nile Valley, preserving the astronomical records and calendars of Amilius the astronomer.[220] They built a city near the edge of the water and the first of the great pyramids,[221] at the center of the plateau now called Gizeh. That pyramid is now known as the 'second great pyramid.'
>
> Time changed, and afterwards catastrophic geologic changes caused the sea to cover the land. Millennia later the water subsided and people re-entered the Nile valley to discover the ruins of the former inhabitants; people who looked to the stars and who became the first of the Egyptian dynasties[222] who built the temple of *Isis*, the Queen of Heaven. Afterward the Great Pyramid was constructed from 10,490 to 10,390 BC.[223]

Egyptian historians believe the Great Pyramid was constructed by *Khufu*, the second king of the 4th dynasty, approximately 2575-2465 BC. Since Breasted had already made up his mind that *Khufu* built the great pyramid, he was not able to recognize that the Inventory Stela was referring to one of the three smaller pyramids next to the temple of *Isis*. It was commonly believed by everyone that *Khufu* built the great Pyramid! They were not open to the idea that it was constructed more than *seventy* centuries before *Khufu*'s lifetime.

In 1889 in *Monuments Divers*, Gaston Maspero wrote concerning the Inventory Stela:
> "The inscription that can be read around the edge of the stone is a dedication in the name of *Cheops*, the founder of the first Pyramid. We see that, while building his pyramid and that of his daughter *Hent-sen*, *Cheops* had restored a temple of *Isis* already existing on the plateau where the Pyramids stand...The names of the divinities of which *Cheops* had noted the altars, the dimensions, the material of their statues, are indeed recalled in the main register of the stone. We will add that the Great Sphinx of Gizeh is among the statues mentioned here. This colossal emblem therefore already existed in the time of *Cheops*. It is therefore older than the Pyramids themselves."[224]

---

[220] The Complete Edgar Cayce Readings on CD ROM, 364-4, paragraph 5, *carrying with them ALL those forms of Amilius [?] that he gained through that as for signs, for seasons, for days, for years...*

[221] The Complete Edgar Cayce Readings on CD ROM, 993-1, paragraphs 19-21

[222] The Complete Edgar Cayce Readings on CD ROM, 364-4, paragraph 5, *mixed peoples, in what later became the Egyptian dynasty. ...*

[223] The Complete Edgar Cayce Readings on CD ROM, 5748-6, paragraphs 7-8,
>   7. (Q) What was the date of the actual beginning and ending of the construction of the Great Pyramid?
>      (A) Was one hundred years in construction. Begun and completed in the period of Araaraart's time, with Hermes and Ra.
>   8. (Q) What was the date B.C. of that period?
>      (A) 10,490 to 10,390 before the Prince entered into Egypt.

[224] Mariette, 1821-1881, Délié, Hippolyte and Béchard, Émile. "Album du Musée de Boulaq [Electronic Version]." (1872) Electronic version published by Rice University, Houston, TX: https://hdl.handle.net/1911/9181.

# THE INVENTORY STELA

The temple of *Isis* was again rebuilt centuries after *Khufu* rebuilt it in the Fourth Dynasty.

In 1908 Maspero wrote:
> "The present stele is not an original dedicated by *Cheops*, but a later copy. If it is the copy of a decayed monument, it probably preserves the arrangement of its original." [225]

In 1953 Salim Hassan wrote:
> "As a matter of fact, the whole stela, in its form, method of inscription, decoration, and the similarity of the writing to that of the graffiti in the temple, all point to it being entirely the work of the Twenty-sixth Dynasty. Maspero states that in his opinion (2), the Inventory Stela is not an original document dedicated by *Khufu*, but is a later copy or perhaps a forgery, made long after the death of *Khufu*, to support some fictitious claim of the local priests. He says: "The temple of *Isis* was rebuilt where it was found during the Twenty-first Dynasty by the Tanite King, *Pasebekhanu*, and the stela must have been made or restored under this King, or perhaps under one of the Ethiopian Pharaohs. If it is a copy of a decayed monument, it probably preserves the arrangement of the original". It is, as Maspero says, quite possible that this stela is, in actual fact, a copy of an older document, such occurrences having been known. A good example of such a restoration is the black Granite Stela of King *Shabaka* (Twenty-fifth Dynasty), which states that the King had found the original document being eaten by worms (a papyrus or perhaps a wooden tablet 1) and" illegible from beginning to end", and he ordered the writing to be made anew "more beautiful than the one that was before" (I). Therefore, we have no reason to doubt that the Inventory Stela is a copy of an older text, and like that of *Shabaka*." [226]

In the tombs of the Kings of Egypt we find the text of a sacred book of astronomy, the *Am Tuat*. Its importance was paramount and was intended to last forever within the tombs of the kings. The names of those kings are *Seti I, Amenhotep II, Tuthmosis III* and *Ramesses VI*. If it is understood that the representations in these tomb paintings are of stars, planets and constellations, one can perceive in the fifth division of the book of *Am Duat* that the position of all of the celestial representations are in the positions of stars on the date of September 21$^{st}$, 10390 BC, which is when Cayce said the Great Pyramid was finished. This marked the completion of Giza and a festival was held that lasted for an entire week, commemorating the New Year. This tomb painting memorialized the beginning of the first official Egyptian calendar. For more on this calendar please refer to our book, *The Coffin Texts Resurrected*, Volume I, by Bunker and Pressler.

---

[225] Maspero, *Guide to the Cairo Museum*, p. 68-69
[226] Hassan, *The Great Sphinx and its Secrets*, vol. 8, p. 116.

# PART V – THE MYSTERY OF THE DEATH AND RESURRECTION OF *OSIRIS*

# THE DEATH AND RESURRECTION OF OSIRIS

## THE LEGEND OF *OSIRIS*

One of the oldest Egyptian legends is the legend of *Osiris* who was murdered and was resurrected. The legend says that his brother Set drowned him. *Isis* and her twin sister *Nephthys* found his body and later, somehow, he was made to be alive again. These are the essential elements in the story. The ancient Egyptians believed that *Osiris*, like Christ, was murdered, died, and was resurrected. This made it easy for the early efforts of the disciples of the Christian teachings to convert Coptic Egyptians to Christianity. According to its tradition, Saint Mark, an apostle and evangelist, established the Coptic Church during the middle of the 1st century (c. AD 42).

The following information may help the reader to more clearly understand the origin of the legend of the death and resurrection of *Osiris*. Looking deeper into the legend, we found the story was built upon astronomy. We're going to show you some examples of the death and resurrection of *Osiris* from the Pyramid Texts, presented by James Henry Breasted.

*How did Osiris die?*

In 1912, Breasted wrote:
> The oldest source, the Pyramid Texts, indicates assassination: "his brother *Set* felled him to the earth in *Nedyt*.

Something that has been felled has been brought down, like a tree that has been felled by a powerful storm. The word fell is also the past tense of fall.

In his book *The Development of Thought and Religion in Ancient Egypt*,[227] Breasted quotes segments of the Pyramid Text:

> Utterance 532
> 1256a. They found Osiris,
> 1256b. after his brother <u>Set had felled him to the earth in Ndi.t</u>.[228]

> Utterance 478
> 972a. Thou art come in search of thy brother, Osiris,
> 972b. after his brother <u>Set had cast him on his side,</u>
> 972c. on yonder side of Ghś.ti.[229]

> Utterance 442.
> 819a. To say: That Great One is certainly <u>fallen on his side</u>; he who is in Ndi.t is thrown down.[230]

---

[227] Breasted, *Development of Thought and Religion in Ancient Egypt*, page 97.
[228] Mercer, *Pyramid Texts*, page 327.
[229] Mercer, *Pyramid Texts*, page 271.
[230] Mercer, *Pyramid Texts*, page 239.

# THE DEATH AND RESURRECTION OF OSIRIS

The first impression is that the Pyramid Texts provided two different places for the death of *Osiris*, *nedyt* (*ndi.t*) and *gehesti* (*ghś.ti*). We wondered if the Pyramid Texts were unreliable, since they provided two apparently conflicting locations for the death of *Osiris*? How was it possible that *Osiris* died in two different places? Thus began our quest to find the answer to the mystery of the death and resurrection of *Osiris*. We needed to understand the ancient Egyptian words *nedyt* (*ndi.t*) and *gehesti* (*ghś.ti*). Since we cannot see the original text, we are left analyzing the words used by the translators, James Henry Breasted and Samuel A.B. Mercer. So we have *nedyt* and alternately *ndi.t*; also we have *geshesti* and alternately *ghs.ti* as our starting places.

From early times *Osiris* was identified with the constellation Orion.[231] Breasted believed that *Osiris* had died, not in the distant sky like Re, but on earth as men die.[232] But if *Osiris* is the constellation Orion and the Pyramid Texts are about the movement of the stars across the sky, then we have our first perspective from which to attempt an explanation for the words *nedyt*[233], alternately spelled *ndi.t*.[234]

Referring to the hieroglyphic dictionary, the word ⟨hieroglyph⟩ *netit*[235] *(nedit)* means the bank of a river or a canal. In this case the bank must be referring to the horizon, which is at the edge of the river *Urnes*[236] that flows through the *Tuat* in the sky. We read in Pyramid Text, line 819, that *Osiris*, "*the Great One, is thrown down on his side.*"[237] The meaning of this statement becomes clearer when we view the stars at midnight and then again at 2:00 a.m., on September 21st, 10,390 BC.

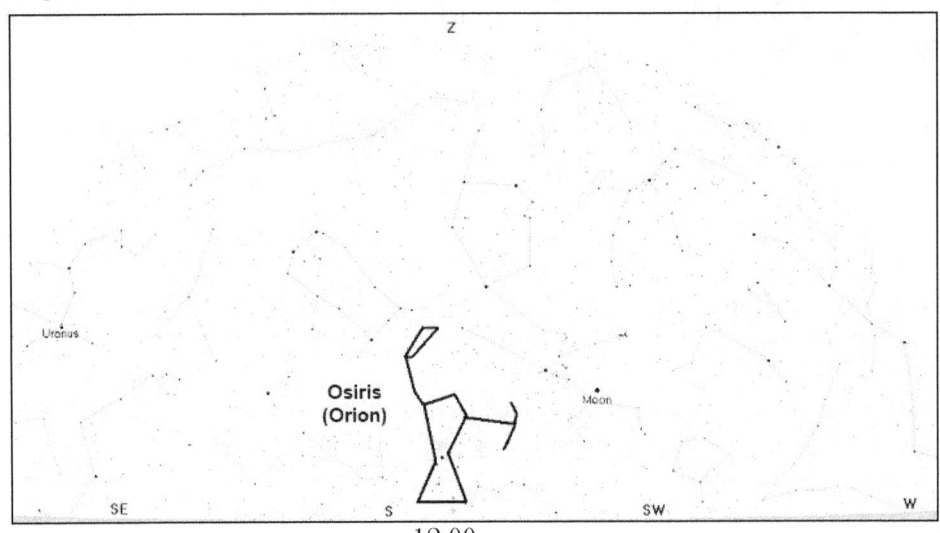

12:00 a.m.

---

[231] Murray, *The Osireion at Abydos*, page 15.
[232] Breasted, *Development of Thought and Religion in Ancient Egypt*, page 78.
[233] Breasted, *Development of Thought and Religion in Ancient Egypt*, page 27.
[234] Mercer, *Pyramid Texts*, the word *ndi.t* is used throughout the text.
[235] Budge, *Egyptian Hieroglyphic Dictionary*, 409A, *netit*, bank of a river or a canal.
[236] Budge, *Egyptian Hieroglyphic Dictionary*, 173A, *Urnes*, the name of a portion of the river in the Tuat.
[237] Mercer, *Pyramid Texts*, page 239.

# THE LEGEND OF OSIRIS

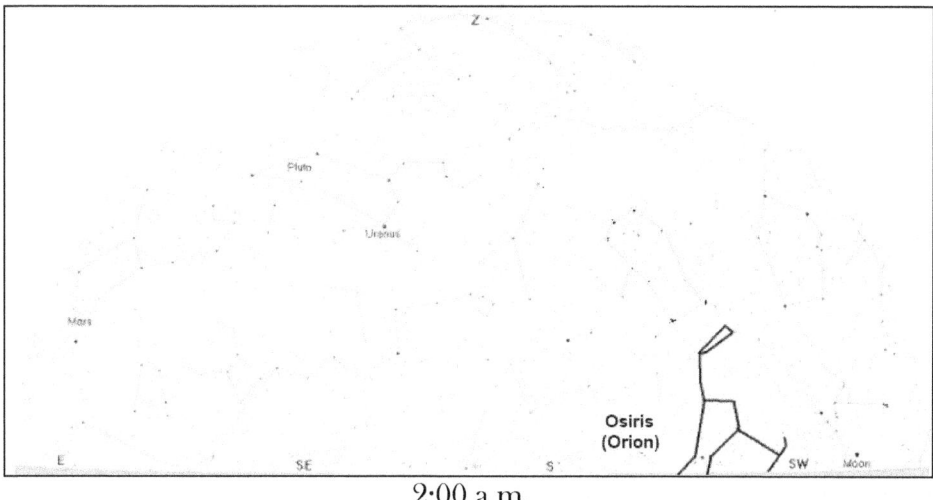

2:00 a.m.

The legend of the death and resurrection of *Osiris* is probably about star constellations. These were the gods of Egypt. The Pyramid Texts, Utterance 442, contains the essential text of this myth.

*Utterance 442.* [238]
  819a. To say: That Great One is certainly fallen on his side; he who is in *Ndi.t* is thrown down.
  819b. Thine arm is seized by *Rē'*; thy head is lifted up by the Two Enneads.
  819c. Behold, he is come (again) as *Śah*; behold, *Osiris* is come as *Śah*.
  820a. lord of the wine-cellar at the *Wag*-feast,
  820b. "good," as his mother said; "heir," as his father said,
  820c. conceived by heaven, born of the Tuat

### *The Death and Resurrection*

In line 819a the *Great One* is Orion, which was identified as *Osiris* from the earliest times[239]. As the constellation of Hydra (*Apep, Set,* etc.) rises, Orion begins its descent from its zenith and begins to fall forward as if it is *thrown down,* apparently caused by the rising of Set (Hydra). The next day the arm of Orion begins to appear above the Eastern horizon just as the sun begins to set below the Western horizon. It could be imagined that the sun is grasping the arm of *Osiris* and raising him up! His resurrection!

                819b. Thine arm is seized by *Rē'*

---

[238] Mercer, *Pyramid Texts*, page 239.
[239] Murray, *The Osireion at Abydos*, page 15.

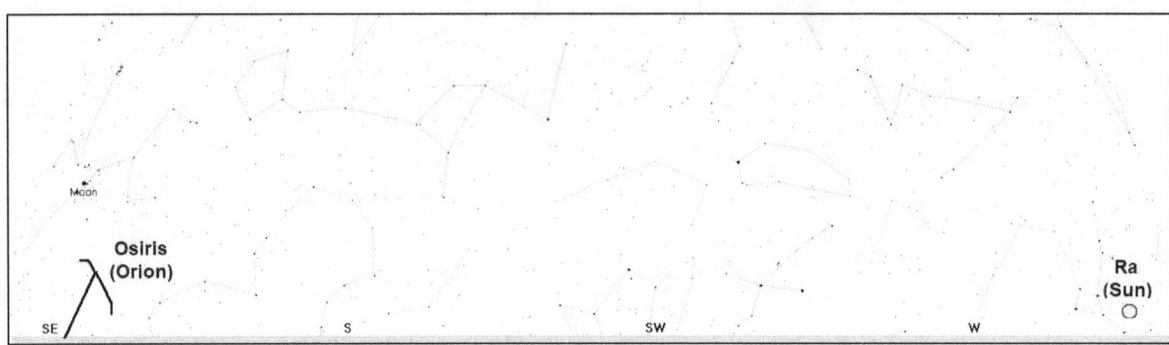

Behold he is come again as Sah (Orion);
*Osiris* is come as Sah.

In the book *Eastern and Western Asia in Antiquity*, Ferdinand Justi comments on Astronomy and provides the Sah-Osiris-Orion identification.

> Among the fixed stars, in the foremost rank stand the 36 or 37 stars of the Equator, which correspond to the 36 decades[240] of the year; every second year has 37, on account of the twice five intercalary days. We possess catalogues of stars in which are found among others *Sopd* (Sothis, Sirius, or Dog-star) ; Sah (Osiris, Orion) ; *Art* (the Hyades) ; *Khau* (the Pleiades) . The solar year contains 365 days; but the Egyptians perceived that its proper astronomical length was 365 ¼ days.[241]

In line 1008c of the Pyramid Text we read that *Osiris* is found upon his side by his sister *Isis* on the shore of *Ndi.t:*

> 1008b. (it is) thy great sister who collected thy flesh, who gathered thy hands,
> 1008c. who sought thee, who found thee upon thy side on the shore of *Ndi.t*,

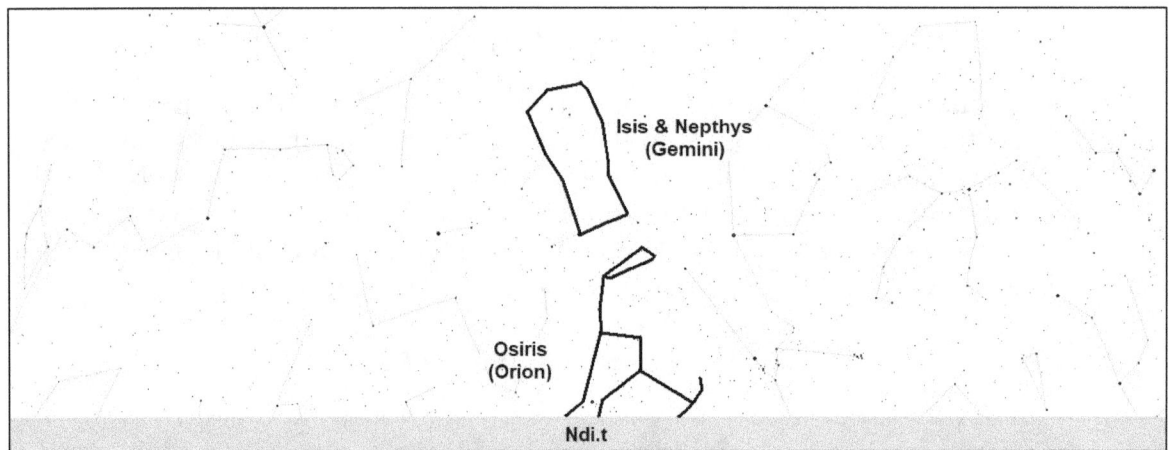

The horizon is the shore (*ndi.t*) of the river that flows in the Tuat in the sky.
*Osiris* has fallen on his side on the shore *Ndi.t*, 2:00 A.M., September 21st, 10,390 BC

---

[240] According to the *Merriam Webster Dictionary*, a decade is a group or set of 10. In this case a decade refers to groups of 10 days.

[241] Justi, *Egypt and Western Asia in Antiquity*, page 115, [Volume 1 of *A History of All Nations*]

# The Legend of Osiris

1255c. *Isis* comes, *Nephthys* comes, one of them on the right, one of them on the left,
1255d. one of them as a *hat*-bird, one of them (*Nephthys*) as a kite.
1256a. They found *Osiris*,
1256b. after his brother *Set* had felled him to the earth in *Ndi.t*,

So it seemed that *Set* was responsible for *Osiris* falling to his death in the waters on the shore of *Ndi.t*.

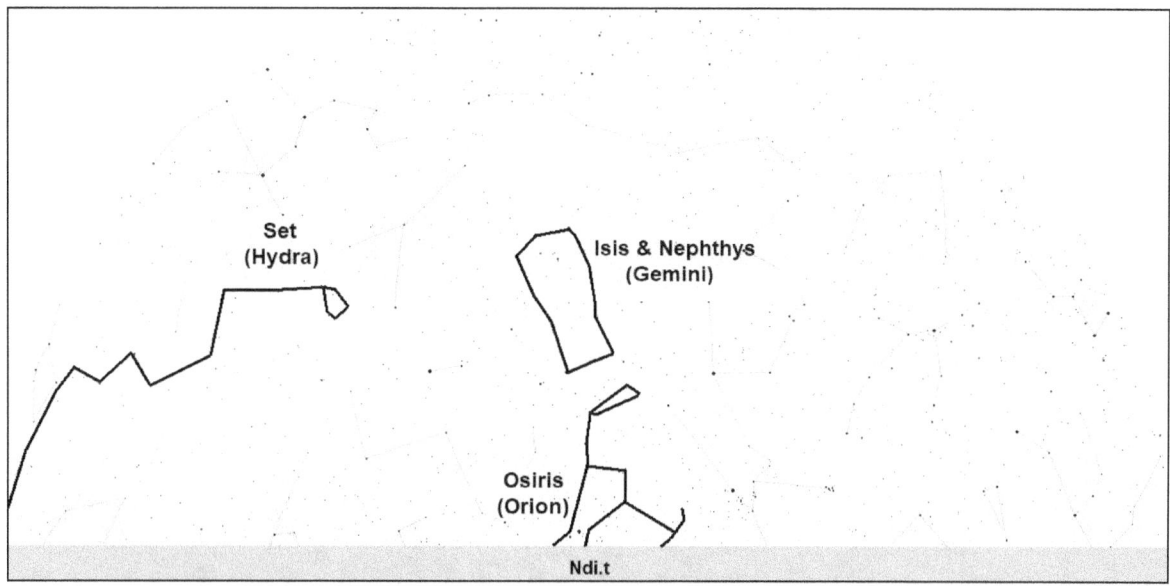

His brother *Set* felled him to the earth 2:00 A.M. September 21st, 10,390 BC

1256c. when *Osiris* (N.) said, "come to me," hence comes his name as "*Seker*."
1267c. Let him be gone; let (him) go to *Ndi.t*;

Because of the rotation of the earth, the procession of the stars appeared to move across the sky. As the constellation of Hydra gradually appeared above the eastern horizon, the constellation of Orion gradually moved toward, and then disappeared below the western horizon. But with the coming of the new day, Orion rose again. This was the resurrection of *Osiris*!

Utterance 576 connects the rising of the constellation Hydra (*Set*) with causing the constellation of Orion (*Osiris*) to fall to his side. Because as *Set* rises, Orion sinks lower in the sky toward the Western horizon (line 1500a).

Utterance 576.
1500a. To say: *Osiris* was placed upon his side by his brother *Set*;
1500b. he who is in *Ndi.t* stirs; his head is raised up by *Rē'*;
1502b. *Osiris* awakes in peace; he who is in *Ndi.t* awakes in peace.

In the Pyramid Texts line 1500a we read that *Osiris* has been placed upon his side by *Set*, but the next line states that *Ra* raises him up. And so we see the very next day, as the Sun (*Ra*) begins to set, the head and arm of *Osiris* is rising in the East.

# THE DEATH AND RESURRECTION OF OSIRIS

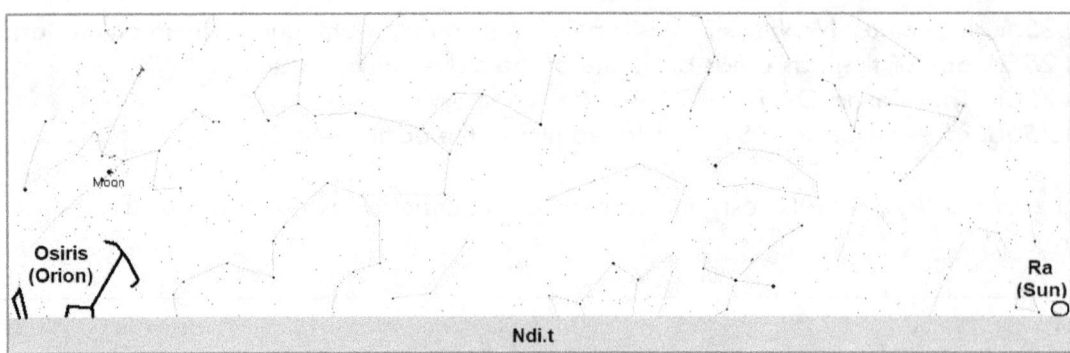

September 22, 10,390 BC 6:50 p.m.

2144b (N. 1029). when they saw Osiris on his side on the shore [of Ndi.t]
2145a (N. 1029). -------- rise up -----------------------
2145b (N. 1029-1030). --------- my brother, I sought thee;
2145c (N. 1030). raise thyself up, spirit." Geb said:

**Utterance 701.**
2188a. To say: The Great One is fallen in Ndi.t; Isis is loosed from her burden (tn).

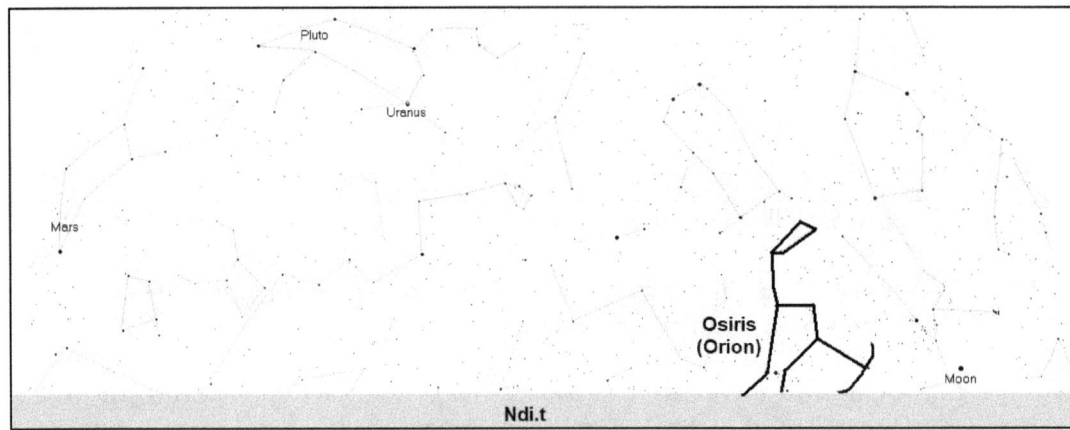

September 21st, 10,390 BC

# THE LEGEND OF OSIRIS

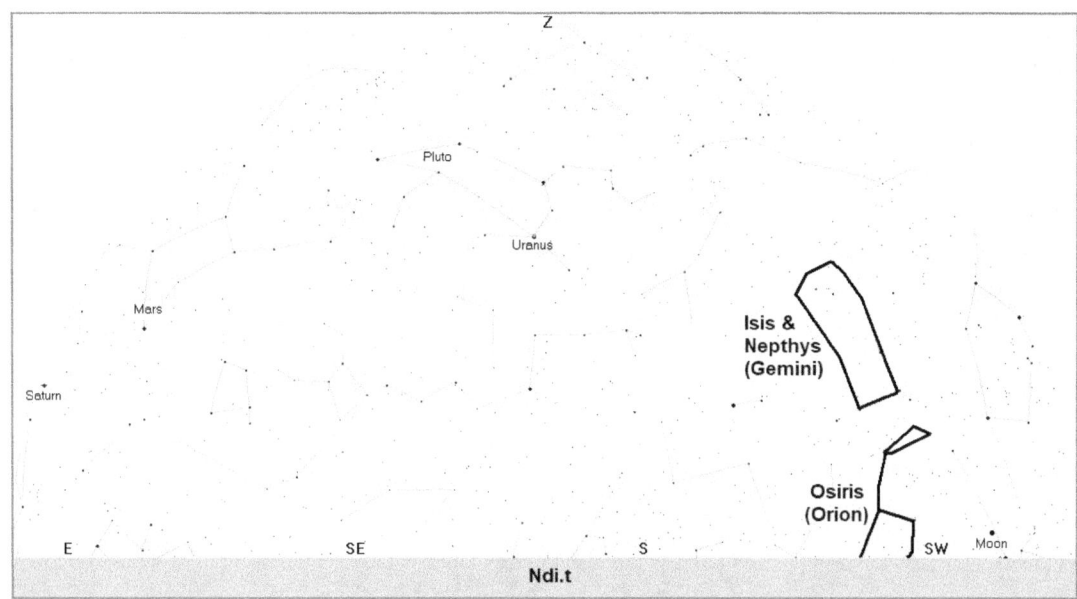

September 21st, 10,390 BC

Utterance 701 (continued)
2188b. Raise thyself up, thou who art in *Ntrw*; raise thyself up
2199a. Thou art come (again) to [thy] (right) state ---------

The text reads "raise thyself up you who are among the *ntrw*." This word *ntrw* also spelled *neteru* means gods, and in this instance, the text is referring to star gods or constellations that raise up from the horizon into the sky.

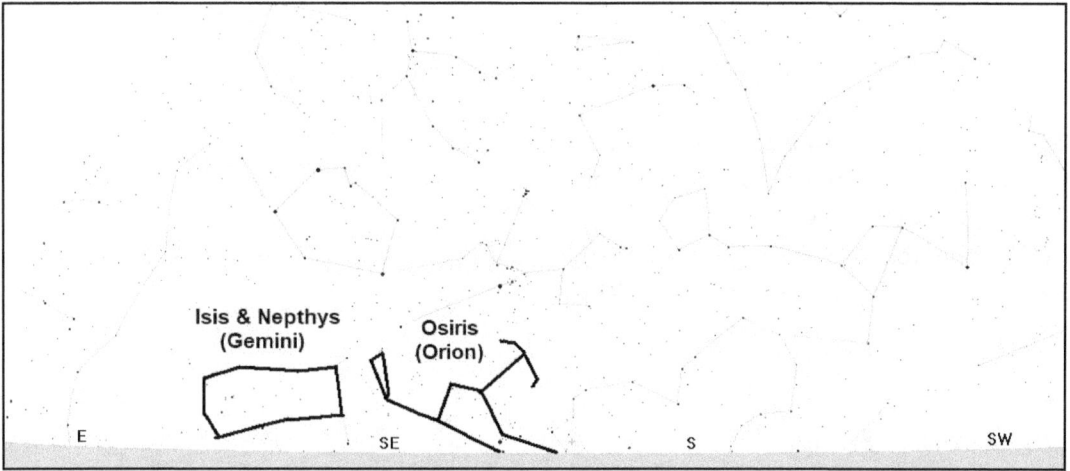

The great and powerful goddesses in the East are the twins of Gemini.
September 22nd, 10,390 BC

2200b. ye great and powerful pair of goddesses, who are on the eastern side of heaven,
2200c. that you both may carry N. and set him on the eastern side of heaven.

# THE DEATH AND RESURRECTION OF OSIRIS

The oldest source, the Pyramid Texts, indicates assassination: "his brother *Set* felled him to the earth in *Nedyt*"[242]; or "his brother *Set* overthrew him upon his side, on the further side of the land of *Gehesti*";[243] Investigation into the meaning of the words *Nedyt* and *Gehesti* revealed that *Nedyt* meant the shore at the edge of a river or a canal. And *Gehesti* meant Gazelle, and was also the name of the ancient Egyptian Gazelle constellation that today has become known as Leo Minor. Just above the Gazelle there are three sets of gazelle hoofprints at the edge of Canus Major called the leaps of the Gazelle.[244]

GEHESTI (*Ghś.ti*)[245, 246]
Gazelle

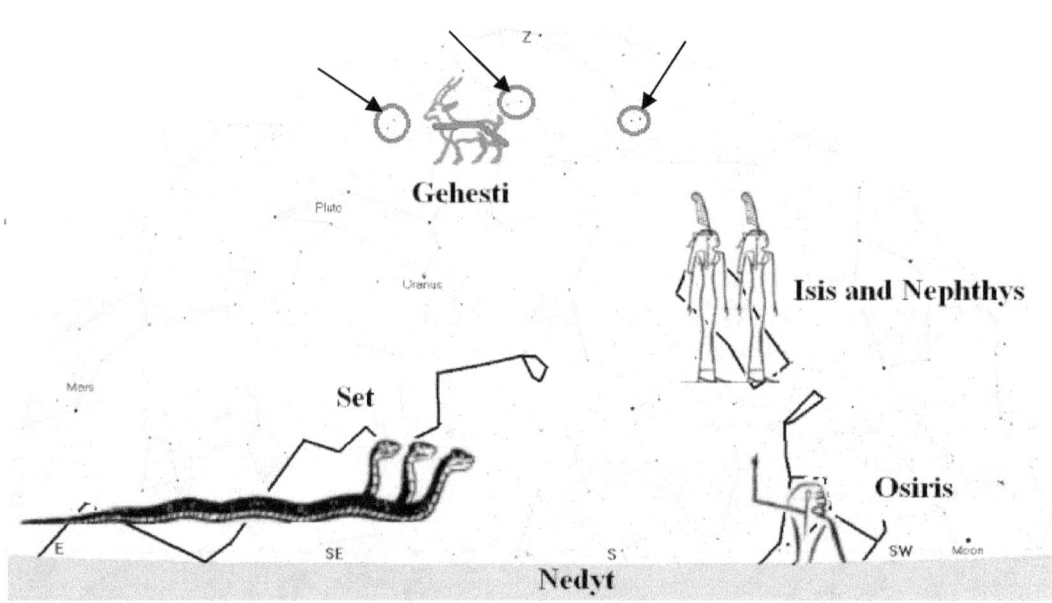

*Osiris* is on his side on yonder side of Gehesti.

972a. Thou art come in search of thy brother, *Osiris*,
972b. after his brother *Set* had cast him on his side,
972c. on yonder side of *Ghś.ti*.
1033b. He found him lying on his side in *Ghś.ti*.
1799b. he found him on his side in *Ghś.ti* [247]

---

[242] Mercer, *Pyramid Text*, page 1256.

[243] Breasted, *Thought and Religion in Ancient Egypt*, page 25.

[244] The ancient Egyptians recognized the small group of stars as the hoof prints left by a herd of gazelles. https://osr.org/constellations/leo-minor/

[245] Mercer, *Pyramid Text*, page 972.

[246] Budge, *Egyptian Hieroglyphic Dictionary*, page 812B, *Ghes-ti*: a gazelle goddess.

[247] In the original hieroglyphs used in the Pyramid Texts, *em* functioned as a preposition and could be used to mean an array of different words, such as: *in, into, from, on, at, with, out from, among, of, upon, as, like, according to, in the manner of, in the condition or capacity of*. In lines 1033b or 1799b the same preposition seems to have been used in both instances. It might have very well been translated, as "at" instead of "in" and still have been correct.

# The Legend of Osiris

Below are two examples of the word Gazelle written in hieroglyphic text, with the English equivalent below.

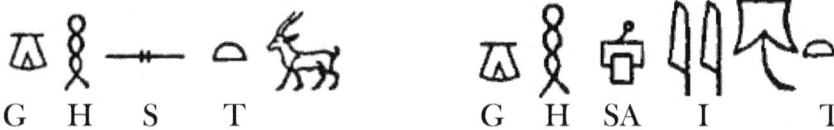

Utterance 670
1975a. They say to thee, *Osiris* N., "thou art gone, thou art come;
1975b. thou art asleep, [thou art awake]; thou art [dead (lit. thou landest)], thou art alive.
1976a. Stand up, [248]

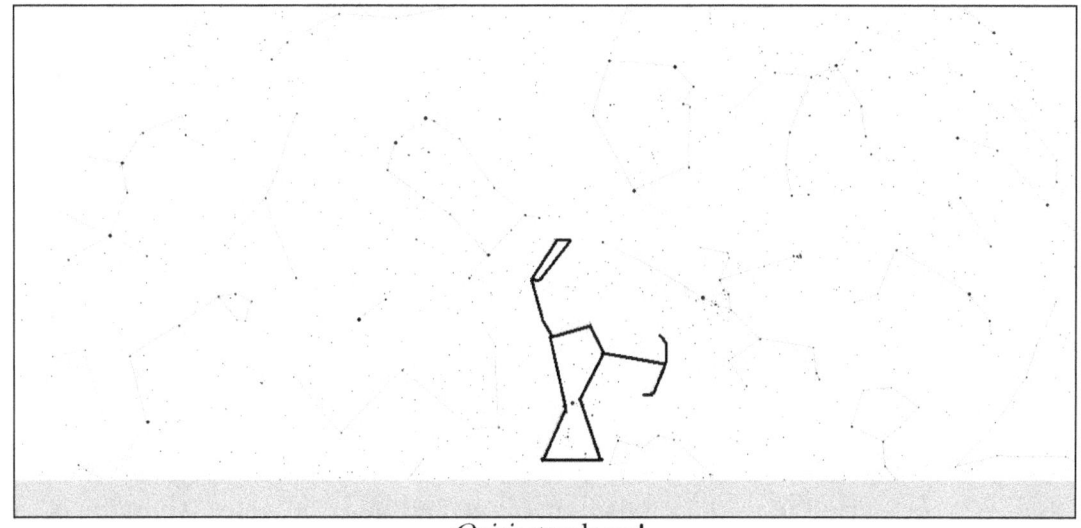

*Osiris* stands up!

1986a. The awakening [of the god], [the rising of the god],
1986b. [for this spirit, who ascends from] the Tuat, (even) *Osiris* N. who ascends from Geb.

And so we may now understand that the death and resurrection of *Osiris* is written in the stars!

---

[248] Breasted, *Development of Thought and Religion in Ancient Egypt*, page *xii*, brackets enclose words wholly restored.

# THE DEATH AND RESURRECTION OF OSIRIS

## FURTHER COMMENTS ABOUT THE DEATH AND RESURRECTION OF OSIRIS

*Isis* was called the mother of the god because she was the mother of *Horus*. In pre-dynastic Egypt, *Horus* was the ancient sky god. Later, as Egyptian religion evolved, he became the son of *Isis* and *Osiris*. To understand this, one must first consider one of the most ancient stories of Egyptian mythology, the battle of *Horus* and *Set*, and then turn to the legend of *Osiris*. *Horus* was the ancient god of the sky whose right eye was the Sun and left eye the Moon. He was the source of light. *Set* was the power in opposition of light and represented the forces of darkness, symbolized in several different forms, one of which was a giant serpent. Each morning the forces of darkness battled the forces of light - *Set* in the form of a giant serpent god of chaos and darkness stood in opposition to *Horus* the sun god, to stop the sun from rising. But each morning *Horus* won the battle against *Set* and the sun rose in the East. This legend of the battle of the daylight and the darkness of night was based upon sunrise, which dispelled the darkness.[249] In this way, this reoccurring astronomical event was woven into a folk tale. During several months each year the largest constellation in the night sky, the giant serpent (*Hydra*) was in the sky before sunrise. So it was that the giant serpent in the sky became the archenemy of the Sun god *Horus*, waiting each morning just before sunrise in the eastern horizon to stop dawn from coming.

*Isis* and *Nephthys* were twin sister star goddesses of ancient Egypt. There are different theories about who they were, but when the great serpent god was in the sky just before dawn, the constellation Gemini, the twins, was over the western horizon just before sunrise. In Egyptian mythology, *Isis* was said to be the mother of *Horus*, the sun god. This may be because Gemini was the last constellation in the sky on the western horizon just as the newly born sun began to become visible in the east. So it was that *Isis* became referred to as the mother of *Horus* and her twin sister *Nephthys* became his nurse. In a Theban papyrus known as *The Lamentations of Isis and Nephthys*, *Horus* [the Sun god] is curiously described as born of the Two Sisters: "Thy son, the youth Horus, the child of (thy) two sisters"[250]

It was also said in Egyptian mythology that *Osiris* was murdered by his brother *Set* and drowned in the water of the Nile. This fable also had its basis in astronomy. Both *Set* and *Osiris* were star constellations and were members of the same family, e.g. the family of star gods. From early times *Osiris* was identified with the constellation *Orion*. *Osiris* was said to be one of the early kings of Egypt. The pyramid texts reveal that in predynastic times it was believed when the king died, he became a star constellation in the sky, just like *Osiris*. The Pyramid texts of *Pepi* reads, "Osiris N. comes to thee as Orion, lord of wine, in the good festival of Uag; he to whom his mother said, 'Become flesh'; he to whom his father said 'Be conceived in heaven with Orion, who was born in the Duat with Orion." [251]

---

[249] Breasted, *Development of Thought and Religion in Ancient Egypt*, page 40: "It is quite evident from the Pyramid Texts that the feud between Horus and Set was originally a Solar incident"
[250] Birch, *Records of the Past,* vol. II, "Egyptian Texts," The Lamentations of *Isis* and Nephthys, page 123.
[251] Murray, *The Osireion at Abydos*, page 15.

## Further Comments

As the serpent constellation[252] rose to its zenith, it seemingly caused the death of the constellation of *Orion* by "pushing" *Orion/Osiris* below the horizon to his death, thus drowning him in the celestial water. After *Osiris* had passed into the underworld, he and *Isis* were reunited (because eventually she also passed below the horizon) and she conceived a child. When the child was born, she named him *Horus* and she hid him in the marshes until he had grown. This too has its basis in astronomy for the marshes in the sky were on the shore of the Milky Way. So it was, in this way in the evolution of mythology, *Horus* became the son of *Isis* and *Osiris*. And the ancient battle between *Horus* and *Set* became the battle of *Horus* the son of *Isis* and *Osiris* taking vengeance upon the murderer of his father.

---

[252] Hydra

# APPENDIX A - COMPLETE TRANSLATION OF THE INVENTORY STELA

# APPENDIX A

Inventory Stela

---

[253] Hassan. *The Great Sphinx and its Secrets*, page 113.

## Daressy's Translation of The Stela of the Daughter of *Cheops*

In 1908 an article written by Georges Daressy was printed in a French publication: *Recueil de Travaux Relatifs à la Philologie et à l'Archéologie Égyptiennes et Aassyriennes*. The title of his article was "*La Stèle de la Fille de Chèops*" We have translated the complete article into English for this book. Daressy's labelling of the sections of the stela differ from that of Hassan. The image below reflects Daressy's identification of the parts of the Inventory as used in his translation.

French assistant curator of the Cairo Museum 1904
Georges Émile Jules Daressy
19 March 1864 - 28 February 1938

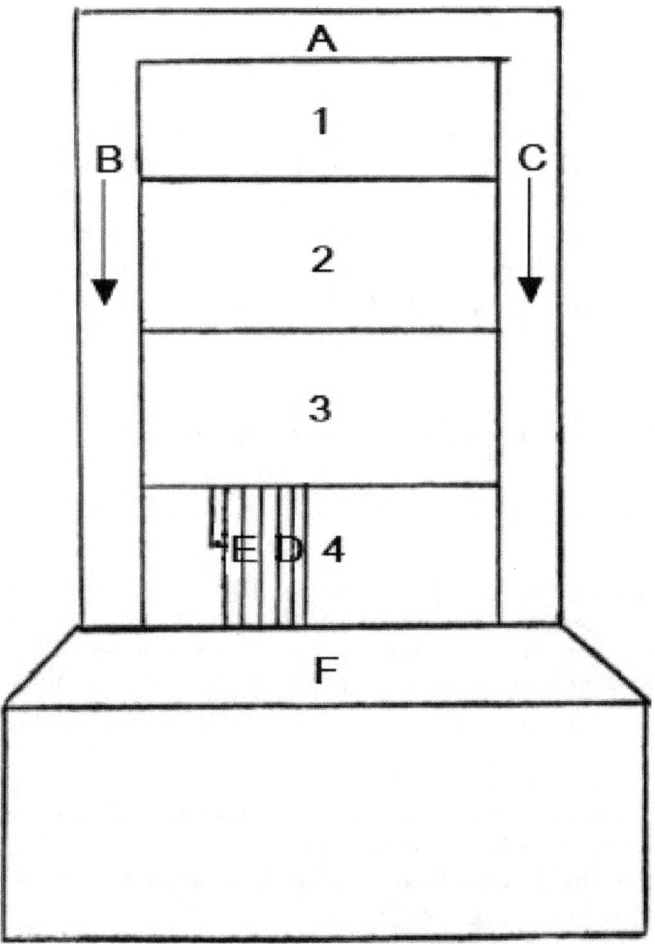

Daressy's translation is laid out in the above diagram

# APPENDIX A

## The Stela of the Daughter of Cheops

In June 1858, Mariette discovered, in the ruins of a temple located at the foot of the southernmost of the three small pyramids, which are to the east the tomb of Cheops, a stela[254] which quickly acquired a great celebrity in archeology, for, after reading his writings, it was believed that it could be said that Giza's great Sphinx far predated Cheops. The mention that this king had built the pyramid of the princess [hieroglyphs][255] beside the temple where the monument was found recalled the passage of Herodosus (II, 126), telling how the eldest daughter of Cheops had built her tomb[256] in a strange way and gave this stela the name under which it is known. The appearance of the monument, the way it is engraved, evidently showed that this was not a work of the Old Empire and that it had to have originated there, that is, during the XXI$^{st}$ dynasty[257], or of the Saïtes; but, following M. E. de Rougé and Mariette, it was suggested that the primitive stela, which had been erased over the centuries, had only been restored, and that the indications which it provided could be dated back to the IV$^{th}$ dynasty"[258]. In the long run, this opinion found challengers, and Mr. Flinders Petrie, in 1883, thought that the inscription had been created from scratch under the XXI$^{st}$ dynasty.[259]

"A more detailed study of the texts led me to conclusions different from my predecessors.[260]

The monument, made of quite fine limestone, 0$^m$ 70 high, 0$^m$ 42 wide, is in the form of a rectangular stela preceded by an offering table, or better under that of a temple of which most of the alcove would have been destroyed; it includes, in fact, a base 0$^m$ 175 high and 0$^m$ 30 wide, surmounted by a vertical part set back 0$^m$ 10, the middle of which is still hollowed out by two centimeters, leaving only a frame of 0$^m$ 04m protruding width at the top and at the sides. The frame and top of the base bear inscriptions, and other legends in the background accompany representations of statues and sacred emblems incised in the stone, in threadlike lines.

The bottom figures are divided between four registers.

---

[254] Entrance No. to the Boulaq Museum 2091; No. 581 of the Mariette Catalog (*Catalogue Mariette*); No. 882 of the Maspero Catalog (*Catalogue Maspero*), page 207, No. 54 of the Catalog of Giza (*Catalogue de Gizéh*). The stele is reproduced in Mariette, Monuments various (*Monuments dicers*), pl. 53; Album of the Boulaq Museum (*Album du Musée de Boulaq*), pl. 27, etc.; cf. Maspero, History, t. I, p. 364.

[255] John Bunker comment: These hieroglyphs are not a royal name, and are not in a cartouche. [hieroglyph] is *hent*: queen, and [hieroglyph] is *sen*: th*ey*, them, their.

[256] It should be noted, however, that Herodotus speaks of the little pyramid in the middle of the three, while the temple is in front of the last one to the south.

[257] The temple was adorned by the kings *Amen-m-ap* and *Pa-seb-khâ-nut*.

[258] E. De Rouge, *Research on Monuments*, p. 46.

[259] Flinders Petrie, *Pyramids of Gizeh*, p. 134, etc.

[260] This is an actual photo of the stela:
https://scholarship.rice.edu/bitstream/handle/1911/9181/MusBo1872_121.jpg?sequence=243

# Daressy's Translation of the Inventory Stela

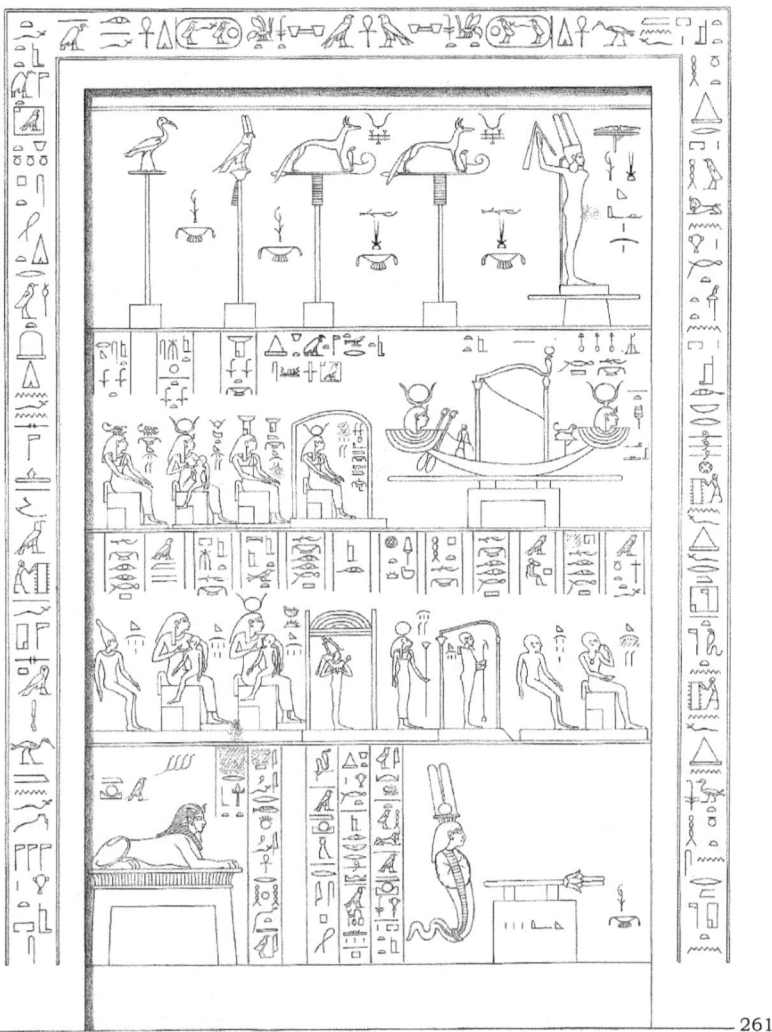

261

First register.

1. The god Min, in his usual attitude, standing on a stretcher. "Min, acacia wood. Height, 1 cubit 1 palm" (0ᵐ 60)²⁶².

2. Jackal, standing on a support, preceded by a uraeus and a coil "Ap-uat, golden acacia²⁶³ wood".

3. Same figure and legend as the previous sign.

4. Falcon wearing disc and two straight feathers, placed on a papyri support form to which is attached a *menat*. "Golden wood".

5. Ibis on a support. "Golden wood".

---

²⁶¹ Illustration added by Bunker & Pressler.

²⁶² I indicate in metric measurements the approximate dimensions given in cubits of 0 "528, palms of 0" 075 and fingers of 0 "019.

²⁶³ For this sign and the following, the looks more like .

# APPENDIX A

Second register.

1. Portable barque of *Isis* whose head overcomes the aegis placed at the bow and stern, in the middle, is a veiled *naos*. [hieroglyphs].264 "Support of the splendors of *Isis* (who wears the seat?), Dofè wood, "Encrusted with stones".

2. *Isis*, wearing disc and horns, sitting in a *naos*. [hieroglyphs] "*Isis*, the great divine mother," regent of the pyramid, *Hathor* in his boat. - Shale[265] "gold plated, uraeus[266] and" horns in silver Height, 3 palms 2 fingers "(0m 264).

3. *Nephthys*, seated. [hieroglyphs] "*Nephthys*, gilded shale, gilded with gold. Height, 3 palms "(0m 056).

4. *Isis*, sitting, suckling *Horus*- [hieroglyphs] "*Isis* mother," shale, black bronze horns. Height, 2 palms 2 fingers "(0m 19).

5. *Selk*, sitting, wearing a scorpion. [hieroglyphs] "*Isis-Selk*," shale, gold scorpion. Height, 2 palms 2 fingers "(0m 19).

Third register.

1. Harpocrates, seated. [hieroglyphs] "*Horus* greeting his father, in ebony, eyes encrusted with stones. Height, 2 palms »2 fingers» (0m19).

2. *Harpocrates*, seated without a seat. [hieroglyphs] "*Harpocrates*, gilded wood, eyes encrusted with stones. Height, 4 palms 1 finger" (0m 32).

3. *Ptah*, standing in a *naos*. [hieroglyphs] "*Ptah*, gilded wood".

4. *Sekhmet*, standing, a papyrus in her hand, wearing the solar disk [hieroglyphs] "*Sekhemt*, black bronze. Height, 3 palms 2 fingers" (0m 264).

5. *Osiris*, standing on the box. [hieroglyphs] "*Osiris*, gilded wood, eyes embedded in stone"

6. *Isis*, sitting, suckling *Horus*. [hieroglyphs] "*Isis*, superior of the great place, black bronze. Height, 3 palms "(0m 226).

7. *Isis*, suckling *Horus*. [hieroglyphs] "*Isis* of the abode of birth," gilded wood. Height, 5 palms "(0m 377).

8. *Horus*, wearing a hat, sitting without a seat. [hieroglyphs] "*Horus* taking the two lands, gilded wood, eyes encrusted with stone. Height, 3 palms 1 finger" (0m 245).

---

[264] The top of [glyph] is mutilated, one would expect to see [glyph].

[265] I do not know of any other examples of this word [glyph]. It is probable that it designates the shale or the saponary stone, if used for the statuettes of divinities.

[266] I take [glyph] for [glyph], the crown of uraeus that generally supports the horns of *Isis*.

# DARESSY'S TRANSLATION OF THE INVENTORY STELA

Fourth Register.

1. On the right, the bull *Apis*, standing, the disc between the horns; the outline of the spots is indicated on the body. "*Apis*."
2. Below, the emblem of *Nefertoum*, two feathers coming out of a lotus, is lying on a pedestal. "*Nefertoum*, gilded wood. Height, 3 cubits" (1ᵐ 58).
3. Afterwards, occupying the whole height of the register, a uraeus with a woman's head, wearing, like *Hathor*, the disk between two long horns and two feathers. [267] "Uraeus, gilded wood. Height, 1 cubit" (0ᵐ 528).
4. On the left, a sphinx is lying on a high pedestal, adorned with a cornice, the legend is and , these two groups are not at the same height. The first sign was taken for a deformation of , and we read "image of *Harmakhis*". I do not see anything else to suggest.

Leaving aside the sphinx, all the other figures are those of rather poor objects, of limited dimensions: a sheet of gold applied to the wood or shale alone gives an appearance of wealth to most of them; rare are those who have a precious metal part. These can not be the essential pieces of the temple furniture, but rather gifts, ex-votos kept in the chapel's treasury and whose stela lists donors for certificates of receipt.[268] "Quantity is far from compensating for quality, and I cannot believe that we have before our eyes the reproduction of statues given by King *Cheops*; this false luxury of gilding is rather reminiscent of the low era and brings us back to the Saïtes.

On the other hand, admitting that the founder of the Great Pyramid[269] bequeathed these statuettes, is there any probability that they still existed at the moment when the current stela was engraved? And from then on, what interest would there have been in commemorating such a poor piece of paper of which there were no traces left? I therefore think that we must give up seeing in these images a figuration of sacred attributes of the Old Empire, and that this part of the stela is entirely from the low era.

---

[267] The name is erased, the alone is clearly visible on the stone.

[268] On the walls of the naos of *Saft el-Henneh* (from the time of *Nectanebo II*) are figured statues of a large number of deities; some are also accompanied by the indication of material and dimension, but at least those with only 3 palms 2 fingers, 5 palms, 1 cubit itself, are noted as gold.

[269] Bunker comment: This reference to *Khufu* shows that Daressy's mind had been imprinted so thoroughly with the idea that *Khufu* built the Great Pyramid, he could not recognize that the reference in the Inventory Stela *(also known as the stele of the daughter of Khufu)* that it specifically identified the small pyramid next to the temple of *Isis* as the pyramid constructed by *Khufu*. There is no text contemporary with the Great Pyramid that says *Khufu* built the Great Pyramid

# APPENDIX A

In the middle of the last register, two inscriptions are engraved in columns. The first (D) is immediately behind the uraeus:

1. [hieroglyphs] [271]

2. [hieroglyphs] [272]

3. [hieroglyphs] [273]

The second (E) separated by an empty column is in front of the Sphinx above its legs:

1. [hieroglyphs] [274] [hieroglyphs] [275]

2. [hieroglyphs] [276] [hieroglyphs] [277]

These inscriptions differ essentially from the explanatory legends which accompany the other figures; we will see later what they are related to.

---

[270] Illustration added by Bunker & Pressler
[271] Direct translation by Bunker: *the tomb of Sphinx of Horus in Horizon upon south of house Isis*
[272] Direct translation by Bunker: *queen pyramid upon north of Osiris lord Restau these writings this*
[273] Direct translation by Bunker: *goddess this of horizon bring her book this*
[274] Budge, *Egyptian Hieroglyphic Dictionary*, 421B, *rut-t:* **quartzite sandstone**.
[275] Direct translation by Bunker: *stone body hard sandstone of body live until eternity everlasting to come*
[276] This group is not very distinct, the stone being worn and chipped.
[277] Direct translation by Bunker: *over in front of the east.*

# DARESSY'S TRANSLATION OF THE INVENTORY STELA

On the upper part of the frame of the stela, is engraved in duplicate *Cheops* (A) protocol:

It is followed immediately, on each side, by an inscription which completes the horizontal line, then descends vertically on the uprights:

On the left (B):

On the right (C):

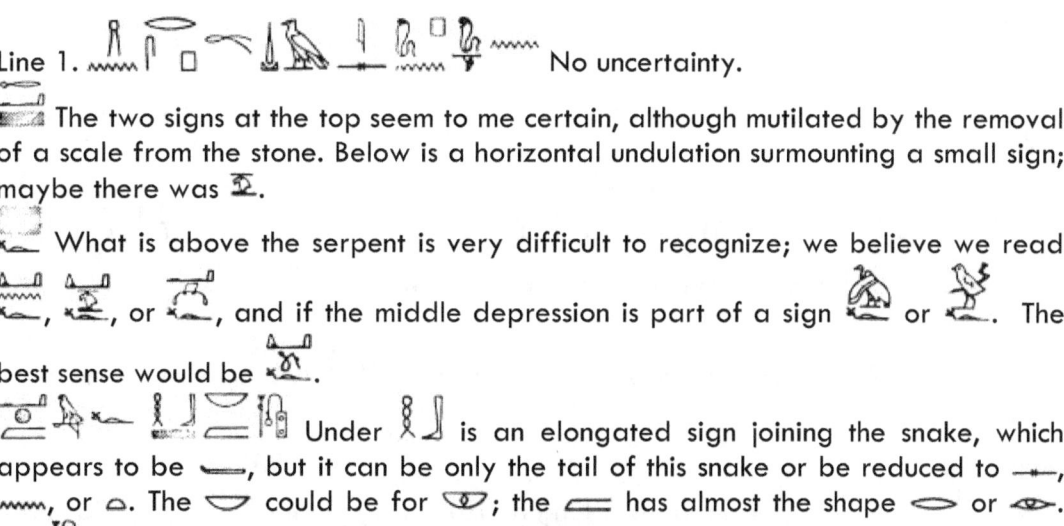

Finally, on the horizontal part of the base, four lines of hieroglyphs (F) were drawn. They are in a very bad state, worn out by the rubbing of the sand, and, except for a few characters which have remained rather clear, we see nothing but silhouettes of signs, without definite outlines; moreover, a breach has removed nearly a quarter of the third line, almost one-third of the last, thus complicating the work of restoring meaning. I managed to decipher part of the text and make a hypothetical reading of the rest; I will indicate some of the readings and point out what I think is going on in the questionable passages, leaving the task of setting the text in its entirety to more skillful people.

Line 1. [hieroglyphs] No uncertainty.

[glyph] The two signs at the top seem to me certain, although mutilated by the removal of a scale from the stone. Below is a horizontal undulation surmounting a small sign; maybe there was [glyph].

[glyph] What is above the serpent is very difficult to recognize; we believe we read [glyph], [glyph], or [glyph], and if the middle depression is part of a sign [glyph] or [glyph]. The best sense would be [glyph].

[glyphs] Under [glyph] is an elongated sign joining the snake, which appears to be [glyph], but it can be only the tail of this snake or be reduced to [glyph], [glyph], or [glyph]. The [glyph] could be for [glyph]; the [glyph] has almost the shape [glyph] or [glyph]. The [glyph] although mutilated, seems to me certain.

All the rest of the line is rough and needs to be studied group by group.

a. [glyph] The top may have been [glyph] or two small signs, such as [glyph], [glyph], [glyph].
b. Akin to [glyph], [glyph], [glyph] and better [glyph].

APPENDIX A

c. There seems to be a circle in the top, two horizontal lines below and a vertical line on the side, and a long sign in the bottom under all, [hieroglyph].

d. The first appearance is [hieroglyph]. Given the wear of the stone, I think it is not impossible to restore [hieroglyph].

e. In the top, ⌑ is almost sure. Below, entangled traits in which I think I distinguish [hieroglyph].

f. [hieroglyph] is certain.

g. Curved line at the top, horizontal line at the bottom, with raised ends, one or two small signs between them: [hieroglyph], [hieroglyph]. Seen in a certain way, one can read [hieroglyph].

h. Group very confused [hieroglyph]. One or two signs at the top, one in the middle, ⌇ or — at the bottom. I suppose [hieroglyph].

i. [hieroglyph] following the ⌇ previous I seem to complete the word [hieroglyph].

j. A very confusing transition that lends itself to all hypotheses [hieroglyph] not to mention other adventitious traits.

I will propose with all reservations to read this half line:
[hieroglyphs].

Line 2. [hieroglyphs] The ↑ is not very clear, we would like to see [hieroglyph] for [hieroglyph], we could read [hieroglyph] or [hieroglyph].

The next group is rough, [hieroglyph] and can give [hieroglyph]. Following, [hieroglyph] seems to me to be [hieroglyph].

[hieroglyphs]. The sign [hieroglyph] is uncertain, but called by sense; the stone gives rather ↑.

[hieroglyph] following is accompanied by two depressions [hieroglyph] which seem to me accidental.

[hieroglyphs] The rough part includes a long horizontal sign in the top: we could read:

[hieroglyphs] for the three vertical bottom signs, we can think of the word [hieroglyphs]. Then comes a gap of five or six groups.

## Daressy's Translation of the Inventory Stela

[hieroglyphs] This last word is a little rough, and the [sign] must be changed to [sign].

[hieroglyphs] The determinative of [sign] is mutilated and looks like [sign]; it had to be [sign] or [sign]. The plural ııı is not very distinct.

The end of the line is fuzzy as a result of stone wear. [hieroglyphs] can be completed [hieroglyphs].

Line 4. The beginning is [hieroglyphs]. In the first group we can see [hieroglyphs], in the second [sign], and look for a meaning like "except the thigh". However there is possibility to read [hieroglyphs] "roasted carcass"; the second word, very erased, still takes the characteristic of [signs]. As a result of the gap of five groups, it is with great difficulty that we distinguish: [hieroglyphs].

[hieroglyphs] This passage does not offer difficulties. The end of the line is, unfortunately, very mutilated.

A first group consists of a word [sign] below which appears to be [sign] crossed by another sign; I transcribe, [sign]²⁷⁸. As a result, I think I recognize the beginning of the text b, [hieroglyphs], but without being able to affirm this interpretation, as the signs are not very [hieroglyphs] distinguishable.

---

278 [sign] *ha*

# APPENDIX A

In summary, here is what is certain in the text F:

[hieroglyphic text]

and how I think I can restore it:

[hieroglyphic text]

The whole documentary importance of the stela results from the way in which these inscriptions are combined. We have already seen that it is almost impossible to consider the figures and inscriptions on the background as a renovation; let us see to what extent the scattered texts can be attached to the protocol of *Cheops* (A). First, we must take B, with the left side having priority according to Egyptian usage. If the stela reproduces the content of an old document, it is in this column that it must be found, and, in fact, I see no reason to doubt that *Cheops* made a donation to the temple of *Isis Hathor* and repaired the building. But, and this is where I separate myself from the previous translators, I believe that this passage is the only one which can be, if need be, attributed to the IV<sup>th</sup> Dynasty[279]; all the rest is the work of the Saite scribe, author of the stela. The connection of old and new texts is in passage [hieroglyphs] renewing what he had "found". The following sentence: [hieroglyphs][280] is the delicate point of the inscription, which sets the time of the

---

[279] It is probable that the decree of Cheops was more developed, and that we have only one excerpt, a summary.

[280] Statement by John Bunker 12/6/2019: These hieroglyphs [hieroglyphs], individually, translate this way: [glyph] *nu*: a demonstrative pronoun, i.e. "these". [glyph] *neteru*: "gods". [glyph] *her*: a preposition, i.e. "at". [glyph] *s-t*: "place". [glyph] *si*: personal and absolute pronoun, 3<sup>rd</sup> person feminine, i.e. "her".. Meaning: "*These gods at her place*". (in reference to statues of the gods in the temple of *Isis*.)

monument. At first glance, one translates: "The approval of the gods is upon his abode," or" "Let the choice of the gods be on his abode!"; but this insignificant formula is not found anywhere, and I think it must be taken with a completely different meaning. ⌢𓏤𓏤𓏤 is the name of 𓅄 of *Amasis*, and I believe that this king was mentioned in an ambiguous manner: "The chosen of the gods being in his dwelling place". Either it was intended to mislead the unaware reader and to let him assume that the whole stela was from *Cheops*, or that he did not want to show the name of *Amasis*, in the spirit of opposition, or at the moment when the cartouches of this sovereign were beginning to be forged, the latter was only designated by one of his ceremonial nicknames.[281]

It seems that the monument was hastily made, the engraver not even having before his eyes the draft of what he was going to draw and improvising the text. No sooner had he started the sentence, than he thought it useful to explain where this chapel of *Isis* is located, using the local topography of his time, and to indicate the neighboring buildings as landmarks. He reported this explanation on the other side of the stela, in C, and made the reminder 𓏛𓍺 to mark where to link this incident. Then, the scribe realized that in his explanation he had skipped an important word, that of 𓅄𓊖 after 𓀀𓏤𓈖; In order to repair his carelessness, he repeated and modified in D the explanatory sentence of the temple's si *Tuation*, before continuing the second part of the inscription, the one which indicates the reasons for the writing of the stela and the circumstances that accompanied it. The rest of the text is on the base and the repairing is still done by repetition: 𓀀𓈖𓊪𓊖 at the beginning of F of the final 𓀀𓈖𓏤𓊖 of D. Finally, it is not impossible to find at the end of this text F the words by which the inscription E starts.

The translation of the whole will thus be established as follows:
"(A) Long live *Horus* slaughterer, King of the South and North, *Khufu*, giving life! (B) He did for his mother *Isis*, the divine mother, *Hathor*, Queen of the West,[282] 'an ordinance consigned to a stela and gave her again sacred offerings. He built his temple in stone, renewing what he had found. (C) The residence of *Isis*, regent of the Pyramid, is close to the sphinx of ...[283], which is northwest of the home of *Osiris*, lord of *Ro-satu*. He built his pyramid near the temple of this goddess, and he built the pyramid of the royal daughter *Hent-sen* next to this temple. (D) The place of the sphinx of *Harmakhis* is south of the residence of *Isis*, regent of the Pyramid, and north of *Osiris* (sic) [284], lord of Ro-satu. The chosen of the gods being in his house, the drawings of the image of *Harmakhis* were brought for the restoration of (F) this

---

[281] The style of the monument agrees with the time so assigned; we find very similar hieroglyphics on some neglected steles of the end of the XXVIth Dynasty, especially on some of the Serapeum.

[282] 𓊖𓊖𓊖 is a fault for 𓊖𓊖𓊖 𓈋 the funerary mountain, the west.

[283] The engraver has skipped the name of *Harmakhis*.

[284] The word 𓊖 was jumped on the stele

## APPENDIX A

colossus, portrait of the very (formidable). He has restored the statue covered with paint (the guardian of the atmosphere, which guides the winds with his gaze[285] "He cut the back of the *nemes*[286] which was missing) in a gilded stone which has a length of 7 cubits (3" 70). (He came to take a turn) to see "the storm on the place of sycamore[287], so named because of a large sycamore with branches struck by lightning when the master of heaven(?) descended on the place of *Harmakhis*, and also this image retracing the blaze(?), ... of all the animals killed at *Ro-satu*. It is a table for the containers full of the remains of the animals that, (except the thigh?), are eaten near these seven gods (?), asking ... (the rays of his face on the stela) traced near this colossus at the time of the darkness. The figure of this god being (cut in) stone, (E) is solid and will subsist for eternity, always, the face looking east. "

Despite the gaps that cut off the text of the base, we see that all the inscriptions were made during a repair of the Sphinx, consisting mainly of refurbishment of the painting and perhaps replacement of the tail of the *nemes*, damaged as a result of a storm that had broken out on the region and during which a neighboring sycamore had been struck down. "If we accept as authentic the content of the inscription B attributed to *Cheops*, we note that it is only a stone chapel of *Isis-Hathor*, Queen of the West, and no other monument; this sanctuary was, perhaps, isolated on this part of the mountain. that the pyramid of *Cheops* and that of his daughter were built near this temple, it could only be later that the local *Isis* received the title of queen of the Pyramid[288] ", which, in fact, is not not attributed to her in the extract from the decree of *Cheops*.

Did this temple of the goddess occupy the site of the one in which the stela was found? There is no document to assert it, and there can only be presumptions for it to be so, for the building is, indeed, north of the Sphinx, but at a distance of 300 meters. If we admit this, considering the importance that the sphinx occupies in the stela, we must infer that this colossal image of *Harmakhis* was considered dependent on the temple of *Isis*, and then there would be no connection between the Sphinx and the granite temple that adjoins it. On the other hand, the chapel of *Osiris* of Rosatu is apparently the same of which speaks the stela of *Thutmose IV*

---

[285] In Makrizi's time, the sphinx was regarded as a talisman charged with preventing the invasion of the Gizéh lands by the sands.

[286] One can still see on the Sphinx that the back of the hairstyle was made of a separate stone.

[287] Of course, there are sycamores in the nearby Sphinx Valley, 220 meters to the south. The offspring of these trees still succeed each other and currently house Bedouin tombs. Here is a grove of sycamores that has survived for more than 2,400 years and has a mention several centuries earlier than that of the tree of the Virgin of Matarieh.

[288] In the Louvre Museum, Historic Room No. 314, a stele from the year 34 of Darius is preserved (see Chassinat, Texts from the Serapeum of Memphis, in the collection of Tracaux, XXII, 173, S CXI), where this *Isis* is also mentioned, at the same time as the cult of the kings of the neighboring pyramids and the Sphinx: [hieroglyphs] etc. It would be no wonder that this *Psamétik-menkh* or his father was the author of our stele.

## DARESSY'S TRANSLATION OF THE INVENTORY STELA

attributing it to *Sokar*: [hieroglyphs], and there is little likelihood of it being the granite temple, because this building is connected by a flagstone path to the buildings placed to the east of the second pyramid and is part of the outbuildings of the eternal home of *Chéfren*. It may be that the mention of this king in the stela of *Thutmose IV*, l. 13, refers to the said granite temple.

Everything in the stela that relates to the Sphinx is therefore from the early days, an addition to the shortened copy of an ancient inscription deemed fit to reproduce in the interest of the temple. This observation made, all the deductions on the prodigious antiquity of the Sphinx vanish, and one is brought back to questioning the monument itself on its age. Given its state of degradation and the successive repairs to the lower parts, we only have the face and hairstyle as an object of research, as M. Borchardt has already done. [289]

The hairstyle is the [hieroglyphs] which, in fact, is in relation with the sphinx, according to the Book of the Dead.[290] The front part which frames the figure and falls on the chest is decorated with equal horizontal stripes, on the contrary, the rear cap bears strips of different width, a large stripe being accompanied by two narrower ones. This arrangement has so far been found only on statues of the twelfth dynasty. Mr. Borchardt could not see it on monuments with a certain date only on images of *Amen-m-Hât III*: more recent discoveries have given us portraits of *Usurtsen II* [cartouche], showing that fashion is a little older, because its *nemes* and the triangular apron offer a similar layout of the bands. At the same time, the features of his figure recall those of the two colossi of Tanis, usurped by Ramses II, who have the same hairstyle. I will therefore also attribute Ginghe's sphinx to the end of the 12th dynasty, to *Usurtsen II* or Amen-m-hath III, rather to the last of these kings, because *Usurtsen* has the elongated figure, *Amen m-haât* enlarged, and what can be distinguished from the features of the colossus is quite reminiscent of the facies of the statue of the creator of the *Moeris*, found at *Hawara*.[291]

It is not that the Old Kingdom has never represented the androcephalic lion. The Cairo Museum has two sphinxes from the Memphite period, but apparently they were kings. One, from Mr. Chassinat's excavations in *Abu-Roach*, is probably in the time of *Dad-f-râ*. He does not have the nemes, or rather his hairstyle does not have that puffy hood, followed by a strangled tail that characterizes him. Of the other sphinx (No. 157 of the Guide) there are unfortunately only the legs, between which is engraved in the basalt: [hieroglyphs]. But it was only under the Middle Kingdom that the sphinx fashion developed and the number multiplied. The

---

[289] Borchardt, *On the Age of the Sphinx*, Berlin Academy, 1897, Appendix Two, page 752 (English translation at https://books.google.com/books?id=C14oDwAAQBAJ&pg=SA8-PA115&lpg=SA8-PA115#v=onepage&q&f=false

[290] NAVILLE, The name of the sphinx in the Book of the Dead, in *Sphinx*, vol. V, p. 193. It is especially the chapter LXXVIII (I, 18, 21, 23) which establishes a relation between the *Nemes* and the sphinx named [hieroglyphs]

[291] Giza Catalog No. 1370; current issue 199. Collection XXX. – NOUV., XIV.

# APPENDIX A

colossus of Giza is indeed an image of the god *Harmakhis*, to which, according to custom, the features of the reigning sovereign have been given; the inscriptions say so, and there was no motive for carving a statue of a king in the middle of the desert, since it is not accompanied by a temple or other monument calling for such an effigy. The sphinxes are rather consecrated to the Heliopolitan deities: *Harmakhis*, *Khépra*, Spirits of An, etc., so it is natural that, under a dynasty that favored the city of the Sun, rebuilt the temple, adorned it with obelisks and from a path of sphinx, the rock of Gizeh (which was probably already attached to an ancient legend) was carved in the shape of the sacred animal, whereas under the Old Kingdom the divine statues seem to have been rather rare.

Stripped of its fabulous antiquity, the great Sphinx is none the less one of the wonders of the world. Considered by the ancients as a kind of Aeolus, as I understand it in the stela, passing in the Middle Ages for a talisman separating the sands of the land of Gizeh, become simply *Abu'lhol* "the father of fear" from his mutilated face he always fixes the east and seems a vigilant guardian of the great Pyramids, imperturbably at his post for eternity.

# APPENDIX B - SELIM HASSAN'S PRESENTATION OF THE INVENTORY STELA

## Selim Hassan's Translation of the Inventory Stela

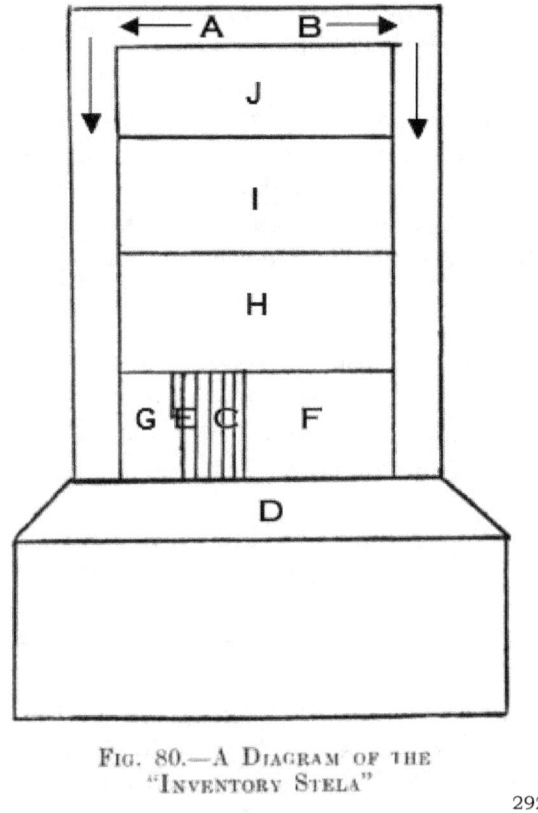

Fig. 80.—A Diagram of the "Inventory Stela" [292]

In *The Great Sphinx and Its Secrets,* Dr. Selim Hassan wrote regarding the Inventory Stela: [293]

> But by far the most important find was the stela which Mariette discovered, and which is now in the Cairo Museum, still wrongly placed among the Old Kingdom objects. It has been given various names, including the "Stela of *Khufu*'s Daughter" and the "Inventory Stela," the latter being the more apt, if less romantic-sounding. It is, in fact, a list of the figures of the Gods which *Khufu* was supposed to have found when he came to repair the temple. This stela[294] which is of fine white limestone, measures 70 cm. high and 42 cm. wide, and consists of a rectangular panel set upright upon a heavy base, and surrounded on three sides by a frame raised 10 cm. from its surface. This frame and the upper surface of the pedestal are inscribed, the text beginning from the centre of the top bar of the frame and extending down the sides (Fig. 80). The inscription (B) on the left-hand side reads: "Live *Horus Mezdw*, the King of Upper and Lower Egypt, *Khufu*, given life. He made for his mother, *Isis*, the Divine Mother, *Hathor*, Mistress of the Western Mountain, a

---

[292] Hassan. *The Great Sphinx and its Secrets*, page 113.
[293] Hassan. *The Great Sphinx and its Secrets*, page 113-116.
[294] Text: MASPERO, "The Dawn of Civilization", p. 413; De Rouge, "Recherches sur les Monuments", p. 46; BRUGSCH, "Thesaurus", Vol. V. Text and translation: DARESSY, "Rec. Trav.", Vol. XXX, pp. 2-10. Translation: BREASTED, "Ancient Records", Vol. I, pp. 83-85.

## APPENDIX B

decree made on a stela. He gave to her a new divine offering, and he built her temple of stone, renewing what he had found, namely these Gods in her place".

-The right-hand side of the inscription (B) reads: "Live *Horus Mezdw*,[295] the King of Upper and Lower Egypt, *Khufu*, given life. He found the House of *Isis*, Mistress of the Pyramid, beside the House of the Sphinx, on the north-west of the House of *Osiris*, Lord of *Rostaw*[296]; and he built his Pyramid beside the temple of this Goddess, and he built a Pyramid for the King's Daughter, *Henutsen*, beside this temple".

The inscription now jumps to the bottom register of the panel where it continues: "The Place of *Hwran* (the Sphinx), *Hor-em-akhet*, is on the south of the House of *Isis*, Mistress of the Pyramid, and on the north of *Osiris*, Lord of *Rostaw*. The plans of the image of *Hor-em-akhet* were brought in order to ..."

The inscription continues in the four lines inscribed on the upper surface of the pedestal; these are very badly worn, but M. Daressy who has made a special study of the monument, succeeded in deciphering most of the signs, and if we may trust his translations, it reads (the inscription is completed in the bottom register of the panel, at "E":-
"... bring to revision the sayings of the disposition of the Image of the Very Redoubtable. He restored the statue, all covered in painting, of the Guardian of the Atmosphere, which guides the winds with his gaze. He made to quarry the hind part of the *nemes*[297], which was lacking, gilded stone, and which had a length of 7 ells (3.70 metres). He came to make a tour, in order to see the thunderbolt which stands in the place of the Sycamores, so named because of a great sycamore whose branches were struck when the Lord of Heaven descended upon the Place of *Hor-em-akhet*; and also this image, retracing the erasure according to the above-mentioned disposition, which is written ... of all the animals killed at *Rostaw*. It is a table for the vases full of these animals, which, except for the thighs, were eaten near these seven Gods, demanding. . . (The God gave) the thought in his heart, of putting a written decree on the side of this (above-mentioned) Sphinx, in an hour of the night[298]. The figure of this God, being cut in stone, is solid, and will exist to eternity, always having its face regarding the Orient."

The main part of the panel is occupied with various representations of sacred statues and emblems, arranged in four superposed registers, and accompanied by explanatory inscriptions:

The Top Register:-
(I) A statue of the God *Min*, standing upon a pedestal provided with carrying-poles. It is inscribed: "*Min*, acacia wood, height 1 ell, 1 hand (60 cm.) ".

---

[295] The Horus name of King *Khufu*.
[296] In our ninth season's excavation, we unearthed the remains of this temple, and its position corresponds exactly with the disposition of the monuments as given in the text of this stela.
[297] *Nemes* - the striped headdress worn by the pharaohs.
[298] As on the Stela of *Thutmose IV*, the God gives his instructions in the form of a dream.

## Selim Hassan's Translation of the Inventory Stela

(2) A figure of a jackal standing upon a support, the front of which ends in a spiral. Before its front legs is a uraeus; inscribed: "*Wep-wat*, gilded acacia wood".
(3) The same as the preceding.
(4) A hawk, crowned with the disk and plumes, perching upon a papyrus-headed standard, to which is attached a *menat*,[299] inscribed: "Gilded wood".
(5) An ibis on a perch; inscribed: "Gilded wood".

The Second Register:-
(1) ... A portable barque of *Isis*, on the prow and stern of which are effigies of that Goddess. There is a veiled *naos* amidships; it is inscribed: "Support for the splendours of *Isis*; gilded wood, inlaid with stones".
(2) A statue of *Isis*, crowned with the disk and horns, and seated within a *naos*; it is inscribed: "*Isis* the Great, the Divine Mother, Mistress of the Pyramid. *Hathor* in her barque; *nen*-stone, plated with gold; head-dress and uraeus of silver. Height: 3 hands, 2 fingers (26.4 cm.)".
(3) *Nephthys*, seated upon a low-backed throne; inscribed: "*Nephthys*, gilded *nen*-stone, head-dress of gold; height: 3 hands".
(4) *Isis* suckling *Horus*; it is inscribed: "*Isis*, Mother, *nen*-stone, head-dress of black bronze; height: 2 hands, 2 fingers (19 cm.)".
(5) The Goddess *Selkt*, seated and wearing a scorpion upon her head; inscribed: "*Isis-Selkt*, *nen*-stone, scorpion of gold; height: 2 hands, 2 fingers (19 cm.)".

The Third Register:-
(1) *Horus* the Child, seated, and inscribed: "*Horus* the Protector of His Father, ebony, eyes of inlaid stone; height: 2 hands, 2 fingers (19 cm.)".
(2) *Horus* the Child, seated, but without a throne, inscribed: "*Horus* the Child, gilded wood, eyes of inlaid stone; height: 4 hands, 2 fingers (32 cm.)".
(3) The God *Ptah*, standing in a *naos*; inscribed: "*Ptah*, gilded wood".
(4) *Sekhmet*, standing and holding a papyrus sceptre; inscribed: "*Sekhmet*, black bronze; height: 3 hands, 2 fingers (26'4 cm.)".
(5) *Osiris*, standing in a *naos*; inscribed: "*Osiris*, gilded wood, eyes of inlaid stone".
(6) *Isis*, seated and suckling *Horus*; inscribed: "*Isis*, Superior of the Great Place; black bronze; height: 3 hands (22.6 cm.)".
(7) *Isis* suckling *Horus*; inscribed: "*Isis*, gilded wood; height: 5 hands" (37. 7 cm.).
(8) *Horus*, wearing the Double Crown, seated, but without a throne; inscribed "*Horus*, who Takes Possession of the Two Lands, gilded wood, eyes of inlaid stone; height: 3 hands, 1 finger (24 .5 cm.)".

The Fourth Register:-
(1) At the top of the space "F" is a figure of the *Apis* bull, standing on a low pedestal. It has a disk between its horns, and its special distinguishing marks are engraved upon its body. It is inscribed: "*Apis.*"
(2) Below the bull is a curious object, consisting of two plumes springing out of a lotus-flower, which is set horizontally upon a rectangular pedestal. It is the emblem of the God *Nefer-tum*, and is inscribed: "*Nefer-tum*, gilded wood; height: 3 ells (1.58 metres)".

---

[299] *Menat* - An amulet worn by some ancient Egyptians for divine protection.

# APPENDIX B

(3) Behind the two preceding figures, and occupying the full height of the register, is the figure of a uraeus having the bead of a woman, and crowned with-the head-dress of the Goddess *Hathor* - a disk between two long horns, and surmounted by two plumes. It is inscribed: "Uraeus of gilded wood; height 1 ell (52.8 cm.)".

(4) In space "G" is the representation of a sphinx, couchant upon a high pedestal, and evidently intended to represent the Great Sphinx of Giza; above it is inscribed: 🏛 which seems to be a corruption of 𓍲 "*seshep*": apparently the first mention of this word as a name for the Sphinx in this district and also 𓅃 𓈌 "Hor-em-akhet".

# BIBLIOGRAPHY

Birch, S., & Society of biblical archaeology (London). (1873). *Records of the past: Being English translations of the Assyrian and Egyptian monuments*. London: S. Bagster and sons. https://catalog.hathitrust.org/Record/000536544

Borchardt, L. (1897). *Über des alter des sphinx bei Giseh*. (Sitzungsberichte der Königlich preussischen akademie des wissenschaften zu Berlin, XXXV, 1897.) Berlin: Koeniglich Prersuuischen Akademie der Wissenschaften.

Breasted, J. H. (1906). *Ancient records of Egypt: Historical documents from the earliest times to the Persian conquest*. (Ancient records.) Chicago: University of Chicago Press. https://archive.org/details/BreastedJ.H.AncientRecordsEgyptAll5Vols1906

Brugsch, H. (1883). *Thesaurus inscriptionum Aegyptiacarum*. Leipzig. https://archive.org/details/thesaurusinscrip12brug

Budge, E. A. W. (1904). *The decree of Canopus*. London: Kegan Paul. https://babel.hathitrust.org/cgi/pt?id=iau.31858006395309&view=1up&seq=11

Budge, E. A. W. (1911). *A hieroglyphic vocabulary to the Theban recension of the Book of the dead: With an index to all the English equivalents of the Egyptian words*. London: Kegan Paul. https://archive.org/details/hieroglyphicvoca00budg/page/n11/mode/2up

Budge, E. A. W. (1971). *Egyptian language: Easy lessons in Egyptian hieroglyphics, with a sign list*. London: K. Paul, Trench, Trübner.

Budge, E. A. W. (1978). *An Egyptian hieroglyphic dictionary : with an index of English words, king list, and geographical list with indexes, list of hieroglyphic characters, Coptic and Semitic alphabets, etc*. New York: Dover Publications.

Budge, E. A. W. (1991). *A Hieroglyphic Vocabulary to the Book of the Dead*. New York: Dover Publications.

Cayce, E. (1993). *The complete Edgar Cayce readings*. Virginia Beach, Va: A.R.E. Press.

Chartrand, M. R., & Wimmer, H. K. (1982). *Skyguide: A field guide for amateur astronomers*. New York: Golden Press.

Daressy, G. (1902). Tombeau ptolémaïque à *Atfieh. Annales du Service des Antiquités de l'Égypte,* 3, pp. 160-180. https://archive.org/details/annalesduservice03egypuoft

Daressy, G. (1908). *La Stèle de la fille de Chéops. Stèle funéraire d'un taureau d'Hermonthis*. Paris: H. Champion. https://digi.ub.uni-heidelberg.de/diglit/rectrav1908/0011

Diodorus & Oldfather, C. H. (1933). *Diodorus of Sicily: The library of history*. Cambridge, Mass: Harvard University Press. https://penelope.uchicago.edu/Thayer/E/Roman/Texts/Diodorus_Siculus/1A*.html

# BIBLIOGRAPHY

Erman, Adolf (1882) Zehn Verträge aus dem mittleren Reich. *Zeitschrift Für Ägyptische Sprache Und Altertumskunde, 20.* https://play.google.com/books/reader?id=kSsGAAAAQAAJ&printsec=frontcover&pg=GBS.PA172

Frazer, J. G. (1919). *Adonis, Attis, Osiris: Studies in the history of Oriental religion.* London: Macmillan. https://www.google.com/books/edition/The_Golden_Bough_pt_IV_Adonis_Attis_Osir/tvQnAAAAYAAJ?hl=en&gbpv=0

Haney, Mark A., creator. (1994) *Skyglobe for Windows* (astronomical software program).

Harley, J. B., & Woodward, D. (n.d.). *History of cartography. Volume two, Book one. Cartography in the traditional Islamic and South Asian societies.* Chicago: University of Chicago Press. https://press.uchicago.edu/books/HOC/HOC_V2_B1/HOC_VOLUME2_Book1_chapter2.pdf

Hassan, S., al- Ğāmiʿa al-Miṣrīya, & Egypt. (1953). *Excavations at Gîza: The Great Sphinx and its secrets: historical studies in the light of recent excavations.* Oxford: Univ. Press. https://www.scribd.com/document/427193836/excavations-at-giza-1936-1937-part-VIII-selim-hassan-pdf

Hassan, S. (1949). *The Sphinx: Its history in the light of recent excavations.* Cairo: Gov. Press.

Herodotus, ., Rawlinson, G., Rawlinson, H., & Wilkinson, J. G. (1889). *The history of Herodotus: A new English version.* New York: D. Appleton. https://www.globalgreyebooks.com/history-of-herodotus-volume-2-ebook.html

Hincks, E. (1838). *On the years and cycles used by the ancient Egyptians.* Dublin: Printed by M.H. Gill. https://www.jstor.org/stable/30078988?seq=3#metadata_info_tab_contents

Justi, F., Stevenson, S. Y., & Jastrow, M. (1905). *A history of all nations.* Philadelphia: Lea Brothers. https://www.google.com/books/edition/Egypt_and_Western_Asia_in_Antiquity/hBo6AQAAIAAJ?hl=en&gbpv=1&printsec=frontcover

Klasens, A. (1952). *A magical statue base (Socle Béhague) in the Museum of Antiquities at Leiden.* Leiden. https://dds.crl.edu/crldelivery/19323

Lepsius, Carl Richard. *Denkmäler aus Aegypten und Aethiopien.* Plates 2, Band 3 [Giza plates only]. Berlin: Nicolaische Buchhandlung, 1849-1859. http://giza.fas.harvard.edu/pubdocs/315/full/

Lieblein, J. D. C. (1871). Hieroglyphisches Namen-Wörterbuch: Genealogisch und alphabetisch geordnet, nach den aegyptischen Denkmaelern hrsg. Christiania: Brögger & Christie.Mariette, A., & Maspero, G. (1889). *Les mastabas de l'ancien empire: Fragment [de son] dernier ouvrage.* Paris: F. Vieweg. https://digi.ub.uni-heidelberg.de/diglit/mariette1889

# BIBLIOGRAPHY

Lockyer, Norman. (1892). "The Astronomy and Mythology of the Ancient Egyptians." (*The Nineteenth Century,* Volume XXXII, July-December, Pages 29-51).

Mariette, A. (1871). *Album du Musée de Boulaq comprenant quarante planches photographiques*. Le Caire: Mourés. https://hdl.handle.net/1911/9181

Mariette, Auguste, 1821-1881, Délié, Hippolyte and Béchard, Émile. "Album du Musée de Boulaq [Electronic Version]." (1872) Electronic version published by Rice University, Houston, TX: https://hdl.handle.net/1911/9181.

Mariette, A., & Maspero, G. (1882). *Le Serapeum de Memphis*. Paris: Vieweg. https://play.google.com/books/reader?id=rrQTAAAAQAAJ&hl=en&pg=GBS.PP7

Mariette, A. (1981). *Monuments divers recueillis en Egypte et en Nubie*. Wiesbaden: LTR-Verl. https://digi.ub.uni-heidelberg.de/diglit/mariette1872bd2

Maspero, G., Quibell, J. E., & Quibell, A. A. (1906). *Guide to the Cairo museum*. https://babel.hathitrust.org/cgi/pt?id=hvd.32044043217710&view=1up&seq=10

Maspero, G., Sayce, A. H., & McClure, M. L. (1922). *The dawn of civilization: Egypt and Chaldea*. London: Society for Promoting Christian Knowledge. https://archive.org/stream/dawnofcivilizati00masprich?ref=ol

Massey, G. (1883). *The natural genesis: Or, Second part of a book of the beginnings, containing an attempt to recover and reconstitute the lost origines of the myths and mysteries, types and symbols, religion and language, with Egypt for the mouthpiece and Africa as the birthplace*. London: Williams and Norgate. https://archive.org/stream/b24885526?ref=ol#page/n5/mode/2up

McCarthy, J. (1900). *The World's greatest literature: Masterpieces of the world's greatest authors in history, biography, philosophy, economics, politics; epic and dramatic literature, history of English literature, Oriental literature (sacred and profane), orations, essays*. New York: Collier.

Mercer, S. A. B. (1952). *The pyramid texts*. New York: Longmans, Green.

Meyer, Eduard, "Aegyptische Chronologie" (1904). *Dr. Kent R. Weeks Book Collection*. 32. https://knowledge.e.southern.edu/kweeks_coll/32

Murray, M. A., & Milne, J. G. (1904). *The Osireion at Abydos*. London: B. Quaritch. https://archive.org/details/osireionatabydos00murr

Naville, E. (1875). *La litanie du soleil: Inscriptions recueillies dans les tombeaux des rois à Thèbes*. Leipzig: Engelmann. https://reader.digitale-sammlungen.de/de/fs1/object/display/bsb11307874_00007.html

Neugebauer, O., & Parker, R. A. (1969). *Egyptian astronomical texts*. Providence: Brown University Press.

Noonan, G. C. (1990). *Fixed stars and judicial astrology*. Tempe, Ariz: American Federation of Astrologers.

# BIBLIOGRAPHY

Payne-Gallwey, R. (1907). *A summary of the history, construction and effects in warfare of the projectile-throwing engines of the ancients with a treatise on the structure, power and management of Turkish and other oriental bows of mediaeval and later times.* New York, Bombay, and Calcutta: Longmans, Greens, and Co.Petrie, W. M. F. (1883). *The Pyramids and temples of Gizeh, by W.M. Flinders Petrie.* London: Field and Tuer.
https://archive.org/details/cu31924012038927/page/n29/mode/2up

Piankoff, A. (1954). *The tomb of Ramesses VI.* New York: Pantheon Books.

Quinn, K. (1978). *Virgil's Aeneid: A critical description.* London: Routledge and Kegal Paul.

Rapoport, Y., & Savage-Smith, E. (2014). *An eleventh-century Egyptian guide to the universe: The Book of Curiosities.*

Reisner, G.A. (April 1918) The tomb of Hepzefa, nomarch of Siút, *Journal of Egyptian Archaeology.* 5: 79-98. http://www.jstor.org/stable/3853727

Rougé Emmanuel de. Recherches sur les monuments qu'on peut attribuer aux six premières dynasties de Manéthon. In: *Mémoires de l'Institut national de France*, tome 25, 2ᵉ partie, 1866. pp. 225-376. https://doi.org/10.3406/minf.1866.1454

Sharpe, S., & Bonomi, J. (1864). *The Alabaster Sarcophagus of Oimenepthah I., King of Egypt, now in Sir J. Soane's Museum, Lincolns Inn Fields.* London: Longman.
dlib.nyu.edu/awdl/sites/dl-pa.home.nyu.edu.awdl/files/alabastersarcoph00shar/alabastersarcoph00shar.pdf

Temple, R. K. G., & Temple, O. (2009). *The Sphinx mystery: The forgotten origins of the sanctuary of Anubis.* Rochester, Vt: Inner Traditions.

Willoughby, D. P. (1970). *The super-athletes.* South Brunswick [etc.]: A. S. Barnes.

Yoo, Sung Hwan, "Patterns of Ancient Egyptian Child Deities" (2012). *Egyptology and Assyriology Theses and Dissertations.* Brown Digital Repository. Brown University Library. https://doi.org/10.7301/Z0SN077S

Zivie-Coche, Christiane M. (1991) *Giza au premier millénaire: Autour du temple d'Isis dame des pyramides.* Boston: Museum of Fine Arts.
http://giza.fas.harvard.edu/pubdocs/193/full/

# INDEX

*An*, the hawk-headed man, 15, 16, 17, 18, 24, 28, 29, 31, 33, 65, 66, 67, 168, 173
Aquila (the Eagle, or Falcon of *Horus*), 67, 68, 69, 70
*Atfieh*
    Ptolemaic tomb at, 31, 34, 35
Balance, 15, 27, 32
    representing the equinox, 13, 27, 30, 36, 64, 67
Bodies without life (Star constellations), 101, 109, 113, 132
*Book of the Dead*, 175
Boötes (the ploughman), 73, 75
Bow, 16, 158
Breasted, James Henry, 175
Bull (see also "Taurus"), 10, 15, 29, 31, 33, 58, 61, 64, 72, 73, 114, 159, 173
Capricorn, 58, 59
Cayce, Edgar, 4, 117, 120, 122, 136, 138, 187
Centaurus, 3, 32, 46, 48, 49, 53
Cetus (the Hippopotamus constellation), 19, 60, 61, 114, 132
Christ (Jesus), 141
Corona Borealis, 73
Cygnus (the Goose or Swan), 67, 69, 70
Daressy, Georges, 85, 100, 107, 108, 155, 172
Dark Ages in Egypt, 41
*Dendera* temple, 3, 4, 57
    rectangular zodiac, 57, 61
Diodorus, 117, 118, 175
Dynasty
    eighteenth, 81
    fourth, 81, 156
    *third*, 81, 120
    thirteenth, 45
    twelfth, 167
    twentieth, 127
    twenty-fifth, 81
    twenty-first, 81, 156
    twenty-sixth, 30, 31, 81
Equinox, 57
    and balance, 13, 30, 36, 67
    autumnal, 4, 9, 11, 14, 18, 20, 22, 41, 44, 47, 57, 60, 64, 67, 72, 73, 76
    spring, 4, 35, 36, 37, 57, 67, 69
Eridanus, 15, 18, 28, 29, 61
Erman, Adolf, 42, 52
Fox, 69
Frazier, James, 43
Gazelles, 128, 148, 149
    cut in pieces, 101, 109, 113, 118, 128
    footprints of, 115, 128
    leaps of, 128, 148
*Geb*, 119, 146, 149
Gemini, 3-9, 64, 147
Great Pyramid, 86, 89, 105, 123, 125
    construction of, 117, 136, 159
Hall of Records
    sealing of, 46
Harmakhis, 85, 108, 159, 165, 166, 168
*Hathor*, 85, 158, 165, 166, 171, 173
    headdress of, 86, 100, 118, 119, 159, 174
    mother of *Horus*, 119
    queen of celestial waters, 86, 100, 103, 118, 119
    temple of (*Dendera*), 25, 35, 75, 164
        ceiling of, 36, 41, 53, 55–62, 61, 63
        zodiac of, 3, 4, 35, 41
*Hent-sen* (*Henoutsen*, etc.), 85, 86, 90, 92, 93, 94, 99, 137, 165
*Hepzefa*
    contract of, 44, 51
    tomb of, 44, 45, 49, 51
Herodotus, 86, 89, 90, 105, 117, 125, 156, 176
*Hesamut*, 19, 23, 132
Hincks, Edward, 42
Hippopotamus, 4, 19, 23, 25, 27, 30, 34, 61, 113, 115, 132
    goddess (*Hesamut*), 23, 32, 132
*Horus*, 21, 31, 32, 34, 60, 70, 85, 86, 88, 100, 101, 106, 109, 111, 118, 119, 125, 126, 127, 134, 150, 158, 160, 165, 171, 172, 173
    birth of, 151
*Horus* and *Set*, battle of, 150, 151
Hours of the night, 57, 53, 172
    10th hour, 76
    11th hour, 73
    12th hour, 77
    1st hour, 58, 59
    2nd hour, 60, 61, 69
    3rd hour, 60, 61
    4th hour, 67, 68
    5th hour, 67, 68, 69
    6th hour, 67, 68, 69
    7th hour, 67, 68, 69, 70
    8th hour, 72, 73
    9th hour, 72
Hydra (*Set*, the serpent), 3, 21, 35, 45, 49, 72, 77, 143, 145, 150, 151
Inventory Stela (*see also* Memorial Tablet), 117, 118, 128, 81-138

# INDEX

and buildings, 125
and *Khufu's* daughter, 85
and *Khufu's* pyramids, 123, 137
and stars, 132
and the Temple of *Isis*, 120, 123, 125
base of, 107
Daressy translation, 154–68
discovery of, 81, 136
lower register, 134
re-copied, 81
text of, 3, 81, 85, 86, 88, 89, 100, 101, 108, 117, 136
Isis, 85, 86, 100, 101, 106, 109, 118, 119, 120, 123, 126, 134, 141, 151, 158, 160, 166, 173
  *as standing serpent goddess*, 134
  *as the scorpion*, 7
  birth of, 47
  chapel of, 165, 166
  *house of*, 85, 88, 108, 118, 120, 125, 134, 165, 172
  *mother of Horus*, 119, 150, 165, 171
  *mother of the god*, 119
  temple of, 84, 117, 120, 123, 126, 130, 159, 164, 166
    *Inventory Stela*, 129
  tomb of, 118
  writings of, 126
Jesus, 141
Jupiter, 58
*Khufu*, 85, 86, 100, 126, 127
  and the Great Pyramid, 90, 120, 159
  books of, 101, 109, 110, 118, 126
  daughter of, 86, 125
    name of, 85, 86, 89, 90, 165, 172
    pyramid of, 86, 88, 89, 90, 101, 105, 117, 118, 123, 125, 165, 166, 172
    *stela of*, 85, 155, 159, 171
  dream of, 84, 105, 126
  Inventory Stela of (see also Inventory Stela), 159, 165, 171
    and the Temple of *Isis*, 129
  mother's tomb, 86, 100, 118
  pyramid of, 123–24, 123, 159, 165, 172
  repair of temple, 84, 120, 171
Leo (the lion), 3, 21, 32, 34, 35, 46, 48, 49, 53, 72, 77, 128, 148
Libra, 67, 69
Mariette, Auguste, 156, 171
  discovery of the Inventory Stela, 3
Memorial Tablet, 113
Menetho, 117
Merer
  diary of, 101, 109

Meyer, Eduard, 43, 44
Milky Way, 151
Moon, 68, 70
  in Libra, 67
*Nedyt*, 141, 148
*Nephthys*, 134, 141, 158, 173
  birth of, 47
*Nut*, 44, 131
  mother of *Horus*, 119
Orion, 10, 13, 150, 151
*Osiris* (Orion), 108, 118, 131, 142, 150, 151, 158, 160, 165, 172, 173
  chapel of, 166
  father of *Horus*, 119, 150
  house of, 85, 86, 101, 118, 123, 125, 165, 172
  legend of, 149, 150, 151
  writings of, 101, 109, 118, 126, 134
*Pedamenope*
  tomb of, 8, 31, 66
  tombof, 67
Pleiades, 27, 28, 60, 113, 114, 116, 132, 133
Plutarch, 42, 43, 44, 117
Pyramid Texts, 119, 141, 142, 148
  and the death of *Osiris*, 141, 142, 143, 144, 145, 148
  and the mother of *Horus*, 119
  and the stars, 142, 143, 150
*Qera* (a storm god), 101, 109, 111, 118, 127
  associated with *Apep*, 127
*Ramesses VI*
  tomb of, 23, 25, 31, 41, 111, 127
Resurrection
  of Jesus, 141
  of *Osiris*, 142, 143, 145, 149
*Sau*, 101, 109, 111, 118, 127
Scales, 13, 15, 24, 27, 30, 68
  parts of, 24
  suspended from the Pleiades, 27
Scorpio, 67, 68, 69, 70
Scorpion, 68, 158, 173
  goddess, 7, 8, 23, 29, 31, 32, 134
  headdress, 83, 158, 173
*Senmut*
  ceiling of, 23, 26, 28, 29, 26
  *Death of*, 64, 65
  tomb of, 8, 26–30, 31
Serqet, 67
*Set* (Hydra, the Serpent), 45, 49, 141, 143, 148, 150
  battle with *Osiris*, 145, 148, 150, 151
  birth of, 44, 47, 48
*Seti I*
  death of, 22
  sarcophagus of, 131

# INDEX

    tomb of, 3, 4, 7, 10, 13, 15, 19, 21, 22, 23, 31, 41, 65, 131, 132
        ceiling, 63
*Shabaka stone*, 81, 138
Solstice, 57
    summer, 4, 57, 58, 59, 60
    winter, 4, 57, 77
Sphinx, 101, 106, 108, 109, 111, 118, 126, 127, 160, 166, 167, 168, 172, 174
    and *Isis*, 166
    book of, 126
    constellation, 41
    dating of, 156, 167
    house of, 86, 101, 118, 123, 125, 172
    of *Harmakhis*, 108
    repair of, 126, 166
    tomb of, 88, 101, 109, 118, 125, 127, 134, 160
    valley of, 108, 166
Spica (star), 72
Sycamore trees, 101, 109, 127
Taurus, 10, 13, 24, 27, 28, 29, 31, 33, 60, 61, 64, 65, 66, 67, 113, 114, 116, 133
Ursa Major (the Thigh constellation or Big Dipper), 113, 114, 132
Virgo, 73
Virgo (the maiden), 72, 73, 77
    rising, 73
Vulpecula (the Fox), 68, 69, 70
Wall of the Crow, 129
Zodiac, 57, 60, 61, 73
    of *Dendera*, 3, 4, 35, 41

## ABOUT THE AUTHORS

John Bunker and Karen Pressler have been researching and writing together since 1993, when they discovered the Edgar Cayce readings and began to study the history of mankind from the remote past, and the lost knowledge from those earliest times. The research has included the study of hieroglyphics, Egyptology, and Astronomy, and their books can be found on Amazon.

Today their home is in rural Indiana where they live in harmony with nature and enjoy boating, gardening, family, and their feline friends.

# NEW FOR *2023!*

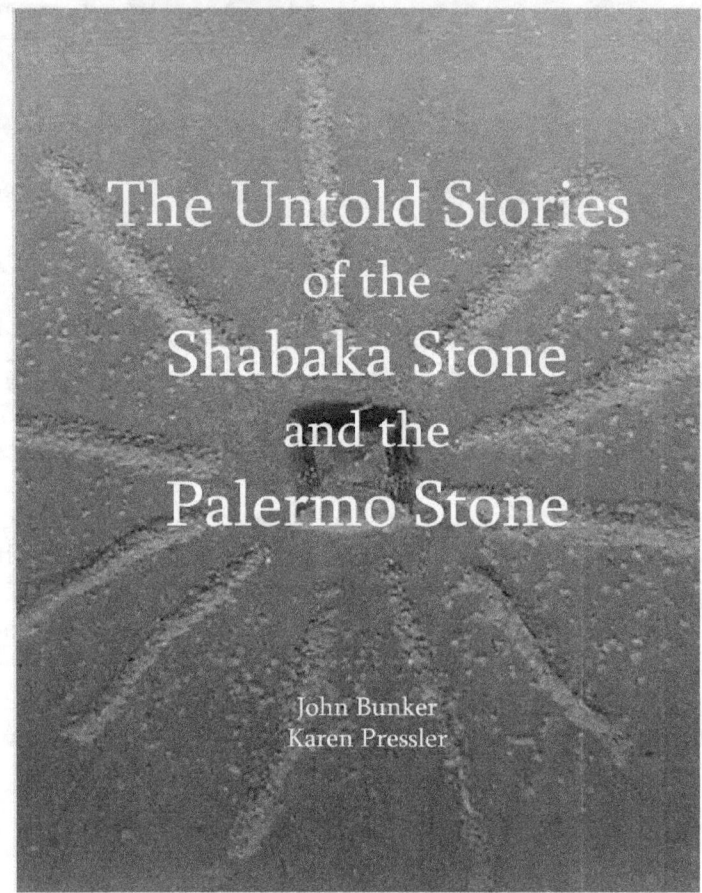

**THE UNTOLD STORIES OF THE SHABAKA STONE AND THE PALERMO STONE**

The mysteries of the Shabaka Stone and the Palermo Stone have attracted the attention of Egyptologists, scholars and students since their discovery and study during the previous two centuries. The impenetrable enigma surrounding them has been gradually chipped away by generations of those who seek to know their meaning. Once again another layer of the shroud covering them has been removed and is presented in The Untold Stories of the Shabaka Stone and the Palermo Stone, piercing the clouds of misunderstanding.

This book also includes the first English translation of Dr. Heinrich Schäfer's 1902 presentation about the Palermo Stone *"Ein Bruchstück Altägyptischer Annalen"*

**ISBN-13:** 979-8-986357133

# OTHER TITLES BY JOHN BUNKER AND KAREN PRESSLER

## EDGAR CAYCE'S SPHINX, THE HALL OF RECORDS & THE HOLY GRAIL

A condensed yet thorough revelation of the exact location of the Hall of Records that Edgar Cayce predicted would be found. This book is a cohesive masterpiece that connects the fragmented bits of information scattered throughout dozens of readings given over a period of many years by Edgar Cayce. You won't be disappointed with this dramatic evidence! The quest for the Hall of Records has become tantamount to the quest of the Holy Grail.

**ISBN-13**: 978-1732579224

## "THE SPHINX AND THE LOST HALL OF RECORDS"
### LECTURE GIVEN AT THE HOUSTON A.R.E. CENTER, JANUARY 17, 2015

This is the complete PowerPoint presentation given at the Houston Edgar Cayce Center in January 2015, complete with lecture transcript. It includes all of the reasoning and proof for the contention that there really is a connection between the Sphinx and the location of the Hall of Records, but current efforts have been guided by a misunderstanding of the clues.

**ISBN-13:** 978-0988500105

## THE ABRIDGEMENT OF THE BOOK OF AM Tuat

It has become clear that the tomb of *Osiris* and the Hall of Records will be found in the upper section of the Pyramid known as Khafre's. The evidence is overwhelming with this fresh translation of the Am Tuat in an astronomical context. Including more analysis, illustration, and supplemental material than ever before, Bunker and Pressler prove that the middle Giza pyramid is much older than previously thought, and exhibits evidence of two entirely different civilizations, hundreds of thousands of years apart. With this groundbreaking research, a new level of understanding humanity's history has begun.

**ISBN-13:** 978-0966977479

## THE COFFIN TEXTS RESURRECTED
### AN ENGLISH TRANSLATION WITH HIEROGLYPHIC TEXT

This volume shows the hieroglyphic text and English translation of each of the first ten spells from *The Egyptian Coffin Texts* 1: Texts of Spells 1-75 by Adriaan De Buck, published by the Oriental Institute and Chicago University Press in 1935. In 1973, nearly 4 decades later, R. O. Faulkner published the first volume of a three volume summary translation of spells 1 to 1185. Now we have begun to take a fresh look at the coffin texts with this translation and commentary, which includes the historical background of the coffin texts as told by James Henry Breasted. The introductory material includes a history of the Egyptian calendar that suggests its beginning may date to the eleventh millennium B.C.E., and commentary on the Pyramid Texts, the Coffin Texts, Book of the Dead, and how some of the ideas from these ancient texts have been preserved in the Holy Bible.

ISBN-13: 978-0988500198

## EDGAR CAYCE AND THE HALL OF RECORDS
### SOLVING THE MYSTERY OF THE HALL OF RECORDS AND THE SPHINX CONNECTION USING ANCIENT EGYPTIAN TEXTS, ASTRONOMY, AND THE EDGAR CAYCE READINGS

The famous psychic and healer, Edgar Cayce, was providing clues in the "life readings" he gave nearly a century ago to the location of a lost Hall of Records. This hidden chamber is said to contain historical archives and artifacts from the most remote times in prehistory. Yet, it remains undiscovered. Most people have assumed that it will be found in a chamber under the Sphinx at Giza, but all attempts to locate it there have met with failure. At last the evidence has been reevaluated outside of the traditional thinking, to reveal incredible new conclusions that are difficult to argue. The sphinx that guards the Hall of Records is not the Giza Sphinx at all, but rather a sphinx star constellation in the night sky. And the Hall of Records is not below the ground, but rather elevated up among the stars at the top of the great middle pyramid at Giza. Finally, we can point directly to a spot and say with confidence, "This is where the Hall of Records will be found." The facts are irrefutable!

ISBN-13 : 978-0966977486

# THE AM TUAT
*By Paul Bucher*
*Translated into English by Karen L. Pressler*

One of the clearest and most complete records of the hieroglyphic texts of the Am Tuat was transcribed about 100 years ago by French Egyptologist Paul Bucher. He worked on a comparison of the Am Tuat from the tombs of Tuthmosis III, Amenhotep II, and *Seti I*, but his published work is not widely available.

This edition compiles two of his previously published works, *Les Textes des Tombes de Thout-mosis III et d'Amenophis II* and *Les Textes à la Fin des Première, Deuxième et Troisième Heures du Livre "De Ce Qu'il y a Douat": Textes Comparés des Tombes de Thoutmosis III, Aménophis II et Séti Ist*. Both are translated here from French to English for the first time. The complete plates of his hieroglyphic transcriptions are also included.

With the ongoing deterioration of the ancient monuments, these early works are becoming more important in the study of the hieroglyphs from tombs such as these. Complete translations depend on complete resources, and comparative studies between the tombs is the best way to truly understanding our ancient ancestors, who have much to tell us.

**ISBN-13:** 978-0988500150

## EDGAR CAYCE AND THE URANTIA BOOK

The original classic, updated with new information! A thorough examination of the evidence of a link between the sleeping prophet, Edgar Cayce, and *The Urantia Book*. For fifty years the channel for the Urantia Papers has remained a complete mystery. Speculation has suggested Wilfred Kellogg as a likely candidate, but evidence has never supported this theory. See the research and decide for yourself.

**ISBN 13**: 978-0966977417

# ENGLISH TRANSLATIONS OF THE MASTERS
## BY BUNKER & PRESSLER

**A FRAGMENT OF ANCIENT EGYPTIAN ANNALS (ENGLISH TRANSLATION OF EIN BRUCHSTÜCK ALTÄGYPTISCHER ANNALEN):**
An English Translation of a 1902 Presentation about the Palermo Stone by Dr. Heinrich Schäfer

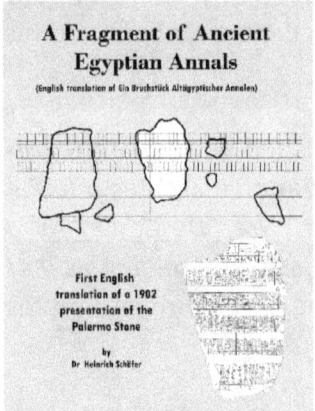

In 1901 three of Egyptology's early pioneers Dr. Kurt Sethe, and Dr. Ludwig Borchardt collaborated in a discussion and study of a fragment of stone that came to be known as the Palermo Stone, because its home was the museum of Palermo, Italy where it was first displayed in 1877. Schäfer prepared preliminary a report of their efforts that was presented at the General Session on March 6, 1902.

ISBN-13: 978-8986357119

**THE PALERMO STONE (Edouard Naville)**

The Palermo Stone is one of the earliest known records of Egyptian history, being a fragment of the Royal Annals, which the Egyptians used to record their most significant historical events annually over the course of many years. One of the first studies of the Palermo Stone was made by Edouard Naville, entitled *La Pierre de Palerme,* published in French in 1903 in a journal of works related to Egyptian and Assyrian philology and archeology. Now, it is again brought to the forefront with the first English edition of this original study.

ISBN-13: 979-8-986357102

## THE TEMPLE PLANS OF DENDERA (Johannes Dümichen)

This book, the first English translation of Johannes Dümichen's critical 1865 work *Bauurkunde der Tempelangen von Dendera*, further opens the discoveries of the original Egyptologists to the English-speaking world. It contains an extensive study of the Hathor Temple at Dendera, previously neglected by other Egyptologists, and particularly a document found preserved in a cavity in the temple wall, which described the restoration carried out by King Khufu of the fourth dynasty. Dümichen's study reveals multiple restorations to the building over a long period of time by various Egyptian kings, and suggests Dendera may date from the time of the Followers of Horus near the dawn of Egyptian civilization.

ISBN-13: 978-1732579248

## TEXTS RELATING TO THE MYTH OF HORUS COLLECTED IN THE TEMPLE OF EDFU (Edouard Naville)

This book contains the text of the original French book, *Textes relatifs au mythe d'Horus recueillis dans le temple d'Edfou*, as well as an English translation on the facing pages. It includes all 25 original plates and Erratum.

[NOTE: this book is not a translation of the hieroglyphic texts.]

ISBN-13: 978-1732579293

## BRUGSCH'S 1883 THESAURUS (VOLUME I): FIRST ENGLISH TRANSLATION

This is the only English translation ever made of Heinrich Brugsch's *Thesaurus* on ancient Egyptian astronomy and astrology. Originally published in handwritten German script in 1883, it was the most in-depth study ever made of the temple of Hathor at Dendera and includes Brugsch's abundant illustrations. Now for the first time it is available to the English-speaking world. It includes Egyptian hieroglyphics, along with a smattering of Greek, Coptic and Latin and several notes from the translators. Over a century has passed since it was first published. This English translation has been motivated by the need for wider access to the works of the original pioneers of Egyptology. Heinrich Brugsch was a leading expert of ancient Egyptian studies who lived during the years of the great masters and fathers of Egyptology and dedicated his life to the pursuit of knowledge and understanding of the greatest civilization on earth.

ISBN-13: 978-1732579279

www.ingramcontent.com/pod-product-compliance
Lightning Source LLC
Chambersburg PA
CBHW082147230426
43672CB00015B/2865